Trier on von Trier

Trier on von Trier

edited by Stig Björkman

TRANSLATED BY NEIL SMITH

faber and faber

First published in 1999
by Alfabeta Bokförlag AB
Box 4284, 102 66 Stockholm
This translation with updates first published in 2003
by Faber and Faber Limited
3 Queen Square London WC1N 3AU

Typeset by Faber and Faber Limited
Printed in England by Mackays of Chatham, plc

Picture Credits: Irving Foto 1, Lars von Trier 2, 3, Danmarks Radio 4, Den
Danske Filmskole 5, Peter Beck Sørensen 6, Søren Kuhn 7, 10, 11, Svenska
Filminstitutet 8, 9, 12, 13, Henrik Dithmer, Danmarks Radio 14, 15, 16, Rolf
Konow 17, 18, 19, 24, 25, 26, 27, 28, 29, 30, Bjarne Hermansen, Danmarks
Radio 20, Morten Constantineanu Bak 21, 22, 23

A CIP record for this book
is available from the British Library

ISBN 0-571-20707-3

2 4 6 8 10 9 7 5 3 1

Contents

Acknowledgements

A big thank you to everyone at Zentropa Entertainments ApS, who helped me find my way through Lars von Trier's cinematic world: to Hanne Palmqvist and Mette Nelund, and especially to Vibeke Windeløv, who went through the manuscript on Lars' behalf. Thanks also to Niels Vørsel, co-writer of a number of Lars' films, and to Jesper Jargil, the maker of documentaries about the filming of *The Idiots* (*De udmygede*, a.k.a. *The Humiliated*) and the installation *Psychomobile #1: The World Clock*, who contributed photographs of the installation. Also to Peter Schepelern for his invaluable assistance in tracing elusive pictures of Lars von Trier's childhood and earliest work.

I would also like to thank Memfis Film AB, Lars Jönsson, Anna Anthony and Emma Sahlin, who provided video recordings of Lars' earliest films and various film-scripts. Also Fredrik von Krusenstjerna for the many suggestions and comments he contributed during work on the documentary *Tranceformer*.

Finally I would like to thank Holger and Thyra Lauritzen's foundation for film research. The grant I received was in large part responsible for making work on this book possible.

Stig Björkman

Foreword by Stig Björkman

I first met Lars von Trier in 1995, when I was making *I Am Curious, Film*, an overview of Nordic cinema in its first century, to mark the centenary of film. Lars was obviously going to be involved somehow. There are few Scandinavian directors – in fact, few directors at all in Lars' generation – who possess such an idiosyncratic talent and innovative style.

I already knew Lars from his deeply original and provocative films. Rumour had it that he was difficult, reserved. Nothing could be further from the truth. Lars proved to be not only unusually approachable, but also someone who was generous with his time and his opinions – as well as being passionate about film. As a result, the day Lars visited Stockholm was extremely rewarding, and we found that we had in common an enthusiasm for a number of films about whose importance and appeal we were fairly unanimous.

Lars was going to talk about Carl Th. Dreyer, and there are, paradoxically, many things that connect these apparently contrasting artistic temperaments. There is a stringency, an implacability and an obsessiveness which, even if expressed in entirely different ways, can be seen as a common factor between them. They are magicians from different eras who, with different means but similar seriousness and passion, have sought out new ways of exploring the nature of film.

Shortly after the day we spent filming in Stockholm, Lars contacted me and suggested producing this book together. It felt like a challenge from the outset. The idea of talking to this director who used film as both his research tool and his source material promised to be both an adventure and a rewarding experience.

In the summer of 1995 we had a first meeting. Lars was preparing for the shooting of *Breaking the Waves* at the time. The book project, and the conversations for it, were initiated some eighteen months later. These conversations have since stretched over a long period. They mostly took place in Lars' home, in a comfortable suburb north of Copenhagen. They also occurred during long walks in the surrounding countryside, an area of almost tropical bounty, with great beech forests, savannah-like grassland and tangled thickets, which called to mind scenes from one of Lars' favourite films from his childhood, *In Search of the Castaways*. In this rebellious landscape Lars spoke enthusiastically about the possibilities of flight via the imagination.

Openness and trust were a given basis for our conversations. I have had the opportunity to read scripts of actual films and of projects that are still at the planning stage. I have also been able to watch Lars in action as a director, during the filming of *Breaking the Waves* on Skye and *The Idiots* close to his home, in the neighbouring community, the Søllerød so detested by the 'idiots' as well as on *Dancer in the Dark* and *Dogville*.

His development since *The Element of Crime* is as daring as it is astonishing, but it is also consequential. Questions, challenges and renewal have been recurrent motivations and arguments in Lars' work in film. Combined, of course, with a considerable dose of provocation. Much of his work has been intended to expand both his and our vision. Some of this desire to continue exploring the medium of film, and his solid faith in the future possibilities of film, is expressed in Lars' final words in *I Am Curious, Film*, where he compares cinema with painting:

'The art of painting must have started when someone drew on the wall of a cave. That probably continued a century or so. It would have started with tiny little lines, then gradually became more complicated. The lines turned into a bison or some other creature. Bearing in mind the position that art has reached now, countless centuries later, we might compare cinema with art. Cinema is a mere hundred years old. And we've just worked out how to draw a bison. There's a long way to go. That's why I'm very optimistic about the future.'

And Lars, with his films, has proved that he is at the forefront of this development. There is every reason to be optimistic about the future of film – and that of Lars von Trier.

1

Lars Trier

Where shall we start? Lars? 'Von'? Or Trier?

You're wondering where the 'von' comes from? You see those big paintings leaning against the wall? I did those when I was about twenty, and I think they're signed *von* Trier. No, hang on, 'von' first appears on that huge self-portrait. I'll just go and check. (*Lars goes over to the wall, where his first works in oil are lined up. He checks the signatures.*) No, these are all signed 'Trier', plain and simple. It was only later that I was afflicted with this terrible case of ego worship.

Wasn't it during your time at the Danish Film School in Copenhagen that you were 'ennobled' – or assumed the name 'von Trier'?

Yes, I started using the name again at film school, because it seemed the most provocative thing I could do. No one really cared how my films looked or how well they did. But this 'von' business, on the other hand, really upset people.

But why assume this aristocratic name at all? And when did you start using it?

About 1975. But it can be traced a lot further back, to my grandfather, Sven Trier. He always wrote his name in Germany as Sv. Trier, because the abbreviation of Sven is Sv. And he was addressed in Germany as Herr von Trier, because people misunderstood the small 'v'. It turned into a funny family story that was often repeated.

1 The artist as a young journalist. In January 1976 Lars von Trier published an article on Strindberg, 'On the brink of madness in Holte', in the local paper *Det grønne omrade*. The article was illustrated with this picture, with the caption 'writer and artist Lars von Trier outside Geelsgaard in Holte, where Strindberg stayed during his creative (and erotic) period of madness during the summer of 1888'.

In the middle of the 1970s I read an awful lot of Strindberg, and Nietzsche, of course. During Strindberg's crisis in Paris – which is always called his 'inferno crisis' – he signed his letters 'Rex', the royal signature. I thought that was pretty funny. I liked that . . . both the craziness and the arrogance of it. So I started adding a 'von' to my name. This sort of thing isn't at all unusual on the American jazz scene. Several people there have used noble titles and called themselves 'Duke' or 'Count' and so on. And later on, naturally, I've had film-makers like Sternberg and Stroheim in the back of my mind. Their 'vons' were entirely made up, of course, but that didn't do them any harm in Hollywood.

So it was a way of 'making a name for yourself'. Did you know you wanted to be 'a name' even when you were young?

No. Well, yes, maybe . . . Of course! Your name is your identity, so I suppose I'd thought about it.

When we started talking about this project, you said you thought the book should be called Trier on von Trier . . .

Did I? I thought you came up with that. I'm sure it was you. Or else it was Peter Aalbæk Jensen's idea. What's your book about Woody Allen called?

In Swedish and Danish it's called Woody on Allen, *because I wanted it to be* Woody Allen *the person talking about the artist of the same name.*

About the artist *and* the phenomenon? Well, maybe *Trier on von Trier* would be a fitting title. I wouldn't mind that. Although the opposite could be interesting as well, *Von Trier on Trier.* Maybe we should do two versions of the book. Or do it so it can be read from both directions, like one of those television guides, where you turn the magazine over to separate the articles from the pro-gramme listings.

This project was your idea to begin with, so I want to ask why you want to do a book of interviews now?

I like this sort of book. For instance, I've read the book that you and a few other people did with Ingmar Bergman several times. There's something about the interview format that gives a certain direction to the content, as well as getting the artist's own words down on paper. I suppose in some ways it's more fun than when the artist writes about himself on his own. Bergman is probably the exception, because he writes very well and describes his life and work in an entertaining way.

So you're keen to speak more in depth about your films and your views on film in general, and about your aesthetic views on film? You think there are things in your past that others could find use-ful?

Well, there's a chance that they might. So why not! Damn it, yes, if I've enjoyed and got something out of reading similar books about other directors, I hope someone will get some pleasure from what I've come up with.

One advantage is that you can digress more. Conversations have no time limit, and they don't have to end with any well-formulated conclusions. I was asked to do that sort of PR work for *Breaking the Waves*, but I turned it down because I couldn't bear it. This sort of small talk feels quite liberating, though.

Shall we go back a bit and do a flashback to your childhood, when you were still just Lars? From what I understand, you grew up in a middle-class, civil-servant family, although both your parents had extremely radical social ideas.

I don't know how radical my father's view of society was. He was a social democrat. But my mother was a communist and a firm believer in liberal childcare and in the child's right to make its own decisions. At the moment I'm in a therapy situation where I'm coming to grips with my mother's way of bringing up her children. But you're supposed to be angry with your parents, aren't you? In the end everything *is* their fault. At any rate, it's their fault that we're here.

What my mother, Inger Trier, wanted to create, at least on the surface, was a free individual. At the same time it's perfectly obvious that she wanted me to live up to a succession of creative and artistic ideals that she hadn't been able to achieve, but which she had worked out for herself, and therefore also for me. It was like an obsession for her. When she was younger she knew left-wing authors like Hans Scherfig, Otto Gelsted and Hans Kirk. Their friendship meant a lot to her at the time, and her social life and interests influenced her subconsciously to create a fantasy in me.

It's been said that she was trying to ensure the survival of her artistic genes by having me. My father, Ulf Trier, isn't my real father. My mother told me that on her deathbed. She had a romance with a man whom she believed had the sort of genes that I would find useful in the future. My biological father's cousin, for instance, was supposed to have good musical genes and was very talented musically. She was aware of this, and I remember that she tried to encourage me to spend time learning music all through my childhood, in spite of the fact that my limited musical talents leave

4

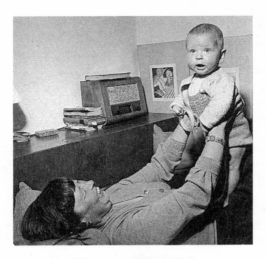

2 / 3 The foundation of Lars Trier's relationship with water. Here together with his mother, Inger Trier.

a very great deal to be desired. But she was always encouraging me to express myself artistically in some way or other. It was obviously very clearly planned on her part. I've always felt under pressure from that, even when it wasn't really there. In retrospect I can see how consciously her plan was executed.

Was your biological father an artist?

No, he was a civil servant as well, but, in my mother's eyes, his family had the capacity for sublime creativity. At least that's what she said on her deathbed – that she had planned everything on that basis. It's a good, juicy story that you could really make something out of. As one of the ingredients in a biography it has its attractions. But I can't live up to Bergman's childhood traumas and his stories about wardrobes – which, according to his sister, were completely untrue.

How did your liberal upbringing affect you? Did you find it difficult, having to make your own decisions in areas that children don't usually have to think about? I also wonder how it affected your friendships with children who might have been brought up in a more traditional way.

I certainly found it difficult. Partly I felt privileged compared to my friends, because I wasn't forced to follow clearly defined rules and regulations. But it was also upsetting, because, apart from my parents, everyone treated me as if my childhood was no different to the other children's. (*Lars' youngest daughter comes in and wants help finding a toy. Lars leaves the room briefly.*) That was Selma. She's got a proper, literary, Swedish name [*after Selma Lagerlöf, the Swedish author*]. But her middle name's Judith, and her sister Agnes' is Rakel. They both share Jewish and artistic names. We do what we can to predetermine our children's futures!

What about your own predetermination? We were talking about your upbringing and how it affected your relations with your contemporaries. Your liberal upbringing meant that you had to make a lot of decisions for yourself at a relatively early age, like whether you should go to school, when you had to go to the doctor or the dentist. You also had to buy your own clothes and other things.

Having that sort of trust can be a positive thing, but there were also a lot of negative side-effects from having to take that sort of responsibility. I was a very nervous child. When I was six I used to lie curled up under the table for hours, terrified because an atom bomb could fall on us at any moment. I was clinically anxious, and I still am – even if nowadays it's about other things.

When you feel that you have complete freedom of choice, you're forever being knocked back when you're confronted with the outside world, where freedom of choice doesn't exist. Naturally, my contemporaries represented that world. The main problem was trying to get these two worlds to connect. I soon became a sort of leader figure to my friends, and I almost felt it my duty to take responsibility, decide what games we should play and so on. It was actually quite a lot of work. Of course, there were a lot of people who didn't want to be part of this, and that led to other problems.

Did you experience this as a source of conflict even then?

No, probably not. But later on I realized that it was a source of extreme anxiety for me, the fact that I lacked a natural authority that could have helped me and guided me in my decisions. I was forced to create an internal authority, and that isn't particularly easy for a child.

Did you go to the dentist, or did you not bother?

Of course I did. And I did my homework earlier and faster than the others, because I didn't have parents who told me when to do my homework. So I used to do it at the bus stop on the way home from school.

I was also tormented by childish fantasies and feelings of guilt. I thought I was responsible for the whole world. I can remember, for instance, a flower that was growing by the side of the road, and the flower had been damaged and couldn't stand up straight. But I managed to lift it up and support it. Every time I passed that flower I had to check that it was still standing, because otherwise the world would collapse.

It's difficult to define and identify clearly the aspects of our child-

hood that we still carry with us, and which affect and colour our adult lives . . .

What I have had problems with is everything in the world that I can't control – things that I'd dearly have liked to be able to control.

But now, looking back, do you think that your childhood and upbringing were positive?

I've got incredible self-discipline, but that's also something that torments me. It's given me an edge, if you like. I'm very reliant on my own abilities. But we're all emotional little creatures as well, so this sort of upbringing had its own problems . . . unnecessary problems.

But you don't have trouble co-operating with other people, from what I understand.

I'm not sure about that. No less trouble than anyone else. Obviously I want to have things my way. And if other people want to do things my way, obviously I don't have a problem with that.

Your father, Ulf Trier, was Jewish . . .

Well, half Jewish.

But I gather that meant quite a lot to you when you were younger, and that through him, and the world of Judaism, you tried to find a sense of belonging.

You could certainly say that I was trying to find a sense of belonging. My family had a fairly relaxed attitude to Judaism. There are loads of Jewish jokes, and there was certainly no shortage of them in our home. But I did feel a sense of security in 'Jewishness'. My parents had drawn up a family tree, and both my mother and father encouraged me to investigate our family history further. I discovered, amongst other things, that we're distantly related to the von Essen family, which amused me mainly because of my interest in Strindberg. [*Siri von Essen was Strindberg's first wife. They were divorced in 1891 after a turbulent marriage, an event that contributed to Strindberg's 'inferno crisis'.*]

But I certainly tried to find a sense of belonging in Judaism, a sense of belonging that it later became apparent that I didn't have any right to at all. I haven't got a single Jewish gene. Well, possibly one or two from my mother's side. But at the time, when I was a teenager, I felt extremely Jewish and went around with a skullcap on when I was in the Jewish cemetery.

Did you go to the synagogue as well?

No, I can't say that I did. Maybe a few times, but I didn't have a particularly religious attitude to Judaism. My father represented assimilated Jewish culture. For the Trier family it was more important to be Danish than Jewish. My father wasn't very religious either. He was probably more rebellious in his politics.

Were you close to your father?

Yes, very. I was extremely fond of him. He died when I was eighteen years old. He was fairly old, about fifty, when I was born. In comparison to my friends I had an old father. There was never any chance of playing football with him, or anything like that. He wasn't physical in that way. But he was very funny, and loved playing tricks. Sometimes when we were out I felt almost ashamed of him. He would limp, or drag one leg behind him, and pretend he was handicapped. Or he would go into the shop windows and hold the dummies under the arm. All the silly things that children hate their parents doing. All the time! It was awful! But he was a reassuring figure, because he knew what he wanted, unlike my mother, who was weak and indecisive.

You left school early, long before most people, and a year or so before the official school-leaving age.

Yes. I remember my schooldays as a deeply unpleasant time. To begin with I went to a terrible school. It was the Lundtofte School, and it was horribly authoritarian. It was very difficult to reconcile the liberal upbringing I experienced at home with the more rigid demands of school. It was practically impossible. I felt claustrophobic almost all the time. All that sitting at a desk, or standing in rows in the schoolyard or corridors, made me very anxious. I would sit and look out of the window, watching the gardener work. I used to dream of becoming that gardener, because he could decide when he wanted to sit down or stand up or get on with his work.

School must have been a source of greater conflict for you than your friends, who probably didn't experience the same freedom from rules and regulations as you did at home.

Of course, and when I complained to my parents, they just said that they couldn't understood how I could bear it or why I didn't just walk out. If my friends had complained about school at home, they would probably have risked getting a slap instead.

So one fine day you got up and walked out . . .

Yes, I suppose I did. But I'd had a lot of problems before that. I was ill. I suffered from migraines during a large part of my childhood . . . I don't know why, but all of a sudden this is sounding like a real Bergman story. (*Laughter.*) I'm sure he must have suffered from bad migraines as well!

How old were you then?

I was in the fifth year, so I must have been eleven or so. You were supposed to stay in school for seven years, I think. I remember having to go to the school psychiatrist when I began to play truant, and he said: 'If you don't go to school, the police will come and get you!' That was his solution to the problem, and he was supposed to be a psychiatrist! His attempts at persuasion weren't terribly pedagogical.

So you stayed at home and played truant more and more, and, in the end, stopped going altogether. How did you manage to make the decision?

My mother solved the problem by organizing private tuition. I studied at home for about six months or so, then my mother gave up. But by then I was old enough to leave school anyway. Going to Lundtofte School was a wholly unenlightening experience. I can probably remember one or two teachers who were vaguely positive.

The rest were terrible, and I just felt I was wasting my time. I don't think I've ever found anything I learnt at that school remotely useful.

After that I studied privately, and eventually I took an exam roughly equivalent to the school diploma. That bit of studying went incredibly quickly – and was interesting as well.

How long after you had left school did you start studying on your own?

Two or three years, I think. There was a long time when I didn't do much at all, actually. I painted a bit sometimes. And a friend and I would paddle out on to some logs in a lake near here. We used to sit there drinking wine and talking long into the night. That took up about three years. My mother thought this was quite all right. That was pretty good. I don't think many parents would react like that.

You've been very open about your childhood and upbringing. Is that because you, as a public person, believe that this discussion ought to be accessible to other people?

You do ask some horrible questions!

But isn't that the point?

It's almost as if you want some sort of political confession from me. You were much more respectful when you spoke to Bergman! 'Herr Bergman, why have you written a book about your childhood? Is it so that other people can learn something from it?' You never asked *him* questions like that.

I don't know what to say. I've probably said so much about my childhood for therapeutic reasons.

I think it's good – and courageous – of you to talk so freely about your background. You seem to have sorted things out for yourself considerably more quickly.

I haven't sorted anything out! The worst thing is not knowing who my real father was. My mother's ideas of childcare were based on a demand for complete openness. Everything was up for discussion, everything could be talked about. There weren't supposed to be any secrets. The fact that she carried her great secret for so long implies that it must have been quite traumatic for her. I'm sure of that. It was completely at odds with everything she stood for.

You say that everything in your home was open, with no secrets. But in one room there was a cupboard that was kept locked. And you've said that that cupboard contained your mother's letters to your real father. Didn't you ever wonder about that locked cupboard when you were younger, because everything else was so open and accessible?

The Danish word for cupboard, 'skab', is interesting. It doesn't just mean cupboard – it can also mean an insect. And the expression 'at skabe sig' means to play the fool, or to make a fuss. If you wanted to, you could make a case for the cupboard actually being an insect in the home.

But somehow or another, with therapy, I've come to the conclusion that my childhood wasn't as free as I used to think, because my mother had the plans that she had regarding me, and led me in the right direction, even if she simultaneously tried to pretend that these plans didn't exist. So this secret might well have suited her after all.

She made a fiction for you and your life, you could say, and has been a sort of director of your life. You could probably say the same of many parents, that they try to create a fiction for their children, and that the children are meant to realize the wishes and dreams that they themselves didn't manage to achieve. But in your mother's fiction this secret occupies an important and intensifying position. It's a mystification.

Of course. My mother was unusually creative.

This sort of mystification is fairly common in film – a secret waiting to be explained, like 'Rosebud' in Citizen Kane. *A lot of film noir is based on that sort of thing too.*

Yes, she must have had a feel for it. Imagine if she'd never revealed the big secret. But she did, and on her deathbed as well! You couldn't get much more melodramatic. Looked at from a cinematic point of view, it was good that the revelation got out. Otherwise there would be no story.

But for you it isn't just a story. It's something that's affected you deeply.

I actually took her confession fairly lightly to begin with. It was so absurd, and so unexpected. Completely. I had never doubted my father or his love for me. It was all unexpected, but at the same time it didn't mean much to me, especially given the upbringing my parents had given me. They thought that environment was more significant than inherited characteristics. They were less important.

The reaction only came later. I almost had a breakdown because of it.

Was it long after? Months, years?

No, it was only a few days later. In a sense I felt that I'd lost both my mother and my father at the same time. To a large extent, that overshadowed my grief about my mother's death.

We're sitting here talking about your childhood home. Now you have moved back here, for the second time. First you moved in here with your first wife, Cæcilia (Holbek). Now you live here with your partner, Bente (Frøge), and your children, the twins Ludvig and Benjamin. What does this house mean to you?

First and foremost, it means peace and security. I've tried to move away a couple of times, but it's never worked. I moved back home time after time. As a young man you want to get away, the further the better. But one day I realized that I couldn't. This was where I belonged. It's neither a slum nor a castle. It has no great dramatic qualities. Its main advantage is that it's where I come from. I've lived here all my life. I don't know if that's positive or negative, but I've had to acknowledge that the house is very important to me.

What is it that unsettles you outside the walls of this house?

I think homesickness has a lot to do with it. I'm speaking from outside my own mental position here. I can understand Tarkovsky making a film like *Nostalghia* in Italy, far from his home. This probably happens in my films as well. Even if I make them in other parts of the world, there are components that can be traced back to the fixed point in my life that's home. Particularly all the water that runs through my films. There's a stretch of water near here where I paddle my canoe. That river meant a lot to me when I was growing up. It's like a nerve, which probably sounds like a worn-out cliché. But paddling along the river, looking at the landscape, with the mills and the old factories, means a great deal to me. Whenever I travel too far from this stretch of water I get unhappy. Water is comforting. Whenever I have to travel, I always want to be near water. It would be very uncomfortable to be somewhere where there was no water for miles.

I think of this landscape as mine, and I know the whole area. A lot of people have moved here since I was a child, but in some sense I feel I have a greater right to be here. I was here first! I feel at home here. I can relax here.

We've made quite a few changes to the house. And we've built a place for me to work in the grounds. I've enjoyed smashing the things that were my mother's favourite possessions. Glass bowls and ornaments and stuff like that. One huge bowl that used to sit on the kitchen table. I smashed that right after my mother died. That was great.

When did you first move away from here?

I was probably fairly old. It was when I was about to start at film school. I was about twenty at the time. Then I moved back after my mother died, together with my wife at that time, Cæcilia. In between I lived in various places in Copenhagen. I've never much liked living in the city. When we divorced, Cæcilia got the house, where she stayed on with our two daughters. Later on she wanted to sell the house, but couldn't find a buyer, so our production company, Zentropa, bought the house. Now that my company has bought the house, I suppose I own it. The strange thing is that the house was also Cæcilia's mother's childhood home. We only found out when some distant relative of hers came to visit. It's like something out of a film sometimes . . .

Do you relive moments from your childhood when you're in the house? Does it bring back memories?

I don't really think about that, but I suppose it happens. The good thing about the house isn't just that it feels comfortable, but that it's adaptable. I can always change things, which I've been doing. The whole house has been rebuilt. Changing the look and the content of the rooms is a symbol of me taking over the house and making it mine. It's always been like that: one of the children inherits the farm and the parents move to a smaller house on the land. Then the inheritor gets to decide what to do with the house and how to manage the land.

I've been worrying about where I'm going to die. Sometimes I imagine myself in a room in some unfamiliar hospital, dying shut up inside four anonymous walls. It's a very claustrophobic feeling. I've tried to counteract and combat that feeling by moving back into this house. Here I am, and here I'm going to stay. I might change my mind about that. But that decision, that certainty, gives me a certain security. I know that I shall never be tempted to move to the United States or anywhere else. And that's an incredibly good feeling. I believe that you die sooner if you don't have a sense of belonging.

At the same time it hasn't been an easy decision. I've got a lot of fantasies and dreams and ambitions. So of course I've felt like living in another country as well . . .

How does a normal day look when you're not working?

When I'm not working?! (*A very long pause.*) I don't know what sort of day that would be . . . I spend quite a lot of time at my computer playing Tetris. I like that a lot. It's a well thought-out game, and it has a calming effect on me. And I spend a lot of time with my family and do normal domestic things. And I do a bit of sport, paddling my canoe. And I watch television, but the amount of programmes on offer now means that I spend most of my time zapping between channels. I'd sooner rent a video.

And a day when you're working?

That's most days, really. I write mostly during the mornings in my little studio in the new house in the garden. In the afternoons I normally go in to Zentropa and work on what needs doing there. Late in the afternoon I generally go out in the canoe. After that I'm pretty tired.

Do you think that every day contains some sort of creative work?

This business of being creative has positive and negative aspects. You get very dependent on the need to create. I suffer from a mass of phobias of different sorts, and when I don't apply my energy to creative work it turns to these anxiety-creating evils instead. Maybe this puts my creativity in a peculiar perspective: it isn't just a need and a desire to create, but, primarily, a means of survival.

Where do you get inspiration from?

That's hard to answer. In your youth you collect a load of themes and motifs from what you read and see, from the interests that you gather together and build up. That's the basis of my inspiration. And that's what it develops from, probably for the rest of my life, I imagine. I'm not the sort of person who goes out into society or off on some journey to look around and get inspiration that way. Not consciously, at any rate.

What if we don't call it inspiration but 'driving force' instead?

I believe that your driving force is connected to your psychological insecurities. It might be a more mechanical driving force, but I think it's the same adrenaline at work. A sort of enthusiasm. But how it arises I couldn't really say.

You're not affected by other art – literature, music, other films? They don't give you inspiration and ideas?

I can't answer that! I'm impossible. I'm not interested in other art in that way. I listen to pop music now and then, but it isn't anything that functions as any sort of driving force.

I think that most of my films have come about as a result of me setting myself a task. I might think to myself, 'Now I'm going to do something funny,' 'Now I ought to do something tragic,' or whatever. And then I ask myself what I think is funny or tragic or whatever. Anxiety-inspiring, for instance. If I wanted to come up with something scary, I'd choose something that I feared myself. I would go through my internal database and pull out something that I could use.

Can you give an example of how the plot of one of your films developed?

(*A long silence.*)

If we take Breaking the Waves, *for instance?*

I can't remember how the story first occurred to me, but it was based on a book from my childhood. I wanted to create an inno-cent heroine. Where could I find an innocent person, and that sense of innocence? I found several references within myself, and others from external influences, possibly from experience of other art forms. And then it occurred to me that Bess should look like this and should behave like this. The construction of the plot, the construction of the intrigue, is almost like solving a rather banal crossword. If I've got this innocent heroine, who should I let her meet, and what shall I let happen to her? There has to be a counter-balance to her, and I can get that from her husband, Jan, who would therefore have to have contrasting characteristics, and so on. Then the process gets extremely banal – it's just a matter of fol-lowing classical dramaturgy. It becomes very mathematical. Or rather, I choose to do it in a mathematical way. Even if I might react against great reams of dramaturgical rules, I still have the basics of dramaturgy within me. Basic common sense is probably an equally valid description of it.

What part of making films do you prefer, if you can differentiate between the various processes?

I can probably say that it would be whatever I have most time to do. Wherever I have most room for manoeuvre. Just following a recipe to the letter isn't very rewarding, and working under time constraints is always frustrating.

My experience of film work has changed a lot over the years. On films like *Breaking the Waves* or *The Idiots*, I've got more out of the shooting and working with the actors. Shooting *The Kingdom* was unpleasantly stressful, so the editing was the best thing with that one. With my earliest films it was mostly the final phase, the soundtrack and mixing, that was most rewarding. That was when I began to get a sense of the whole that I had been aiming to create in the films. In my first films I never had enough room for manoeuvre during the recording. With them the process of working on the scripts was more rewarding than the actual realization of them.

2

The First Films

Going back in time again, you were allowed to borrow your mother's cine camera when you were fairly young, and started making films with it. Did you know then that you wanted to get into films when you grew up?

Well, I suppose I did. Films were already in the family. My mother's brother, Børge Høst, was a successful documentary director, and he supported my ambitions. I felt a need to describe my own reality. You could probably also see it as escapism. When life gets too threatening, you have to create some sort of fantasy existence, a life where you can control the things you can't control in real life. That's a fairly good reason for creating fictions, I think.

This desire, this need to create another life for yourself – through film – was something you felt early on, then?

Yes, fairly early. I was probably ten or twelve when I started making films. And it was fairly clear to me that that was what I wanted to do with my life. It was fun trying to come up with a story and all the other stuff involved in films, the technical side of things. But when it comes down to it, it's about building up your own universe, something that you can regulate and control. It's incredibly satisfying. And very puerile as well. A lot of children create imaginary worlds where they're in charge. It's no insult to say that a lot of artists base their work upon childish desires. Childishness has its own merits, I'm absolutely convinced of that.

Directing films is also about creating a world of your own. The main task of a director is to persuade everyone involved in the film, both in front of and behind the camera, to join in his game, to agree to his terms. As a child you soon realize that you can't just tell other children what they have to do and then imagine that they're going to want to play the game because of that. It's better to find a way of convincing them that they're joining in because they want to. This game – making films – means that you have to be fairly manipulative.

I think I've got a lot better recently at persuading people that they want to join in the game. Especially where the actors are concerned, where co-operation is the name of the game. But it's still my game that we're all playing in some way.

What would you say is your best quality as a director?

My stubbornness. And having an idea of what sort of thing is remotely manageable.

And your worst quality?

(*A very long pause.*) It depends what you mean by worst. Whether you mean what my own handicaps are, or the way I affect other people. In both cases I think it might be my impatience. But if I was more patient, maybe my work wouldn't be as stringent as I would like. Stringency is something I value a lot. And I think my imagination is far too limited. It's too egocentric, which limits it a lot.

Did you see a lot of films as a child? Did you go to the cinema much?

I don't think I went more than my friends did. But my interest in film developed thanks to my uncle. I was particularly fond of editing together the different scenes I had filmed, and my greatest wish in those days was to have my own editing table. While my friends were dreaming of bikes or horses or cars, I was dreaming of an editing table. A proper Steenbeck, a professional editing table.

You wanted to make 16mm films?

I didn't care what format it was. The important thing was being able to edit sound *and* pictures. I was already fairly obsessed with the technical side of things. And my mother's camera, a little

Elmo 8mm, could do loads of different things. It could run backwards, could be set at loads of different speeds, and it could take single frame shots and double exposures. It was fantastic! And, of course, I had to try everything out. Video's a bit boring in comparison to old cameras like that. They presented a more fundamental, mechanical challenge. They were great fun. Later on my mother gave me a projector with sound. The soundtrack was on a magnetic strip on the film reel.

You've kept all those old films, and they're great fun to watch. In one of them there's an image in particular that struck me. It's a long close-up of yourself. It looks like you were trying to see your reflection in the camera. Do you remember that?

Yes, I remember it. It's a strange shot. There's a series of fairly diffuse, improvised images that I've kept, which I keep thinking of editing into something. Among them are a few black-and-white shots of me, where I'm sitting and feeling my face and doing odd things with my fingers. I can't remember exactly when I took those images. I had so many complicated ideas about what I wanted to do.

When did you get really interested in film?

I must have been fairly interested the whole time, enough to want that Steenbeck editing table, for instance. I used to sit there with a little hand-held monitor, looking through the film, and I had a fairly primitive editing set-up using glue. The joins in the film were always thicker than the rest of the film, so it would jump a bit in the projector when the join went through. It was bloody irritating. And sometimes the film got stuck, and burned through.

At some point I bought an old 16mm projector in a camera shop for 150 kroner (£14). A huge black machine, no sound. And then I got a few films from a friend of my mother's who worked at Statens Filmcentral [*a Danish distributor of short films*]. Among them were two short bits of film that I edited together. One was a documentary about cockroaches, and the other was part of the trial of Joan of Arc. The scene where she's being interrogated by the judges, I've seen it thousands of times. I put them together as a sort of edited montage. I hadn't the faintest idea then that it was one of Dreyer's films. I also coloured in some of the scenes by hand.

4 The actor Lars Trier in the Danish-Swedish television series *Hemlig sommar* (*Secret Summer*) from 1968, together with Maria Edström.

So you decided to get involved in film . . .

I think I was seventeen the first time I applied to the Danish film school. And they turned me down. But before that I'd done some acting in a television series for children and teenagers, a Danish-Swedish co-production. It was called *Hemlig sommar* (*Secret Summer*) and was directed by Thomas Winding. During the recording I was mostly interested in the technical side of things, and when I visited the studio about six months later I was allowed to help set the lighting and so on. And I thought this was all pretty exciting. I was twelve when I was in *Hemlig sommar*, so I must have been thirteen or so when they let me help out in the studio.

I remember bumping into Thomas Winding at a cafe in Copenhagen, when I was just getting going with *The Element of Crime*. And he said to me, 'If you only want to provoke people with a load of dead animals, you might as well not bother.'

Did being in Hemlig sommar *make you want to continue with film?*

Yes, I got extremely interested in the technical side, the camera tracks and all that. It fuelled my desire to make films myself. I became rather influenced by Thomas Winding and came up with a few projects involving his characters. But it still wasn't me. It was all a bit too Teutonic, a bit too dramaturgical.

And then you went to study film.

Right. I'd tried a bit of everything. But most of the time I was trying to make my own films. I joined a group of amateur film enthusiasts called Filmgrupp 16. They had cameras that they hadn't used for years. I became a member; I think the annual membership fee was 25 kroner! And suddenly I had access to equipment. I started shooting a couple of 16mm films straight away. I took other work to pay for the film and other stuff I needed. One of the jobs was on a building site, putting up the huge aircraft hangars at Værlose. The doors of the hangars were huge, and when they were open, they were precisely the same format as CinemaScope!

Thanks to my uncle I also got a bit of work at Statens Filmcentral. It was sort of consultancy work, looking through films that had been sent in and working out whether they deserved to get distribution. In the evenings I had access to the editing tables at Filmcentral, so I could sit there editing my films. It was very handy.

During that time I managed to put together two films, both about an hour long. One was called *Orchidégartneren* (*The Orchid Gardener*), and the other *Menthe – la bienheureuse*. It was recorded in French, in spite of the fact that I can't speak a word of French. I made it after seeing *India Song* by Marguerite Duras, so of course I had to film it in French. In *Menthe* I did my first experiments with back projection. I tried it later on in some of my work at film school as well. It's an exciting technique. It's like doing a laboratory experiment out in the field.

Cinematic technique interested you a lot at the beginning of your career.

That's right. I remember that we did some pretty funny titles for *Menthe*. They were revealed as the camera slowly moved along a woman's naked body. That sort of camera movement was extremely difficult to do, so I came up with a steel construction to attach the camera to, which meant that we could move as slowly as we wanted, centimetre by centimetre. Technique, and the things it can lead to, fascinated me. In those days technique meant something different. Now you can do whatever you want to on film electronically. It's all done in laboratories and special-effect studios. And it's become a lot duller. The idea of workmanship has vanished completely. I think it's pretty natural to want to turn away from technical effects.

Were The Orchid Gardener *and* Menthe *based on your own stories?*

I wrote a couple of novels that were never published, and *The Orchid Gardener* was based on one of them. It was a very exhibitionistic film. I appear in Nazi uniform and then as a transvestite in the film. I was really going for it. But David Bowie was my great idol and role model at the time, which is pretty obvious from the film. My curiosity has always made me want to try different things. I wouldn't like to call them experiments, though, or classify my earliest films as experimental.

Menthe was a somewhat eccentric reworking of *The Story of O*, and, as I said, it was very influenced by Marguerite Duras. *India Song* was a revelation. It's one of the few films that have really influenced me.

What was it about Duras that influenced you most?

When you get the idea that a film has come from nowhere, that it wasn't made here on earth – that's fantastic. I can't express it any other way. I felt like that when I saw *India Song*, and possibly even more so when I saw Tarkovsky's *Mirror*, which I must have seen at least twenty times and which I'm completely obsessed by. I've seen a lot of Marguerite Duras' other films, but they haven't had the same effect on me as *India Song*. Nor did *Hiroshima mon amour*, which she wrote for Alain Resnais.

As a director Duras often used narrative techniques that you've used as well, particularly the way the plot is driven by one – or more – narrative voices. There's a hypnotic quality in these voices, like the voices in The Element of Crime *or* Europa, *which is also very suggestively charged.*

Yes, I'd emphasize the suggestive element. *India Song* is an incredibly atmospheric film where plot is less important. Full of symbolism, you could say. But I didn't feel any need to interpret the symbolism – or the symbolic language – of *India Song*. The film was majestic, and the atmosphere incredibly beautiful.

Have you seen the companion piece to India Song, Son nom de Venice dans Calcutta desert? *There are no actors – it's mostly long camera shots of building façades and grand interiors. But behind that you hear the voices, music and sound effects from* India Song.

It sounds interesting – a sort of iconography. It's a fascinating idea, using fragments of images and setting them to a soundtrack. *Mirror* is constructed in a similar way, with newly shot footage mixed with archive material and documentary inserts.

Are there other film-makers you came across when you studied film history who affected or fascinated you?

Of course, above all Jørgen Leth and two of his films, *Det perfekte menneske* (*The Perfect Human*) and *Det gode og det onde* (*Good and Evil*). The latter influenced me a lot. It's a film I keep coming back to. I must have seen it at least twenty times.

What was it about those films that fascinated you?

To begin with, they were very untraditional; they didn't tell a story in the conventional sense. I was very interested in advertising imagery in those days, like Jørgen Leth. Photographs from *Vogue* and magazines like that. A sort of still life, using people. And Jørgen Leth's films approached the same aesthetic as those pictures. But I don't want to define them narrowly by implying that they're just about aesthetics, because Leth's films mean a lot more to me than that. They convey atmospheres and experiences and events that aren't just aesthetic. It was liberating to see films that were different to most of what Danish cinema was coming up with. I thought that Danish films in those days, the mid-1970s, were incredibly boring.

I remember another film from that period: *The Night Porter* by Liliana Cavani, with Dirk Bogarde and Charlotte Rampling. I've just seen it again on video, and these days it's the sort of film you'd probably classify as kitsch. It's got a sort of basic comic tone that I didn't notice when I saw it the first time. It's very Italian in style and atmosphere.

I met Liliana Cavani once. It was just after *The Element of Crime*. There was going to be a big EU meeting in Paris about European cinema, and I was invited by Jack Lang, the French Minister of Culture at the time, to go along as a representative of the Danish film industry. Everyone was there! I sat opposite Antonioni during the meeting, alongside Bertolucci and Ken Loach. Bergman had been invited from Sweden, but of course he didn't come. But everyone else was there. It was a pretty interesting experience for me, considering that I'd just finished film school and made my first film.

The first day I was sitting eating breakfast on my own. They had organized the catering in an office in the Ministry of Culture. The socialists had just come to power. I was squeezed in by a wall, and noticed that there was a picture by Picasso behind me, which they must have borrowed from the Louvre. If I'd stretched out my arms, I could have hit a Picasso with one arm and Braque with the other!

I was staying at a hotel near by, and I had the room above Liliana Cavani. One morning I rushed off to a flower market that was close to the hotel and bought a bunch of lilies on my Danish expense account, knocked on her door and thanked her for *The Night Porter*. But she was furious. She thought it was a commercial, imperialistic piece of crap, something she'd just done for the money. Later she had gone on to make more sincere, left-wing films that were more to her own taste. She honestly thought *The Night Porter* was a piece of shit, though she did take the flowers, albeit not with any great enthusiasm.

But I was very struck by *The Night Porter* at the time, with all its symbols and signs. I probably pinched quite a bit of it for *The Kingdom*. In spite of everything, it was an interesting film. The show trial of the former concentration camp boss showed how deeply ingrained Nazi attitudes were. And Dirk Bogarde was brilliant in the role. Liliana Cavani was hopeless at directing people, but Bogarde managed to create a character in spite of her. It's still a film that's meant a lot to me. As I said, I was very influenced by David Bowie at that time, and he used to go about in a Nazi uniform. I was trying to imitate him. It was all part of my rebellion against my mother, I think, this business of ostentatiously going about in military uniform. She'd been in the Danish Resistance during the war.

You've mentioned before a film that influenced you a lot when you were younger: a Disney film called In Search of the Castaways. *You said at the time that that film had been the inspiration for most of your films.*

Yes, I liked that one a lot. And I can recognize that a lot of images come from that film. There's one scene in it where they survive a flood by climbing up a huge tree. It's an unforgettable scene, and it embodied a sort of childhood dream. I used to build tree houses when I was little, and I was very good at climbing trees. I loved it. So that scene from *In Search of the Castaways* was the inspiration for both *The Element of Crime* and the final scenes in *Europa*.

It's certainly a very poetic scene. The children escape into the top of the tree, where a lot of animals have also gathered.

And the scene where they escape on some sort of cliff is very good. There's another film I remember from that period. I might have been a bit older, but it was one of the best films I've seen – John Schlesinger's *Billy Liar*. It's a brilliant film.

What is it about it that you like?

Its imagination. And the rebellious streak in the central character's daydreams. All of a sudden he's standing there with a hand grenade, throwing it at an old lady. At the same time he works for an undertaker, and is supposed to hand out calendars for the company, which he doesn't bother to do. He flushes them down the toilet during his lunch break. I was very fond of *Billy Liar*. There are a few films that have stuck in my mind like that. I've only seen *In Search of the Castaways* once, but those images from it are etched on my memory.

Have art or literature inspired you in a similar way? Are there works of art or books that have lived on in your memory like these films have?

I read quite a lot when I was younger. Strindberg especially. But perhaps art has been more important. I was very taken with Peter Watkins' portrait of Edvard Munch in the television programme he did. It was a revelation. When I saw it I had to go and paint – and scrape the paint with the handle of the brush as well. Strindberg's and Munch's madness was the height of artistic romanticism for me then. It's interesting that both Strindberg and Munch came to Copenhagen to be cured by Professor Jacobsen, who was the great Danish psychiatrist of the time. He was an eccentric who used to go about in a cape. I once met a Swedish woman who was so old that she had been treated by him. But Strindberg's novels got much duller and Munch's paintings were far less interesting after their meetings with Professor Jacobsen, so he was a bit of villain in my eyes. They might have felt better, but their art was damaged by those consultations. Strindberg wrote a couple of his best plays, *The Father* and *Miss Julie*, here in Denmark, and Munch had already painted his remarkable schizophrenic works before he came here. Then he turned into a sort of Norwegian Carl Larsson. No, artists are meant to have it bad, because it makes the results so much better!

You painted for a while yourself when you were younger . . .

Well . . . I might have painted ten or fifteen pictures, then I stopped, after painting a huge self-portrait, two metres by three in size. After that there was nothing left to give! But I think I managed to paint my way through most of the '-isms' within painting during that period. I started with expressionism and went through impressionism to naivism. But I never really had time to try modernism and abstract art. I was very fond of Chagall, who was also my mother's favourite artist. His work can be a bit too sweet and nice, but I like that easy style with figures floating in the sky.

I was very fond of Fellini when I was younger. His lightness, his ability to get his characters to take flight – even literally. *Amarcord* was a wonderful film, I thought at the time, funny and full of fantasy and told with wonderful imagery. I can't really stand him any more.

I think Fellini is a director you abandon as you get older, even if *La Dolce Vita* and *8¹/₂* are still films I have a high regard for.

One thing about La Dolce Vita *which isn't always stressed enough is Fellini's journalistic way of telling stories. He films small reports and essays, and then puts them together to make a big, generous, multi-coloured fresco.*

That's true. And it explains why his films can be so uneven. Like *Roma*, which has some scenes that I was very taken with, but others which are quite indifferent. Like those frescoes in the underground, they're mostly rather saccharine. When his symbolism becomes too obvious, it's hard to put up with. It's better when there's a bit of mystery to it.

I also like the Italian way of recording sound. When I was at film school, I wanted my films to be dubbed *all'italiana*, i.e. slightly out of sync. And all atmospheric noises had to be very stylized. So if two people are in a car, the noise of the car shouldn't sound natural, but like a dubbed and flattened buzzing noise. Like in Rossellini's *Viaggio in Italia*, another film I'm very fond of. I was completely obsessed with it for a while. And also *La Notte* by Antonioni. An ambitious film, with an atmosphere all of its own. The fog over the golf course, for instance! A wonderful, idiosyncratic and personal film.

But there aren't any films like them any more. It's impossible to find films with that incredible wealth of expression nowadays. Maybe I just don't see enough films, and there are still films like that but I've managed to miss them. What I miss today is a sense of joy in narration, in invention. And a sense of mystery, above all.

Joy in invention. Isn't that what you're trying to do, to rediscover the medium of film again?

Yes, I suppose I'd like to. Whether or not I manage to is another matter. Now I'm older I'm more interested in older films. When I see an old film with a sense of style, it cheers me up. I recently saw Ken Loach's *Family Life* again. That was great. Or Jan Troell's *Utvandrarna* (*The Emigrants*). That's wonderful. Take a scene like when Karl Oskar (Max von Sydow) is travelling through America. You see him in several camera pans that suddenly stop and get cut in half. That's a pretty unusual arrangement – very unusual images.

Perhaps that's because some modern, anachronistic detail would have appeared in shot otherwise . . .

That's a terrible thing to suggest! But that's probably because you're Swedish. I don't know what it is that makes me feel so light-hearted when I see that film. Perhaps it's because it's got such a fine sense of style.

That's certainly something lacking in films today. A lot of what's made is shaped in a very conventional mould, or else put together in a sort of MTV-style with fast editing and a thumping rhythm. Or there are very stylized films that are almost entirely form and very little content. I miss the awareness and feeling for form that so many directors in the 1940s and 50s had, both in the USA and in Europe. Perhaps it will come back. But that was an incredibly fertile period for film. I saw a film from the 1970s on video the other day – *Five Easy Pieces* by Bob Rafelson. A wonderful film! Really wonderful! I'd never seen it before. Then I saw his *The King of Marvin Gardens*, which I couldn't stand. It was so banal and mannered, whereas *Five Easy Pieces* had a spontaneity and lightness to it. It feels like everyone involved said: 'OK, let's make a film together,' then they went on to make *Five Easy Pieces* quickly, lightly, and with a sense of fun. This business of taste is funny. It's so precise. You might think, 'This is good and proper,' but that's only what you think. I think most people who watch films can't tell the difference between one and the other. I mean, this question of style – I don't think it bothers most people. They just think a film is boring or not boring.

When did you start to notice the difference yourself? When did style and taste become important to you?

I'm not entirely sure, but I think it was when I started making my first 8mm films. I think I looked at them with a certain awareness. I tried to make my own camera crane. I had grand plans for how it would look and how it would be built. I filmed camera shots riding my bike in one of my first films. I mean, if you're twelve years old and making films and getting interested in how to get good camera shots, then you're probably already fairly aware of how films look.

Do you watch a lot of films these days?

No. That's the whole point. I hardly see any new films. I don't think much of films that are fashionable today. Like *Brazil* by Terry Gilliam. I hated it! Or those Frenchmen who made *Delicatessen*. I couldn't stand it. It's mannered and superficial, and it doesn't say anything to me. *Delicatessen* is grotesque without having the generosity or colour or intoxication of the truly grotesque. But you get that in Fellini. *Brazil* was a film I couldn't watch all the way through. And I feel the same about Peter Greenaway's films. They're films without mystique. The aesthetic is so heavy and obvious that the films are anchored to the floor. Yet I still get compared to these directors now and then.

You got into film school in Copenhagen in the early 1980s.

Yes. Like I said, I tried before, when I was about seventeen. I applied again, and this time I got in. Something that was obviously in my favour this time was that I'd already made a couple of films. I think *The Orchid Gardener* managed to convince the entrance board that I had potential.

I came up with a good idea when it came to the final entrance test. Applicants were given a camera and three minutes of film, and in three hours we had to come up with a short film, which we had to edit directly in the camera. In other words, we had to take our pictures in the right order, as we wanted to see them in the finished film. I wasn't really thinking artistically about what I was going to do. Instead, I was wondering what all the others were going to do. I thought that they would probably go to the main square in Kristianshavn near the film school and film some poor Greenlanders sitting there drinking, or to the park to film people out walking their dogs.

I was fortunate enough to have a car at that point, so I thought I would drive somewhere else and film there. I could spend an hour getting there and an hour getting back, so I would have an hour to film something. So I went off to Skovshoved, which is a residential area with a lot of rich people's mansions. I remember it was a brilliantly sunny day, and the streets and roads out there were completely deserted. So I took pictures of those mansions, with the occasional gardener or someone in a swimming pool. I made a sort of 'Peeping Tom' report, and I thought it was pretty good. The film was quite funny and, above all, it was different to what all the others presented. It was a tactical manoeuvre. So I got into the school! The people who got in with me were an eccentric bunch, so I was lucky there. But I don't look back on it as a particularly happy time. I was fairly depressed and had a few physical problems, mainly with my stomach.

In an interview many years ago now you said that it wasn't thanks to the school but rather in spite of it that you learned anything.

Yes, schools can work like that as well. I was probably antagonistic to a lot of what was said and taught at the school. But in order to break the rules, I had to know what they were first. It was idiotic. It was a waste of time. I already knew how I wanted things. In spite of everything, I'd managed to make two hour-long films before I got into the school. Of course, there have been interesting films made by people who went to film school and learned how to cross-edit and how to avoid crossing the axis when you're filming a situation with two people in front of the camera.

What did those years at film school give you?

Well, to begin with, I didn't have to pay for the films I wanted to make! I had an almost fetishistic attraction to the technical side of things, and at film school I suddenly gained access to more advanced and professional equipment. It was wonderful to be able to get my hands on all that equipment! I could see before me all the endless possibilities that this technical equipment suddenly offered me. I regarded film school mostly as a workshop. I could learn by experimenting and testing out different techniques. I got much more out of the film exercises than the theoretical part of the course.

I was very rebellious and got into arguments with most of the lecturers. I thought they were idiots. The one I got on best with was Mogens Rukow, who taught scripts. He took me under his wing a bit, because he thought what I was doing was pretty unusual. But I was in constant conflict with the direction teachers, Gert Fredholm and Hans Christiansen. They really didn't like what I was doing. They wanted to see a completely different type of film. Not conventional film exactly, but some sort of hybrid. It should be nice and tidy and proper and . . . I don't really know what sort of film they wanted, or what they themselves made. But, to me, they both stood for mediocrity in their attitude to film.

We also had teachers for art history and musical theory, but I never understood the point of that. An appreciation of art was surely something we should have developed before we got to film school. People who apply to and get into film school are adults, after all. If you accept people who have a certain level of experience and things they want to do, it's a bit late to start teaching them that sort of thing. I don't think they should try to teach what films should contain. They should teach technique. The students themselves ought to contribute the content. I'm far more inclined towards a workshop sensibility. A workshop where students get the chance to make as many films as they can. I'm not very fond of schools . . .

You've said that when you were bored at film school, you made sure you always had a book by de Sade with you, or Pauline Réage's The Story of O.

That's probably true. At one point I wrote a script for *La Philosophie dans le boudoir* by the Marquis de Sade. A grand drama in three acts, splendidly vulgar. I thought I might use it to practise on. But Gert Fredholm, who taught direction, told me to destroy the script. It wasn't enough that I couldn't make the film. Any evidence that a script like that had been written at film school had to be destroyed! I made a short film based on a story by Boccaccio instead. A lot of what I first did at film school was only done to be contrary. The tasks we were given were so stupid. It felt like being back in nursery school again.

You were fairly interested in erotica and erotic stories at that point. Do you think that erotica has been depicted in film in a sensual and convincing way? Is there any particular film, or films, that you've found stimulating?

Erotically stimulating?

Yes.

33

(*A very long pause.*) No, I can't think of anything at the moment. I was very fond of *The Night Porter*, but that was more on a theoretical level. It wasn't very erotic in a stimulating way. It was far too fragrant for that. *The Story of O* wasn't very successful as a film. As a novel, though, you could probably say that it's stimulating.

Why do you think it is that films that are supposed to be erotic – and I don't mean porn films – are so unerotic?

Well, erotica is something that's more fun to do than to watch. But one great characteristic of film is its capacity and possibility to create erotic people. There's a whole host of erotic women on film. And not merely in erotic films. But film is so good at creating erotic images, with sensual and charismatic actors at their centre.

Can you name any actresses who've got this charisma?

I think Charlotte Rampling radiated sensuality. I was mad about her. Dominique Sanda was incredibly beautiful. Catherine Deneuve, she's magnificent. There are a lot of French actresses who have that erotic magnetism.

You've named three European actresses. Is there anyone in American cinema who's appealed to you in the same way?

Some of the great stars had that sensual charisma. I think Katharine Hepburn had it, and Marilyn Monroe, of course. We could probably look up a list of actresses and find loads of them. Because what film offers is the chance for them to build on their erotic potential. There's an extremely strong sexual undercurrent to most female acting on film.

Max Ophüls once said, 'Making films is easy, you just need a beautiful woman and a mobile camera and you follow her as closely as possible.'

There's a lot in that. I saw Maurice Pialat's *Loulou* recently, with Isabelle Huppert and Gérard Depardieu. It's a brilliant film. And I remember when I first saw Huppert's début film, *The Lacemaker*, by Claude Goretta. I thought, 'That insignificant girl, she can hardly be the lead.' But after seeing it all the way through I was

5   Trier in a leather jacket during filming of *Nocturne*.

quite captivated, almost obsessed by her. Jeanne Moreau was another brilliant actress.

If we return to your time at film school – what else is there to say about it?

Mainly that there I came into contact with a cameraman called Tom Elling and an editor called Tómas Gislason. We formed a triumvirate who worked well together. The collaboration we set up was extremely important for me, something that developed and continued on my first feature films. It started with a short film called *Nocturne*, which was my most visual adventure up to that point. Today it looks like an MTV clip, but at the time it had a sense of freedom about it. The film was highly influenced by Tom Elling and his experiences. Tom was a painter before he started film school. After *Nocturne* we did a film that probably wasn't much good, *Den sidste detalje* (*The Last Detail*). It was a sort of gangster pastiche, partly inspired by Jean-Pierre Melville. But we carried on our collaboration later with *Befrielsebilder* (*Liberation Pictures*) and *The Element of Crime*.

35

What did your collaboration with Tom Elling and Tómas Gislason give you?

An awful lot. I was able to put into practice a lot of the theories they had. Tom had spent a lot of time on what you could characterize as symbolic painting. We worked a lot with symbols and symbolic language, and we had complex theories about the symbolic content of separate shots. We developed structures and contours in our images. We drowned some scenes in water or poured oil on the walls to make things clearer. The sort of thing you do in painting or sculpture. We were extremely interested in getting a patina on the things we filled our shots with. We spent a lot of time getting that patina on things. In *The Element of Crime* our interest in patinas became almost overwhelming. Niels Vørsel once said something about 'the danger of nature'. That fascinated us, the collision between nature and culture. Our point of view was purely visual, and greatly influenced by Tom.

Tómas, on the other hand, had a lot of theories about editing. Above all, he had got very involved with eye scanning – where the focal point for the eye should remain in the same place in two shots after you edit them together. These were theories we took with us from film school, but we tried to use them in a creative way. We had them as a starting point. Purely technical details were what inspired us. And that was something they weren't keen on at film school. You shouldn't start out with technique, but with content, or rather the message. You should start with the message, then create a story around it, and then – eventually – spare a thought to style.

You mentioned Niels Vørsel, who has been one of your closest collaborators and co-writer of a lot of the scripts for your films. Was he another person you came into contact with at film school?

No, he was actually an extra on my exam project at film school, *Liberation Pictures*. We had a mutual friend, and, through him, he ended up in the film. One day we bumped into each other in a cafe, and he started discussing a project with me. He wanted to film Wagner's *Ring* in the Ruhr. As far as I could make out, it would be filmed from the autobahns and would be projected on to huge screens so it could be seen from the autobahns. It was a huge, bizarre project, and I said it sounded extremely exciting. But I'd just got funding for a script for a detective film and suggested we work on that instead. So we went on to write *The Element of Crime* in a couple of months, if I remember rightly.

Had Niels Vørsel already published anything at that point?

He'd published one small book, *J.B.*, which was almost a conceptual publication. And he'd written some radio plays. He was also in *Epidemic*, but you know that.

Of course, he and his wife, and you and your first wife, Cæcilia Holbek . . .

Yes, she's the nurse. If there's anything she's never been, it's that. During the time we were married, I think at most she might have given me a cup of tea when I was ill. But only once!

But you and Niels have collaborated on a lot of films now. How do you work? Do you each sit alone and write, or is the collaboration more direct?

We sit together and work. To begin with he used to sit at an enormous IBM typewriter, but he's had to give that up for a computer. When we wrote *The Kingdom*, Niels did a lot of the research as well. That was the bulk of the work on that one, so we had to divide it between us. But usually we work by writing a treatment, a synopsis together first, then we share the work between us and write separate scenes on our own.

Together we've written what we call a trilogy, *The Element of Crime*, *Epidemic* and *Europa*. And then *The Kingdom*. And we're also working on the project that I'm calling *Dimension*, a film that will take about thirty years to complete. We started recording in 1992, I think. All my little 'film family' are in it. Eddie Constantine was in it to start with, but of course we can't have him any more. In December 1996 I filmed a few scenes with Katrin Cartlidge, Stellan Skarsgård and Ernst-Hugo Järegård. One idea behind it was that I'd work with actors who I'd just used in a current film.

Can you say anything else about the project?

Well, the idea is to make a film by recording two minutes per year up to the year 2024. We haven't got a script, we just improvise the action each year. It's a pretty weird project. It's always annoyed me that you usually make people up in films to make them look younger or older. With *Dimension* I wanted to do something where time was a central theme. The project is regarded as being well nigh impossible. The scenes are so short. But, one way or another, it will also be about how difficult it is to make a film like this one.

Do you edit each instalment the year you film it and add it to what you already have? Or are you saving the editing for later?

Originally we weren't going to edit the sections as we went along, but we've ended up doing that after all, mainly to get financial backing for the project. The Film Institute has been very understanding about the project, and we've also got a grant from Statens Filmcentral. I suggested at one point that they could give us a production grant equal to what a normal Danish film would get, which we could put in the bank, financing each year's recording with the interest. I mean, put the money in some sort of fund, and then, when the film was finished, give the money back to the Film Institute. But that wasn't possible because of the Film Institute's rules and the agreements they have with the government. So we have to apply for funding each year. And so far we've got it. It's probably hard to stop a project like this once it's started. Otherwise we'd have to throw away everything we've already recorded.

And you'll be unveiling the finished piece in 2024?

Yes, why not! As long as I'm still around. You'll probably get to see it as well. How old will you be then, seventy-five or so?

No, eighty-five, if you have the première in the spring. Otherwise I'll be eighty-six.

Well, we'll have to arrange a special screening where we can wheel you into the cinema and ensure you can see the screen properly.

But you ought still to be around then. You'll be a pensioner – sixty-eight years old.

But I'm convinced I'll die of cancer any moment. I've got a whole load of phobias about cancer these days. Haven't you?

No. I haven't actually got that many phobias.

Well, I've got more than enough to go round. The best thing about cancer phobias is that they swamp all the others. Now that I'm worried about dying of cancer, there isn't so much room for the other phobias. There's a certain logic to it. At the moment I'm suffering from crushing cancer phobia. The problem with a phobia or an anxiety of this sort is that it isn't creative. You don't get anything out of it. You ought to be able to turn the anxiety into something else, because there's a fair amount of energy in it. But it just creates apathy instead.

You've said that your work is a way of confronting your phobias and anxieties. Can you develop that a bit more?

The phobias that I suffer from can obviously be used to my advantage sometimes. A person who's afraid of the dark will probably make a better horror film. But mostly phobias just make you uncomfortable. At the moment I'm so self-obsessed that I imagine my own death five or six times a day. It's pretty pathetic . . . There he goes again, the idiot, fantasizing about his own death again, half a dozen times a day!

I've spoken to Ernst-Hugo Järegård about this a few times. We're both terrified of dying. I think I'm most afraid of the process itself. Ernst-Hugo's fear was different. He couldn't imagine life without Ernst-Hugo Järegård! I once said to him that seeing as we've experienced our own death night after night, and been so terrified of it in advance, then we're going to be really well-prepared when we're finally confronted with death for real, because we've suffered so many rehearsals of the event itself.

The worst thing is that you don't get anything out of all this anxiety. It has the sort of power that it would take to climb a mountain or go off exploring or something like that. But anxiety gives nothing in return, even though it demands blood, sweat and tears from me when I'm trying to get through a difficult night. When the morning comes, it's all gone. There's no visible evidence of what I've been through. I haven't managed to plant a

flag at the top of a mountain. It's all a pretty pathetic performance.

But you can become immortal through your films . . .

I can become immortal through my films . . . (*Laughter.*) But that's
not much good to me now. Immortal is putting it a bit strong, too,
but it's possible that someone in the future will dig out an old film
and think he's found something interesting. I probably still think
that immortality comes from a stable, sound basis, not from the
opposite. If something has characteristics that make people think
of it as worthwhile, then it has to contain energy that isn't just negative. That's what I think, anyway.

Nevertheless, Dimension *is a project that ought to keep you alive
for a while. The film could be your life insurance.*

That all depends on what you mean by life insurance. It could be
insurance against dying. But I imagine you're referring to usual
insurance terms, where those who are left get some money.

*I mean that the film might act as insurance for you, that you have
to stay alive until the project is finished.*

Yes, I can imagine that. I'll do practically anything to convince
myself that I've still got some life left.

3

Liberation Pictures

SYNOPSIS

The first day after the liberation of Copenhagen, May 1945. A group of German soldiers is gathered in an unspecified location, characterized by water and fire. These men, the war's losers, are killing themselves or saving their comrades from the humiliation of being captured by the Allies. Even Leo, the film's main character, wants to commit suicide, but at the vital moment his revolver merely clicks. He writes a letter to his Danish sweetheart, Esther.

We find Esther in a house on the edge of the city, where the liberation is being celebrated. She is embracing a black American soldier when she catches sight of Leo, who has crept into the house. When they are alone, she criticizes Leo for taking part in an act of torture. A young boy from the resistance was blinded. Leo denies being involved, and says the SS were behind the act. Esther points out his culpability, but promises to take him to a hiding place in the forest anyway.

In the forest Leo remembers his childhood. People are moving through the trees, and Leo is lured into an ambush. He is captured by resistance fighters, and Esther blinds him before he levitates up into the sky. Behind the windscreen of a car we see Esther's tear-streaked face.

* * *

LARS VON TRIER: This is a long film, a film with long scenes – particularly the final scene. It takes a long while for the image to fade. I remember there's a little dog in the scene, which stands nodding its head, because there are explosions in the distance. It took a long time before it was still again, and then I let the image fade.

No, it doesn't fade. But you let Kirsten Olesen look into the cam-
era, and there's a sense of you saying 'thank you', because the scene
is over now. But the camera's still reacting, you get a sense of
Kirsten emerging from her character, and you break the fiction. I
was going to ask you about this final image later, but we might as
well start with it instead. Was it an idea that was formulated at the
editing table, or had you planned to do it like that from the outset?

I'd planned to do it like that from the start . . . Yes, that's what we
came up with at some point. We've got the long drive in the car,
and that shot from the ground, which I think we managed very
well. It's an effect that succeeded, I think. Whenever I had a particular aim with something technical, or with some technical special effect, I always planned it so it was obvious how it had been
done. I did it like that even in my first films at school. If there was
a mirror in the scene, I would often move the camera so that the
whole film crew appeared in the mirror. I liked that, that the camera became visible at a certain point.

That was typical of Godard in his earliest films. Is he a director
who's influenced you?

No, he hasn't meant that much to me.

Liberation Pictures *looks like it was a fairly expensive production*
for a film-school film. Was it hard for you to get it off the ground?

No, we made it pretty quickly. The film probably just looks expensive. Its production values are high when you consider the budget we
had to stick to. We were lucky to find an old factory where we filmed
the whole of the first part of the film. It was very suggestive, with its
old ovens and so on. And we made a few improvements of our own.

Did the film school have any opinions about the film before it was
made?

Not that I remember. We had a long discussion about the long
crane shot at the end of the film. Edward Fleming, who is also a
director, played the central character in the film and didn't want to
go up in the crane. And we were supposed to have a sunrise in the
background. And the forestry official who helped us up in north

6 Lars von Trier testing the camera crane for the long, unnerving crane-shot at the end of *Liberation Pictures*.

Zealand where the film was recorded suggested having the forest in the background as well. But when we finally got the crane set up, the sun rose on the wrong side. We'd read the map wrong. So we've got Esprup Lake in the background instead. And it was very nice, even if it wasn't meant to be like that to begin with. But we thought, what the hell, we'll take it as it is. So we tied Edward Fleming to the crane, and I went up with it, 28 metres, because the cameraman didn't dare go up. We had to get it done quickly. We had to get the shot in one take to get both the sunrise and the mist that was drifting over the ground. And it was proper mist, not something out of a machine.

So we did the long, slow ascent. I'd promised Edward not to lift him more than ten metres above the ground. At the end of the shot he opened his eyes and looked down. And he said, calmly but very sternly: 'We're going down now!'

So that was one phobia you could deal with?

Yes, fear of heights is one of the few phobias I don't suffer from. I can hardly see a crane without wanting to climb up it. Situations that I can control and make decisions about don't really bother me. When we filmed *The Element of Crime*, I was always up high. Either that or down in the sewers. We paddled round in the sewers and floated around in them. Or else we were up in tall cranes instead.

Yes, and in Epidemic *you've got a long scene where you're hanging from a rope under a helicopter, flying over the countryside.*

Yes, but that wasn't bad either.

Liberation Pictures *takes place during the days following the liberation of Denmark from German occupation, and the central character is a German soldier. Why choose him as the main character?*

By Danish standards it was pretty provocative to view the surrender from the German point of view. People were used to seeing it from the Danish perspective. But then we got to see some documentary footage of captured Danish collaborators, '*stikkere*', and of some Germans as well. Those pictures were shot with great awareness of the camera's role, of who it was who was documenting the whole thing.

But you wrote the story together with your two closest colleagues on the film, the cameraman Tom Elling and the editor Tómas Gislason.

Well, I'm not sure about that . . .

That's what it says in the final credits.

Well, we did the storyboard together, and some of the story probably came about while we were doing that. But I don't think we wrote the script together. It's possible though. In any case, we did an extremely detailed storyboard before we started filming.

And the film follows the storyboard?

Yeah, most of it.

This sort of preparation, is it something you've done since then?

Yes, up to *The Kingdom*. I stopped after that. *Breaking the Waves* came about naturally without any storyboard. You can't predict anything when you work with a hand-held camera. But even at film school I was very choosy about camera movements. I'd set myself a mass of rules. Panoramic shots and tilts, horizontal and vertical camera movements, they weren't allowed. I thought camera movements that weren't in parallel were unattractive. I didn't like altered perspective. Nor did I want to combine crane shots with panoramic shots. The camera's gaze should be along pure, clean horizontal or vertical lines. I remember having a very good second cameraman on *Europa*, who wanted to do some small panoramic shots to settle the image. But I said no. I could easily have fixed the camera stand so that it couldn't move horizontally. I was very conservative on that point, until I moved on to using a hand-held camera, which is considerably more anarchic.

Had you felt obliged to establish rules like this for yourself before?

Yes, I felt I had to. It just came naturally. But by setting yourself rules, you also choose a style. I used a lot of parallel camera movements at a lot of different points. It was a bit like a cartoon. We did a lot of work with motifs in the foreground but also in deep perspective. Important things were going on in the background, and the action could shift between the two. It was very consciously constructed.

You also created similarly complex shifts in the soundtrack, where voices could overlap. The dialogue in some scenes is occasionally interrupted by a narrator moving the action of the film forward.

That was something I developed at film school, which I first used in *Nocturne* and then continued in *Liberation Pictures*. Everything was synchronized late. What interested me was that body language was a separate thing and that the voices didn't match it. It helped to create the sense of unreality that I was after in these films.

When we recorded the narrator's text for *Europa* with Max von Sydow, I made him lie down. That way, his voice assumed a completely different tone. We worked in the same way with Michael Elphick in *The Element of Crime* when we recorded his internal monologue. A lot of what I was doing then was based on theories.

45

In many of your earlier films you used internal dialogue to tell the story. Have you got a theory about that?

Interior monologues have always seemed to me to have a dream-like quality. They also say something about observation. The person who is speaking – or thinking out loud – has observed something. It's a stylistic touch which has a lot in common with the Raymond Chandler films of the 1940s.

And with film noir.

Of course.

You use this narrative technique in Liberation Pictures *as well.*

Yes, and there are several scenes where it's raining, which is another typical film noir trademark. Rain can be very evocative, and it can emphasize things and generally make a scene more intense. They hated rain scenes at film school. But I argued with them and pointed out the practical advantages of filming so many shots with rain. If it rains during recording, you don't have to postpone the shoot. That was the sort of argument they could accept.

But you must have used rain machines as well?

Of course, and the fire brigade too. I exploited the fire brigade as much as I could during my earlier films. Constant floods!

You seem to enjoy getting the actors soaked . . .

Yes, you get to see the outlines of their faces and bodies in a clearer way. Especially in black and white. It always looks great.

As far as colour's concerned, you divided Liberation Pictures *into three acts. First one that's reddish-orange, then a yellow, then a green. How did you come to tone the film like that?*

I don't really remember. But I suppose I thought the red tone gave a sort of 'inferno' look. There are a lot of fires early on. We just set fires at various points in the scenes. It's pretty exaggerated, but in its own way it's actually quite beautiful. There are loads of torches, and it was years before I could see another torch. I'm still not very fond of them.

I don't remember why we chose to film the second section in yellow. I think the wind was important. In the first section the elements were fire and water, and in the second air. I don't think anyone would get an awful lot from me remembering why the second section is yellow. But this business of tinting black-and-white film is an unashamed imitation of Tarkovsky, a bit like his *Mirror*. When we tried out different colours, we found that orange-red is an extremely good colour, because it gives a particularly strong sense of colour as it contains both yellow and red.

The film is pretty cerebral in character, even down to the choral music accompanying the visuals.

That was also inspired by Tarkovsky. He used Bach. I just went a step further and chose a choral piece. It made the film even more overblown, but I still think it's a good piece of music.

Do you listen to music much?

No. These days I mostly listen to disposable, modern pop music. But I've spent a lot of time on music in the past. I went through a phase of listening to a lot of impressionistic music, and piano music as well. That was partly thanks to that film about Delius by Ken Russell. That was a great film, without doubt the most disciplined thing Russell has done. It got me interested in Delius's music. Russell made films about several composers, *The Music Lovers* and *Lisztomania*, and so on, and they were really dreadful. But *Delius* was an extremely good film, and it was black and white.

The central character in Liberation Pictures, *Leo, tries to contact various German cities. He calls out to them. This happens again in your trilogy about Europe, with* The Element of Crime, Epidemic *and* Europa.

That's Leif Magnusson, the director, sitting down in one scene and trying to contact Germany by telephone. '*Fräulein, geben Sie mir bitte Berlin,*' he begins. But he can't get a connection, so he lists all the cities he wants to contact. '*Lüneberg an der Heide, Essen im Ruhrgebeit . . .* ' When you see or hear the names of these cities, they summon up images. It's a very visual thing, talking about cities, because a lot of cities have some sort of soul attached to them, whether or not you've actually been there. Cities are like people. Take a film like Bergman's *The Silence*. You get that sense of atmosphere in that. The fictional city in that, which seems to be in some East European country, really does have a soul, albeit a particularly depressing one.

What is it that fascinates you so about all these German cities' names? They appear as a kind of catechism in Epidemic *and the other films as well.*

These cities and their names have an almost mythological quality for me. It's also to do with Germany, like *The Element of Crime* and *Europa*. There's a Teutonic cultural quality about it. I can't really explain it very well. But there *is* a fascination, which you should probably ask Niels Vørsel about, because it's more his fascination than mine. There's a terribly depressing film noir feel to it all. There's a similar mystical content in all the American cities that the film noir genre is anchored to. The effect just gets more extreme with these German cities' names. When you pile on night, darkness and rain or fog . . . 'It's always three o'clock in the morning,' as someone says in one of those films.

That was Niels Vørsel's favourite scene. He didn't write *Liberation Pictures* with me, of course, but he particularly liked that scene. The camera takes a symbolic tour of the floor of the factory where the scene is set, a tour which is supposed to give an impression of the geographical positions of these cities. It's quite a smart idea, I think. When we get to Lüneberg an der Heide, the heath landscape is symbolized by some sand on the floor. It was one of the most successful scenes in the film. I'm very fond of shots like that, with a mobile camera pointing straight down, vertically, because your usual vision is compromised and you don't know what's up or down.

We planned that scene for a long time, weeks before we filmed it. We planned the scenography on a large table, and it included most things – water, vegetation, wind. In one place where we'd poured some sand we hid some small lights that shone through it. It's a very dreamlike image. I'm very fond of model landscapes. I tried to do something similar in *The Element of Crime*, but we

48

didn't have time. But at film school we had all the time in the world. We could carry on tinkering as long as we wanted.

How long did the filming itself take?

Not very long. About a week or so, I think. That's not long at all, but then the film is only an hour long. But we did spend a long time preparing it.

The locations in Liberation Pictures *are often very spacious, and the rooms and layouts are also difficult to identify and get an idea of. How did you find and choose the locations, and what sort of qualities were you looking for?*

The locations – perhaps we ought to call them the film's spaces – are also significant for the plot, not least because it was important not to reveal exactly how they were constructed and how they were connected to each other. The film explores these spaces in the way that other films try to explore the psychology of the plot or the central character. And when you explore psychology, you don't start by showing and explaining connections and circumstances; instead you give a series of pieces of the puzzle which eventually give a more complete and clear image. It's not much fun to give a quick overview of any psychology. I tried to use these spaces in a similar way.

But I have to say that the spaces in *Liberation Pictures* lack coherence. They don't exist in reality. They're more embodiments of an idea than realistic locations. The first location, with Leo and the German soldiers, was put together from lots of different rooms. We created a location that existed only for the camera. It gives quite a claustrophobic feeling, although I think 'claustrophobia' is a dull word, or definition, in this instance. But there is a conscious lack of any sort of overview. We chose what the viewer sees and what he can't see. We're compromising the signals.

It's a bit like trying to film Napoleon and his army of 100,000 men. I can do that by showing one soldier who has got separated from the ranks, and then put the sound of marching in the background. You can get an impression of a whole other dimension from a single detail. I think that's the best thing about the opening scene of *Liberation Pictures*. We picked out a few details, which give the impression that we're in a huge labyrinth where a whole mass of different things are happening. It's a bit of a trick really!

So do you remember how you constructed the location?

I've always wanted to work mathematically and symmetrically. We drew up a storyboard and made various plans for how the camera movements would happen, and so on. Then we built up the various elements of the décor in relation to that. I can't really remember – and I'd rather not remember – but I think we were fairly systematic about it.

In classical drama people talk about the unity of plot, time and space, but you don't really bother much with that. There's unity of plot, but unity of time and space is something that you seem to have consciously avoided in your first films.

I don't know how conscious it was. But, to put it another way, I've never been in any doubt as to how things should be expressed and embodied in my films. Not at all. That doesn't mean it's a wholly conscious decision on my part – rather the opposite. Things just had to be the way they were.

The way you deal with space in Liberation Pictures *recurs in* The Element of Crime *and* Europa. *The locations lack clear boundaries, which gives the viewer a sense of unreality and insecurity . . .*

And that *was* a conscious decision, that was what I was trying to convey to the viewer. When I make leaps in time in *The Kingdom*, the intention is the same. There, where I want to open up the unknown and the unsettling and the frightening, it's very important not to show clear spatial connections or how the different locations are connected to one another. That's why I only chose to show parts of the rooms in that.

But in these earlier films, in *Liberation Pictures* and *The Element of Crime*, I wasn't trying to convey a sense of fear, but of disintegration. My old dislike of panoramic shots and tilts also meant that the spaces became more confined and less realistic. If you follow a character walking through an apartment, you can't help seeing the whole apartment. But if you have fixed shots and parallel movement, you limit the scope of vision and therefore also sensory perception of the location.

It's also a narrative technique that can be effective in a story with a lot of suspense.

Of course, the images can compensate for whatever the plot lacks in terms of intrigue.

This sort of technique also allows you to play with illusions and even perceptions of time and surprise the viewer. There's one scene in The Element of Crime, *for instance, where the main character is on his way to a brothel. It's a very long scene, filmed in a long camera shot, where, to begin with, we follow him entering a building. Then we lose him for a while, while the camera goes past some clothes lines and sheets swaying in the wind. And when the camera comes to the end of its run, he's suddenly there again, but facing the wrong direction, so we get the impression that he's in two places at the same time.*

Don't ask me why I did that scene. It's a long time since I saw the film now, several years. But it might be fun to see it again.

One problem is that we decided in advance exactly how a scene should look. Then we'd get to the location and it would turn out to be bloody difficult to get the scene exactly as we'd planned. But the results of that can be interesting as well, when you do your damnedest to achieve your idea no matter what it costs, because you – and the actors – are forced to carry out gestures that aren't always natural in that situation. But they can also be more interesting to look at than if you'd chosen the simplest and most realistic way. If you plan to finish a long scene with a close-up of a pair of legs, for instance, and this then proves impossible unless you put the character on a table. But that creates an absurd situation that I think has its own advantages: suddenly someone's standing on a table without the slightest explanation. So in a choice between the natural and the construct, I've often chosen the latter.

This sort of attitude can infuriate the film team. One technician walked off the set once. We were going to have curtains in Osborne's office in *The Element of Crime*, but it turned out that they couldn't be hung inside the set. I said that it didn't matter; we could hang them outside instead. 'But it's raining outside,' he said. 'Great,' I said. So he left. He couldn't deal with that sort of thinking. Curtains have to hang inside a window. But I think that absurdities like that can only help to enrich a film.

Liberation Pictures was filmed very quickly. One reason for that must have been these extremely long scenes?

Of course, you've experienced that yourself. When everything's been planned and is in place, you get quite a lot of time to do the actual filming. The same thing happened when I was filming *The Kingdom* 2. After a load of short scenes filmed on a hand-held camera, I could allow myself one long scene where we followed the actors through a very long take. And suddenly we'd gone through eight pages of the script. And suddenly the job's done! And the producer ends up swearing!

The strange thing is that most producers are afraid of long takes. They seem to think that they take more time, and even that they cost more, when for the most part it's quite the reverse. A producer counts the number of pages in a script and reckons that the director ought to be able to get through three or four scenes a day. That's according to the conventional view of multiple shots and the division of scenes into long shots, half shots and close-ups. But with long takes you can easily get through eight or ten pages a day.

Yes, and you have the scene changes in the script as soon as you change location. And the producer does his calculations according to the number of locations. But sometimes they can be linked or combined. That happened on *The Kingdom* 2. I had a load of scenes in the doctors' room, for instance, or in the corridor or the wards. Thanks to the steadicam, we could move freely between all these sets and could easily get through ten or twelve scenes in a single take. So what the producer thought would take three days to record, we managed in a morning.

What do the actors think about these long takes?

I think they like them in principle, because they get to act in a context that isn't usually available. In *The Kingdom* there's not a lot that's particularly well defined. In my earlier films everything was much more planned and calculated in advance.

I remember that some of the more complex scenes in *Europa* were extremely demanding for the actors. Particularly one scene with Ernst-Hugo Järegård, when we started the scene with a model train, then continued in a single shot across the model railway, out through the roof, in towards a train that was travelling parallel to the model train, and into one of the carriages where Ernst-Hugo was going to deliver his long monologue. This was all filmed in one single long take without any edits. The camera was on a crane, and the carriage where Ernst-Hugo was standing was shaking and swaying, and it was lit by special lighting effects to make it look as though it was in motion. This meant that Ernst-Hugo had to stand on a little platform one and a half metres off the ground and sway as though he was in the train, at the same time as performing this long speech. And every time he began his speech I'd say, 'Thank you,' because there was always something that had gone wrong in the introduction to the scene. He was absolutely furious in the end, I remember. We did a lot of different takes of that scene, because of course it also happened that when we finally got the chance, Ernst-Hugo muddled his lines. I remember joking with him, when we'd finally got the scene after a day's work, saying: 'I should have gone for Max von Sydow instead!' He wasn't very impressed with our technical arrangements and camera movements. He was only interested in his performance, which he was on the point of losing his grip on. But I got on very well with Ernst-Hugo. We hardly ever argued.

I'm still very proud of that scene. It was terribly complicated, but good fun to do. Originally we were going to do it with back projection, but then the technician who helped us with those scenes suggested that we record the shot for real. I misunderstood him and thought he meant the back-projection. But he didn't. But it did give me the idea of doing the scene without any trickery, by building a train carriage directly linked to the model railway. So we did it, and built a roof with hatches in for the camera to go through. So the camera goes from the model, up through the roof and out towards the train in the studio. And it was surrounded by smoke and specially lit to give the impression that the train was moving. The camera moves along the carriage towards the compartment window, where Ernst-Hugo delivers his monologue. And when he pulls down the blind in the window, the light effects play on the blind, while the carriage carries on rocking.

Do you remember how many times you had to shoot that scene?

It took a whole day, if I remember rightly. But that's what we'd planned for.

A lot of the scenes in Europa *are pure trickery.*

Well, I wouldn't say that exactly . . . They were attempts at Hollywood solutions to problems of scenery. Henning Bahs, Dreyer's old collaborator, was the scenographer on *Europa*, and he had loads of ideas and solutions to the problems the scenes posed. I've actually always wanted to make a film in a single shot, like *Kvindesind*. It would be fun to try once. It would also be a lot easier to do.

There's Hitchcock's Rope, *of course . . .*

Yes, but that was a disappointment, because the film doesn't use the idea for anything special. It would be fun to move freely through a large landscape, and maybe even go indoors as well. Hitchcock confines himself to a small apartment. I don't think that that particular film and that story were best suited to that sort of experiment.

Have you seen Jerzy Skolimovski's film Walkover?

No, I haven't seen that one.

It consists of maybe twenty scenes, about four minutes each, about as long as a camera could take in one shot when the film was made in the mid-1960s. It's about a boxer travelling from one place to another for a boxing match, and a lot of it is filmed with a handheld camera. From what I remember, there's a scene where he gets on a train – and the photographer gets on after him.

There's a brilliant but simple scene in Orson Welles's *Touch of Evil*, where he goes into a lift while the other actor runs down the stairs and stands there waiting for the lift when the doors open.

That was a great idea.

Perhaps we should get back to Liberation Pictures. *What's your attitude to symbols? If we take the beginning of the film, you have a whole series of shots of little birds.*

Those birds have a direct connection to the plot. Leo says later in the film that he can talk to birds. And I thought these close-ups of little birds had such a good, melancholic feel to them. That's about all there is to say about symbols, in my opinion. I've got nothing against symbols, as long as they don't have to be analyzed. Symbols lose their potency if everything has to be explained. If 'the bird' represents something different, it doesn't make it more interesting. The image of a bird represents so much more. I'm against explanations that diminish an experience.

It's worth asking why you have to use symbols at all. Words are just as good. Things can be exactly what they appear to be, and function as symbols at the same time. People often try to simplify things by trying to find hidden symbolic language. Everything is symbolic, you could say. Symbols in films don't interest me much. I'd sooner talk about 'pure greatness'. That appeals much more.

Do you read what critics and other people write about your films?

Yes, I read reviews with my eyes closed, preferably. I look at the title, then shut my eyes so I can't see anything else. I've read some of the analysis that people have done in the realm of film studies. After all, I read film studies myself at university. The sort of essays and analysis they write there are of most interest to the people writing it. I can't remember ever reading any film analysis that made me think, 'Of course, that's what it's all about!' But I think it's excellent that people are trying to reveal a film's significance and complexity and its wealth of expression. But it's nothing that I have any use for.

The main conflict in Liberation Pictures *concerns a betrayal, and betrayal is a recurrent theme in your films . . .*

I'm afraid it is. The story told in *Liberation Pictures* is terrible. But it's true, that's what the film is about – betrayal.

How did the story come about?

I don't remember. I've suppressed that completely. I don't know how it came about that the film dealt with Nazism. I can imagine – thinking about the co-operation we had with the film school – that I was given a basic outline of the story, and then went to Tom (Elling) with it. And that would have suggested a number of locations, which we would later try to tie together in some sort of context. Instead of a normal location he would suggest, for instance, the factory location that we have in the film, and point out all the advantages and possibilities that it offered. That's something I learned from and used in my later films.

Perhaps that's to do with his background as a painter.

Definitely. Certainly his way of seeing things from a different perspective.

In Liberation Pictures, *betrayal by a woman is the decisive dramatic conflict. In* Europa, *betrayal is again a constant theme, and there again it's a woman who stands for the betrayal . . .*

Yes, they're always doing that! I've been betrayed by women myself. And it turned out that my mother was responsible for the greatest betrayal of my life. There's also a literary tradition of treacherous women. Treacherous men are really incredibly banal. With treacherous women the dramatic impact is more apparent. Women are mothers as well, and mothers are people you ought to be able to rely upon. And when you can't trust them, the consequences are that much worse. The tragedy is more obvious when it's women who are treacherous.

The whole film noir genre is based upon portraits of treacherous women.

Yes, the women there are relentlessly and carelessly treacherous. The men are more clearly defined: either they are heroes or villains. But the women are always changing sides.

Liberation Pictures *also reflects gender conflict. At one point Esther (Kirsten Olesen) says: 'You're so useful. I could use you.'*

Yes, well . . . It's so embarrassing to hear the dialogue. Really embarrassing!

Why?

It's so pretentious. And poor. It's what I like least about the film. It's so bad! *The Element of Crime* suffers a bit from the same thing, but not as badly as *Liberation Pictures*. 'I could use you'! No, it's terrible, really terrible! Complete nonsense. Rubbish! I hate everything that's said in that film. It's dreadful. With the possible exception of the story about the birds, because that's quite poetic. The lines aren't so clumsy, and Edward Fleming delivers them very nicely.

Nocturne suffers from exactly the same sort of pretentious dialogue. But thank God I got over that after *Breaking the Waves*. The good thing about *Breaking the Waves* is that the characters speak about the things that the film is about. Everyday things, like how to do things. If Jan is ill, what do I do to make him better? It's nice when the characters talk about the subject of the film, instead of sitting there reflecting about a mass of idiotic ideas. I can't stand that any more.

The soundtrack to *Liberation Pictures* was pretty OK, from what I remember, with the music and sound effects. But that makes the dialogue even worse.

If Liberation Pictures *in part depicts gender conflict, that makes your casting choices more interesting. In the female lead you cast Kirsten Olesen, a professional actress with a lot of experience of both film and theatre. As the male lead you have Edward Fleming, who is mainly a director, and has also been a ballet dancer. In terms of their acting experience, there's already an imbalance in favour of the female character.*

You could say that, purely about the acting. I didn't get on terribly well with Kirsten Olesen. We did *Medea* together later as well. She didn't really understand what it was we were doing, and she didn't bother trying to understand either. That was particularly true of *Medea*, but also with *Liberation Pictures*.

Liberation Pictures was fairly unusual in that it was a film-school movie. Kirsten also had to do some fairly unusual things in the film. She sings one of Brahms' *Lieder* in slow motion and had to dub the song with a speeded-up Mickey Mouse voice. Edward Fleming was gay as well, which gives added support to the women in this particular instance of gender conflict. I think Edward was extremely good in the role. He has a strong, expressive face and was very good at portraying a conflicted German soldier.

Maybe we could return to my first question, which I was going to ask last, about the final shot of Kirsten Olesen in the car. Was the sense of alienation that you achieve by her looking into the camera planned or a complete coincidence?

I can't answer that, but I was pleased with it. Didn't Pasolini end one of his films like that? I was very keen on Pasolini for a while, particularly that trilogy he did towards the end of his career, with *The Arabian Nights* and *The Canterbury Tales*. And *Theorem* was a wonderful film. *Salò* was interesting as well. He was fairly daring with that one, it's a really extreme film. It's a good thing that there have been such colourful characters as Pasolini in film. Film would be a lot poorer without them. Like Fassbinder. It's a good thing that there have been all these gay men.

All these homosexual directors made a huge impression. And created some very powerful films. Both Fassbinder and Pasolini were extremely strong characters, who went considerably further in their art than many others have dared to go. Perhaps I know Fassbinder better thanks to Udo Kier, who has been in a lot of my films and who visits me here every now and then. He lived with Fassbinder for several years. I haven't always been that keen on Fassbinder's films. I admire a lot of them, and I think that *Berlin Alexanderplatz* is a masterpiece. But I respect the way he chose to live his life, as well as his work as an artist. Pasolini has probably meant more to me.

While we're on the subject of homosexuals, I once happened to mention on the radio that I had great respect for homosexuals as directors, as far as their work in films was concerned. But, I said, they were useless as critics. About eighty percent of Danish film critics are homosexual, and there was a huge fuss and debates on the radio. You can't say things like that!

You once described one of your films as 'a heterosexual film'. Why did you do that?

In conjunction with my first trilogy of films I wrote several short manifestos to each film. In one of them I spoke about 'heterosexual film' – I don't remember if it was in conjunction with *Europa*. I think, for me, 'heterosexual' stood for polarization. You can't deny that within contact between men and women, there are two different poles. I was really just trying to make a comparison.

MANIFESTO 1

Everything seems to be all right: film-makers are in an unsullied relationship with their products, possibly a relationship with a hint of routine, but, nonetheless, a good and solid relationship, where everyday problems fill the time more than adequately, so that *they alone* form the content! In other words, an ideal marriage that not even the neighbours could be upset by: no noisy quarrels in the middle of the night . . . no half-naked compromising episodes in the stairwells, but a union between both parties: the film-maker and his 'film-wife', to everyone's satisfaction . . . at peace with themselves . . . but anyway . . . We can all tell when The Great Inertia has arrived!

How has film's previously so stormy marriage shrivelled up into a marriage of convenience? What's happened to these old men? What has corrupted these old masters of sexuality? The answer is simple. Misguided coquetry, a great fear of being uncovered (what does it matter if your libido fades when your wife has already turned her back on you?) . . . have made them betray the thing that once gave this relationship its sense of vitality: *Fascination*!

The film-makers are the only ones to blame for this dull routine. Despotically, they have never given their beloved the chance to grow and develop in their love . . . out of pride they have refused to see the miracle in her eyes . . . and have thereby crushed her . . . and themselves.

These hardened old men must die! We will no longer be satisfied with 'well-meaning films with a humanist message', we want more – of the real thing, fascination, experience – childish and pure, like all real art. We want to get back to the time when love between film-maker and film was young, when you could see the joy of creation in every frame of a film!

We are no longer satisfied with surrogates. We want to see religion on the screen. We want to see 'film-lovers' sparkling with life: improbable, stupid, stubborn, ecstatic, repulsive, monstrous and *not* things that have been tamed or castrated by a moralistic, bitter old film-maker, a dull puritan who praises the intellect-crushing virtues of niceness.

We want to see heterosexual films, made for, about and by men. We want visibility!

Published 3 May 1984 at the Danish première of The Element of Crime.

4

The Element of Crime

SYNOPSIS

For the past thirteen years Fisher, a policeman, has been living in Cairo. He visits a psychiatrist in order to talk, under hypnosis, about his latest job, which he has been working on for the previous two months.

A serial killer is on the loose in Germany. He has assaulted and killed a number of young girls. The murders are being described as the 'lottery murders'. All the girls who have been murdered have been lottery salesgirls. Fisher is working under the authoritarian Commissioner Kramer, but chooses to consult his old teacher, Osborne – now a pensioner, and author of the book The Element of Crime. *Osborne doesn't seem to be in full command of his faculties, but puts Fisher on the trail of a suspect, Harry Grey. Osborne maintains that Grey died in a car chase, but Fisher is convinced that the mysterious and elusive Grey is still alive.*

Fisher embarks on an affair with Kim, a prostitute, who gave birth to Grey's child. Together they set out on the trail of the murderer. Fisher suddenly uncovers a possible pattern to the killings. Six girls have been killed, and with an anticipated seventh murder, the scenes of the crimes would make up the letter H on the map. Fisher attempts to lay a trap for Grey at the possible last crime scene with the help of a young girl who has apparently already been contacted by Grey. While Fisher is waiting for Grey with the girl, he loses an amulet in the shape of a horse's head. Similar amulets have been found beside all the earlier victims. The girl becomes frightened, believing Fisher to be the murderer. When she tries to escape, Fisher suffocates her, thus fulfilling the pattern of the crimes in place of Grey. Fisher escapes, though, because Commissioner

Kramer claims that Osborne, now mentally ill, committed the crimes. Osborne is found hanged.

* * *

About a year after Liberation Pictures *you had the chance to make your first feature-length film,* The Element of Crime . . .

It came about quite by chance. The Film Institute had got a new film consultant, Christian Clausen, who wasn't very popular within the film industry. He had previously been a production assistant. A lot of directors decided not to co-operate with him. So I thought that this could be a chance for an opportunist like me. So I took a walk across the little bridge between the film school and the Film Institute with my project. And Christian Clausen didn't have any other projects. He thought *The Element of Crime* seemed a thoroughly odd film. After pointing out that the abbreviation of 'point of view' ought to be spelt POV and not POW as I had written, he approved it.

I don't think he ever really understood the film. The only thing I remember is him being thrown out of the première in Cannes for not wearing evening dress and turning up in jeans and demanding to be let in. But he gave the film his support, and I'm grateful for that.

The Element of Crime *was produced by Per Holst, a former director himself, and later a very successful producer, of Bille August's* Pelle erobreren *(Pelle the Conqueror) amongst others. How was your collaboration with him?*

The film was originally going to be produced by Gunnar Obel, an extremely colourful producer with whom I've worked a lot since then. But he wanted to cast a couple of popular Danish actors in the leading roles, Ole Ernst and Anne-Marie Max Hansen. He described in very colourful terms how he imagined them fucking on the bonnet of a car in one scene. And the film wouldn't be called *The Element of Crime* but *The Inspector and the Whore.*

Which is the title of the film that never gets made in Epidemic . . .

Exactly. But after a few meetings with Gunnar I said I didn't think we could work together. He also distributed porn films.

7 *The Element of Crime*: Michael Elphick (Fisher) and MeMe Lai (Kim) exchange acting stories with their director, here in the role of the hotel receptionist 'Schmuck of Ages'.

I know. It was Gunnar Obel who distributed my film, Kvindesind, *in Denmark, although perhaps it doesn't fit into that category.*

He used to take his son with him when he was going to buy porn films. His son was maybe nine or ten years old at the time, and he had to sit and watch the films alone if Gunnar got too tired or had to leave the room to go to a lunch appointment. And his son had to decide which films they should buy in. Gunnar is a quite remarkable character, and I liked him a lot. He's a strange mixture of different things. He's from Jutland, and is both a racist and a real charmer. And extremely paranoid. He installed bullet-proof glass at his holiday home because he was afraid of Muslims. I borrowed the house once, and found a loaded pistol under the pillow. He didn't want to live in Copenhagen after they started talking about building a mosque in the city, which never happened in the end. He really did cut an odd figure in the Danish film industry. When I broke off our collaboration he said he'd see to it that I never worked in the Danish film industry again. He had some serious mafia tendencies. But we worked well together after that. He was co-producer on *Europa*. He was a fantastic personality. Peter Aalbæk Jensen, my colleague and producer at Zentropa, does his best to be an equally colourful producer, but he can't match up to Gunnar Obel.

No, Per Holst took over as producer of the film. He's also an odd character. Have you worked with him?

No, only with Nina Crone here in Denmark.

I don't know her, but they're all mad, each in his or her own way. The job must make you mad. Per Holst was quite difficult to understand. He's one of those people you don't know if you can trust, because it's hard to interpret exactly what they're saying. But his great advantage was the boundless enthusiasm that he for some reason showed towards my project. He was always encouraging and supportive and generous with resources. If I asked for five cars for a scene, he would say that we ought to have ten, and helicopters and stuff as well. The film ended up over budget, but he was fine about it.

You chose to film it in English. Why?

To begin with, I think English is a good language for film. All the films I like are in English. And most of the films I don't like are in Danish! *The Element of Crime* can be seen as a sort of latter-day film noir, so English was more suited to the film than Danish. And in the back of my mind I also had an idea that it might get noticed outside Denmark if I filmed it in English. Which happened, of course. There's nothing to say that just because I make films in Denmark I have to make them in Danish.

Was it complicated, filming in English? I mean, did anyone on the production team oppose doing it in English?

Considering that it was being supported by the Danish Film Institute, it wasn't that complicated. 'Well,' they said, 'so you want to film in English. OK, get on with it.' The only thing that was a problem was the agreement between the Institute and the government. In the agreement it says that films have to be filmed in Danish to be considered Danish. So we thought about doing a Danish version and an English version. But we only completed the English version. We took the risk.

But there were problems after the film was finished. The Film Institute withdrew their initial support, so all of a sudden Per Holst was standing there owing the Institute ten million kroner. But at the same time Per Kirkeby, the painter and film-maker, was voted on to the Film Institute's committee. Both Tom Elling and Niels Vørsel knew him. I asked for and was given a long meeting with him, and we fell out badly. I thought that as an old rebel, he would understand and take our side. He later wrote a letter saying that he'd never had such an unpleasant meeting before. He armed himself with all the arguments of the powers that be and defended the entire system. It was quite remarkable. Since then we've got on much better. Our collaboration on *Breaking the Waves*, where he was responsible for the chapter illustrations, was extremely rewarding.

I was regarded with suspicion by all sorts of people in conjunction with *The Element of Crime*. A lot of Danish cultural figures got in touch with me and asked if I was seriously interested in making films. They thought the film was destructive, and questioned both my desire and aptitude for film-making. It was around the time when punk broke through, and punk music was regarded as terribly destructive at the time. People didn't see it as an expression of a fundamental and spontaneous desire to express something.

Making *The Element of Crime* was great fun. All that technology, and all those props – helicopters, and loads of horses. It was also reported later, by animal-welfare activists, that we had all these dead or half-dead horses. But they were horses that were going to be put down anyway and thrown to the lions at the zoo, so why couldn't we use them in our film instead? And if you want to talk about symbols, then people who do harm to horses really are evil. Horses are friendly, useful animals – a working animal that by definition is good. Killing cattle isn't regarded as anything particularly bad, because they're going to end up in an abattoir anyway. But horses are supposed to die of old age.

I've been in touch with Friedrich Gorenstein, who collaborated with Tarkovsky on the script of *Solaris*. He has a theory that

Tarkovsky died because in *Andrei Rublev* he had a horse dropped from a ladder. He was convinced it was a punishment from God.

In conjunction with The Element of Crime *you published your first film manifesto, where you summarize the meaning of film in a single word: 'fascination'.*

Yes, I liked the idea of manifestos, this business of putting things in context. Like the Surrealists' manifesto. I'm very fond of that. And the Communist Manifesto isn't bad either . . . But it's a dangerous word, fascination. I have a terrible habit of falling for certain words at certain points. But I remember the creation of *The Element of Crime* as total fascination. It was incredibly exciting. We were working with a completely professional team for the first time, where a lot of people kept their distance from me and the cameraman, Tom Elling. We were both newcomers, whereas they knew how to make films and how films ought to be made. That caused a few problems to begin with, but we're both extremely stubborn. So in the end we managed to create a film that didn't look like all the others.

Sometimes we had to be devious to get them to do what we wanted. We'd give them the instructions for a scene, and they would light it as they were used to doing. Then we'd say that that wouldn't do at all, that it was completely wrong, and that we'd have to start again from scratch. This was repeated a few times, and a lot of them got furious. We also worked with an electrician who'd worked on *Liberation Pictures* and who had worked on a feature film in the meantime. He kept wanting to use blue strip-lighting. He thought it would be suitable here, bearing in mind the film's basic and recurrent yellow tone. And I thought it was one of the ugliest ideas I could imagine. So I kept getting rid of the bloody light. I remember him getting so angry that he broke the lamp in protest.

Now and then the producer called us in for conciliation meetings. He thought we ought to talk about the problems we were having. A lot of the crew thought we were arguing too stridently about how we saw things.

I'd like to return to the lighting and sound of the film. In my early short film, *Nocturne*, we used monochrome lighting, a strongly filtered light which means that all the nuances in colours disappear. We went to a lighting company and they told us about sodium lamps, which were available in high- and low-pressure versions. One was entirely monochrome, and the other gave slightly greater colour reproduction. So we used that type of lighting on the film instead of the usual floodlights. The only problem with them was that they couldn't tolerate water. Too much moisture and they exploded. This happened again and again, because the film is saturated with water from beginning to end. The broader shots were recorded on black-and-white film and tinted afterwards, because we couldn't cover such large areas with sodium lighting alone, but all the closer shots were recorded using sodium lamps. This also meant that we could put in a blue lamp, or some other colour, and get different lighting effects – in other words, moderate the yellow lighting with other coloured elements. I don't think that sort of experiment had been tried before in Danish cinema before we did *The Element of Crime*. It was a lot of fun, but bloody difficult!

Another good thing was that you could see the effects of the experiment immediately. The sodium lamps suppressed or extinguished all other colours. So we went round the locations in this monochrome light. It was a real 'happening'. It was at its best in the sewers where we installed sodium lamps. And we had Wagner playing during the recordings – the whole film was dubbed later. It was pretty insane.

We would row about in a rubber inflatable through raw sewage. There was a sort of dam-room that we wanted to fill with water. But we only got sewer water, so we had to use hoses to get rid of the shit. I remember that it was pretty much only our old friends from film school who helped out on those scenes. The professionals sat above ground sunbathing the entire time. The assistant director on the film, Åke Sandgren, who was a contemporary of ours at film school, Tom Elling and one other member of the team were down there filming in the shit. It was fantastic. Not many of the locations we used in the film exist any more.

You set up a very suggestive atmosphere in The Element of Crime. *You get a sense of it right at the start, in the scene with the dying horse, for instance, and in the images of Cairo in the prologue.*

Yes, they're unusual, suggestive – amongst other things, you see a parachute hanging outside a window. They were filmed using 8mm, if I remember rightly, and were done by a homosexual architect who died of Aids soon after. Yes, *The Element of Crime* was a bizarre project from beginning to end.

The film is called The Element of Crime, *with the definite article in the title. Was there any particular reason for that?*

The title is linked to a book written by Osborne, one of the central characters in the film. The book is called *The Element of Crime*, and it proposes the thesis that crimes occur in a certain element, a locality that provides a sort of 'centre of infection' for crime, where, like a bacteria, it can grow and spread at a certain temperature and in a certain element – moisture, for instance. In the same way, crime can arise in a certain element, which is represented here by the environment of the film. 'The element of crime' is the force of nature that intrudes upon and somehow invades people's morals.

In the beginning of The Element of Crime *we hear a narrator's voice say: 'Europe has become an obsession for you.'* The Element of Crime *is also the first part of a trilogy about Europe, followed by* Epidemic *and* Europa. *But to a fairly large extent, Europe seems almost synonymous with Germany for you.*

It probably is to a Dane. Because if you look down towards Europe, the first thing you see is Germany. Seen from Denmark, Germany *is* Europe, which is obviously an unfair view. There's also a fairly large country called France, and a boot-shaped country called Italy, but they're more difficult to see from the Danish horizon.

In the opening scene of the film, which can be seen as a sort of prologue, the Egyptian psychiatrist says to the central character, Fisher: 'It's hard for you to remember, to get into that belt of memory,' and he goes on to say that that's why they're going to use hypnosis. You seem to be very interested in supernatural powers like this. In one central scene in Epidemic *a young woman is unexpectedly and bizarrely hypnotized, and in* Europa *Max von Sydow's hypnotic voice leads us through the whole film.*

Yes, I think hypnosis is extremely exciting, and film is itself a medium with a hypnotic effect.

Have you tried being hypnotized yourself?

No, but I've tried suggestion. I'm afraid of letting myself get into hypnosis, because it makes you lose control. But I've tried hypnotizing other people.

Who? Your actors?

Yes, it's happened with a few actors. In *Epidemic* I had a black actor, Michael Gelting, who played a priest. (He also has a small part in *The Kingdom*.) In one scene in the film he has to stand in water almost up to his head. He also has to deliver a long monologue, and he was very worried about forgetting his lines. So I hypnotized him into believing that not only would it be very nice in the water, but that contact with the water would help him remember his lines. And it worked. He calmed down after being hypnotized, and got through the scene without any problems.

You've also pointed out that Dreyer used to hypnotize his actors.

Yes, I heard that from Baard Owe, who played one of the leads in *Gertrud*, and who I worked with on *The Kingdom*. Dreyer used to say Mass in a foreign language, which Baard Owe thought might have been Hebrew. It's quite likely, because Dreyer had learned Hebrew when he was working on the script of his film about Jesus. There's also a very hypnotic atmosphere in *Gertrud*. It's a brilliant film, but it was panned here in Denmark. It's one of my absolute favourites.

'What's the story?' asks the voice at the beginning of The Element of Crime. *So, what's the story? What do you think the film is about?*

The Element of Crime was an attempt to make a modern film noir, but a film noir in colour. I thought it would be terribly difficult, because there was a risk of it being far too coloured. I tried to counteract that in my use of colour and in the choice of locations. The film, after all, is filmed in a Europe that is under the threat of nature. I haven't seen the film for a long time now . . . What's the film about? Well, what can I say? There's an element of intrigue, with a couple of obscure ideas about switches of identity . . .

The film sometimes reminds me, in both style and content, of Orson Welles' Confidential Report, in which Welles plays the unscrupulous business magnate Mr Arkadin, who hires a detective to uncover a big-time swindler, who turns out to be Arkadin himself! The film portrays an investigation that leads to an unexpected solution, and a revelation not wholly unlike what happens in The Element of Crime. *There's a switch of identity, and guilt-transferral similar to what happens in your film.*

I might have seen it, or maybe part of it, but I don't remember it as a particularly noteworthy film. I've got my own Welles favourites. *Touch of Evil* is a fantastic film, a cinematic gem. I often return to it – Tom Elling and I have watched it together several times. I've got a certain weakness for *The Lady from Shanghai* as well, possibly because of all the back projections and tricks with mirrors. The scene in the hall of mirrors is pure genius, which Woody Allen was inspired by in *Manhattan Murder Mystery*. And Rita Hayworth is magnificent in it.

    Citizen Kane has never really appealed in the same way. I can admire it. I think his experiments with deep-focus photography are interesting. But here, and in *The Trial* as well, he comes across as far too plastic. The décor looks plastic and constructed. When Welles tackles Kafka it over-eggs the pudding, because Welles has so much of Kafka in him. When an American tries to be European, I lose interest. I prefer a slab of pure Americana like *The Magnificent Ambersons*. But you talking about *Confidential Report* has reminded me that I must have seen it. I just don't remember the plot.

Confidential Report *is also sprinkled with a collection of extremely bizarre bit parts played by several of Welles' talented actor friends – Akim Tamiroff, Michael Redgrave, Suzanne Flon and others. They aren't wholly dissimilar to the impartial figures who populate your film. I'm thinking of Janos Hersko (the head of the Dramatic Institute in Stockholm) or Stig Larsson (Swedish author and film-*

maker) or Astrid Henning-Jensen (an older director) who make similar 'guest appearances' in The Element of Crime.

I hadn't thought of it in connection to Welles' film, although I know he often had 'ghosts' in small roles in his films.

There are also certain parallels between The Element of Crime *and* Touch of Evil. *They both take place in a nocturnal no-man's-land, a border area between reality and dream – or rather, nightmare. It isn't hard to find points of contact, not least in the final scene, where Lt Quinlan's best friend gets him to reveal his duplicity on a hidden tape-recorder.*

That's true. It's reminiscent of the scenes I shot at the dam at the end of my film. It's not far from here, and recently I've started canoeing. I often go past that dam. It's a very strange structure. I also think it's extremely beautiful, and very effective in *The Element of Crime*. It's got something almost mythological about it. You're quite right, I can see and recognize the parallels between my film and *Touch of Evil*. And if they are there, then I'm glad. I'm happy with that.

Do you remember why you chose Janos Hersko and Astrid Henning-Jensen for The Element of Crime?

We went on an exchange trip to the Dramatic Institute in Stockholm once, where we showed *Liberation Pictures*. I remember that the students only had one question after the screening: why? I talked about 'art for art's sake', which was very unpopular at that point. Then I met Janos. I've always been predisposed to like exotic personalities, and he's certainly one of them! So he appeared in *The Element of Crime*, and later also in *Europa*. I didn't really know Astrid, but she had been a guest lecturer at the film school, and I thought she had a wonderfully expressive face. Behind the evidence that her experiences have left on her face you can still see traces of the little girl.

There's a scene where Janos Hersko, playing the pathologist, says: 'It's a very beautiful corpse. The corpse is impersonal, but it interests the scientist.' You could say that via the film you're acting as a scientist investigating boundaries and emotions.

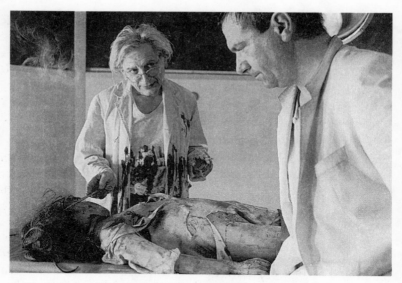

8 *The Element of Crime*: Janos Hersko as the pathologist, with a fresh corpse and Michael Elphick.

That's true, I also feel like a scientist. I have a strong sense of it, that I behave like a scientist, investigating film.

But could you also say that you differ from other scientists by being more conscious of the results your investigations are going to lead to? Researchers in other areas are perhaps less sure of the goal, of what their work will lead to.

A scientist doesn't just throw himself into a project without having a pretty good idea of where it will take him. If he chooses to investigate the cosmos, he can take it for granted that there are going to be comets and planets. A scientific investigation often has its basis in seeking to prove a theory or refute one. It's the same with me. I've allowed my imagination and my fascination for things to direct me, but I've always had a theory about what the end result is going to look like.

But, despite this, have you ever been surprised by the results? For instance when you made The Kingdom, *which was an entirely new style and way of working for you?*

74

Yes, I was mainly surprised that it was so rewarding to change technique.

The other main character in the film, Kramer, says at one point: 'It sometimes helps to study the geography of a crime.' Can you say something about how you created the geography of the film? I understand that the designer, Peter Høimark, found and created a lot of suggestive and expressive locations?

We didn't actually collaborate that closely. He's quite a feverish person. He often got very excited. And film work is often pretty stressful. I think he mostly felt that he had to follow orders, which wasn't always easy. Take the scene where we had to create a pit for victims of foot-and-mouth disease, for instance, where we had to place a corpse under a mass of dead animals. I'd ordered thirty animals for that scene. When I got there, there were two horses, three pigs and a cow that stuck its tongue out at me. I said that that wouldn't do, that we'd ordered thirty animals. But Peter replied that we couldn't afford them because the film was already so expensive. It was one of the most demanding and complicated scenes in the film, a long scene involving a helicopter and a load of divers. I wanted to stop filming because the basic requirements weren't there. We had to cut the animals up to make it look as if there were a lot more of them. I remember that night scene very well indeed, because we only had that night to do it in. The helicopter could only fly until sunset, and the pilot sat there constantly pointing at his watch, while we were working frantically to get everything right. The flares that were supposed to light the scene weren't there, and the person responsible for them came running in at the last minute, just before the sun went down, and got them set up. So we had just enough time for one take, but from what I remember we persuaded the pilot to let us do another one. The result was bloody good in the end.

The preparatory work to find locations was pretty extensive, and we found loads of places we liked. Taking them as our starting point, we rewrote the script where there was a good reason to do so. For instance, we wrote that the hospital was in a cellar. So that was how we decided which locations to use. Most of them worked well, others less so. Then we had the props to furnish the locations with, hammocks and old oil lamps and other crap, to give a certain atmosphere. They were the sort of props that were supposed to suggest a nomadic lifestyle, things that were easy to pack away and move.

Peter Høimark wasn't entirely responsible for the scenography. We had another designer, Jeffrey Nedergaard, who designed a lot of the locations. For example, he was completely responsible for Osborne's office, which was a remarkable set. It was set up in a location with a very high ceiling, divided into different levels with platforms jutting out and so on.

The architecture in that room also contributes a lot to the sense of unreality in many of the locations. The walls are strangely angled and you can't quite get your bearings in it.

We also added an oily patina and other reflective materials to give the impression that nature was taking over. Everything was damp and the walls were dripping. When I saw *Alien3*, it struck me that the environment it was set in was almost exactly like the one we created for *The Element of Crime*. It's interesting that something that was regarded as an avant-garde film ten, twelve years ago can now be linked to a purely commercial product.

The scenography of the film doesn't just consist of environments, of rooms, furniture and props. It also contains people and other living matter.

You could put it like that. You could say that the people aren't used for anything other than part of a fairly comprehensive scenography. There's not a lot of conventional acting in the film.

I don't really mean the central characters, Fisher, Kramer and Osborne, but all the bit parts and extras in the film, all the people wading through water or lying on the ground and so on.

You're right, we did a bit of 'furnishing' with human bodies as well. There's an odd thing about the actor who played Osborne, Esmond Knight. It turned out that he was blind, which none of us had any idea about. We had done the casting in London and knew his sight was bad, but it turned out that he was totally blind. He'd lost his sight during the Second World War and walked with a white stick. So in his scenes someone had to lie on the floor and move his legs when he had to move!

Esmond had been a close friend of Laurence Olivier, who had always given him small parts in his films. A bit like Fassbinder and his actor friends, who could count on getting bit parts in his films. He'd also worked on a lot of Michael Powell's films, and one by Hitchcock. He'd been a pilot, so when you had to tell him where on a plate a piece of food was, if you said 'Five o'clock position' he always put his fork in the right place.

Esmond must have been over seventy when we made the film, and one good thing about him was that he used his handicap to his own advantage. He would put his hands on women's breasts and say: 'Oh, so it's you, dear!' I was walking past his dressing room once, where he was standing with the wardrobe manager, Manon Rasmussen, and I heard him say: 'Oh, Manon, do you know what the word "extrovert" means?' 'No, Esmond, I don't,' she replied. He put his hands on a carefully chosen part of her anatomy and said: 'This is extrovert!' And she let out a shriek. He was great fun! He also had a glass eye which he would take out every now and then and put on the shoulder of some woman in the team, saying: 'I've got my eye on you.'

How did you find the rest of the actors on the film? Most of them must have been new acquaintances to you, because they were mostly foreign.

We cast the film in London. We got hold of a casting director who gave us suggestions of different actors. It was fantastic, because we met about twenty actors a day, who would come to our office in London for interviews. That's how they do it in Britain and a lot of other places. You can't imagine it ever happening in Denmark. Here you contact the actors themselves about a part, and they either accept or they don't. Anything else would be unthinkable. But in London we met loads of actors who were already well known from television and so on.

It turned out that the actor playing the central character, Michael Elphick, had attended the same school as our casting director. He was fairly well known, because he'd played the lead in

9 *The Element of Crime*: Kim (MeMe Lai) and Fisher (Michael Elphick).

a television programme called *Private Schultz*, which was pretty good. We didn't know for a long time whether he would take the part, but of course he did in the end. But I don't think he's particularly proud of his work on *The Element of Crime*, because I've since seen his CV, and it doesn't mention the film. But he was very nice, even if he had certain dependency problems while we were filming. It didn't affect his performance though, rather the reverse. It suited the story and the setting of the film.

And the female lead, MeMe Lai?

We came across her in London as well. We were after an actress with an Asian background. What I remember best about her is that she had had a breast implant to make her bust bigger, which I found out after our first day of filming with her and Michael Elphick. After the take they were both sitting on their own crying. MeMe was crying because she thought her breasts were now far too big, and Michael was crying because he thought he'd been too tough on her in the scene. It was a fairly shocking introduction to my life as a grown-up film director. 'Is this how it works?' I wondered.

One important aspect of writing a script is the characters' names. And the characters in The Element of Crime *have very telling names – Fisher, Harry Grey, and so on.*

I think the name Harry Grey was inspired by some character in Joyce. Niels Vørsel was very fond of *Ulysses* and *Finnegans Wake*. There's a quotation from *Finnegans Wake* in the film: 'Harry me, marry me, bury me, bite me.' I can't remember why we chose the name Fisher for the detective. I think he was called Mesmer in the first draft.

The name Harry Grey has other associations. Harry Lime from The Third Man, *for instance, and Harry Morgan in Hemingway's* To Have and Have Not.

Of course. Osborne's not a bad name either. I've heard that if you want to do a religious reading of the film, Osborne is the Father, Fisher the Son. In which case Harry Grey – H. G. – must be the Holy Ghost. But that's an attempt to rationalize things in hindsight. I never had any thoughts along those lines.

You can also see Fisher as a fisherman trying to haul in his catch.

Yes, it's possible that we intended that sort of association. But mostly we liked being able to give him the nickname Fish.

You mentioned the quotation from Finnegans Wake, *and the film includes a whole host of similar quotes. There's one from Coleridge's 'The Rime of the Ancient Mariner': 'Water, water everywhere and not a drop to drink.'*

Yes, that's mainly there as a joke, because Michael Elphick wanted a drink so badly, but wasn't really after water. Coleridge's poem is about a sailor at sea, surrounded by water he can't drink. In Michael's case, he was surrounded by water, which wasn't what he wanted to drink at all.

But I love that sort of quotation. We had one scene with Osborne, where he was going to quote from an old Danish nursery rhyme, '*Far har køpt den, jeg har døpt den, mor har sytt av tyget.*' It was impossible to quote it in Danish, but it was completely impossible to translate into English. So in the film it became:

'Mom does it, Dad does it and horses have a try.' There's a sexual connotation there, and the fact that horses evidently have trouble.

Some of the quotes were in the script, but some of them were thrown in whenever we found something we thought was fun. When Fisher throws his pistol out of the window, for instance, he shouts: '*Tora, tora, tora*,' which is a reference to an old war film about Pearl Harbor, of course.

Over the years a lot of people have offered different interpretations of The Element of Crime, *and references have been identified, not only to other film-makers like Welles but also to philosophers like Nietzsche and works like T. S. Eliot's 'The Waste Land'. What do you think about these attempts to interpret your film?*

As soon as people come across anything mysterious, they start looking for a way of contextualizing it. But I can't do that for them, because I haven't got the answers myself.

The best bit of *The Element of Crime* was putting together the initial intrigue for the plot and filming the ending. It was pretty scary with that bungee jump at the end of the film. When we made the film, bungee jumping was still an unknown quantity. All we knew was that people had started doing it in Latin America, where it all began.

I'd seen that sort of jump on some documentary when I was younger, and I thought it could be fun to try something similar. Especially from a construction crane like that, looking like some sort of prehistoric creature. One funny detail was that a couple of years after making the film I got a letter from someone offering to jump from the Eiffel Tower, if I was prepared to film it.

Creating the introduction was fun, and also the ending, but the bit in between wasn't as much fun. The plot itself is fairly theoretical. It's about one man, Fisher, pursuing another man, Harry Grey, a criminal, and during this journey he gets so affected by the fate of his quarry that he slowly begins to assume his identity. He assumes 'the element of crime' which governs Harry Grey, and makes it his own. It's an interesting thought, but a stupid idea to base a film on! *The Element of Crime* is more literary in form than cinematic. And in large parts of it the locations and the atmosphere are more interesting than the story. I think the middle section

80

is the least successful, certainly when compared to the beginning and ending.

But somewhere in this central section the female lead asks Fisher: 'Do you believe in good and bad?' Isn't that what a lot of your films are about, the struggle between good and evil?

'Do you believe in good and bad?' . . . I should have made her shut up! But, of course, a lot of my films are about that, and it's also what my life is about, to a large extent. I was brought up not to believe in 'good' and 'evil'. I was brought up to believe that there was an explanation for everything. Absolute extremes like 'good' and 'evil' don't exist – instead, there are things like mistakes and misunderstandings. Religion formed no part in my upbringing, and religion, of course, cherishes concepts like 'good' and 'evil'.

Fisher represents the humanists who've often had central roles in my films. And everything keeps going wrong for them! He's working from the assumption that good and evil don't exist. But they're there all right, in strength. I can't really say whether they're represented by people or nature. The question of good and evil is pretty central really, which is all the more reason why she should have kept her mouth shut.

Fisher's reply is: 'I believe in joy.'

Yes, well. 'Joy'. We laughed when we filmed that, and said: 'Who the hell is Joy?' But, yes, he says, 'I believe in joy,' but at the same time looks deadly serious. There's not the slightest sign of any joy in this film.

What preparations had you done before beginning The Element of Crime? *The form, the style, anything you'd jotted down on paper before you started filming?*

Anything?! We had a storyboard that we followed to the letter, and the film is largely edited according to the sketches we drew up beforehand. There were hardly any changes. We worked a lot with what's called eye scanning, which is judging the visual concentration point of one scene, then making sure that the next scene is edited so that the concentration point is in the same place, so that the eye isn't exposed to too much irritation or doubt about what the important element of a scene is.

At the end of the film Fisher says: 'You can wake me up now.' Do you see the whole film as a dream?

No, the whole film is conjured up with hypnosis. It begins in Cairo, where Fisher is hypnotized by the fat therapist, who has a small monkey on his shoulder. That was probably Tom Elling's idea. He was very fond of cartoons, and he thought that now we were in Egypt, the psychiatrist ought to have a monkey on his shoulder. It was actually a bit of a nuisance. It scampered about trying to bite us whenever it could.

But film as dream, what's your view on that?

There are popular theories that film is closely connected to dreams. But I regard film and dreams as two entirely separate media, if we can call them that. Film is as far from dream as it is from reality. Whether or not film is somewhere between the two is probably a matter of opinion. There are dream sensations that I can easily connect with some films. Charles Laughton's *Night of the Hunter* is one of them, in my opinion. But saying that a film is a dream, I think that's a simplification, an exaggeration.

Eventually The Element of Crime *made it to the Cannes Film Festival, where it was awarded a technical prize. You weren't entirely happy with that.*

Well, I don't know. The jury that awarded the prize was a group of very friendly and pleasant people. I got the same prize for *Europa*, actually. But I thought that *The Element of Crime* was more than a purely technical achievement. So I don't know if I was happy about it or not. One of the members of the jury was Dirk Bogarde, who's supposed to have thought the film was crap. He thought the way we'd made it was atrocious. Which was interesting considering the fact that he'd worked with Fassbinder on his version of Nabokov [*Despair*]. Later on I wanted him to be in *Europa*, but he obviously wasn't interested.

But the screening in Cannes, and launching the film there – and the prize – was quite an achievement for you, which has obviously had significance for your later work.

Of course, because the film was sold to a lot of countries, which meant a lot to me. Gilles Jacob was responsible for the film being considered there, and I've had a good relationship with him since then.

But the recognition that followed the film's success in Cannes, did it help you or were there certain disadvantages to it? I suppose I'm wondering whether you felt under increased pressure, or that people had greater expectations of you as a director now?

Not here in Denmark. No one really took much notice of the prize, although it did mean that they had to treat me with more respect because the film had got such wide distribution abroad. So in that way I suppose it helped me.

Actually, there's a funny story about *The Element of Crime* at Cannes which is also a bit weird. As the film's director I was invited to the festival, but I didn't want to go without Tom Elling and Tómas Gislason. So in order to get them there I exchanged my plane ticket for three second-class train tickets. There was a huge fuss about it, because the Film Institute weren't in the slightest bit interested in sending anyone except the director and a few of the actors.

So there was a press conference, where we were pretty provocative. I happily admit that. A lot of people were irritated at our behaviour, and several people protested against our presence at the festival. A couple of the actors were there as well – Michael Gelting, the black actor, and Esmond Knight. Michael sort of looked after Esmond. They'd stuck together during filming as well, but Esmond didn't have a clue that Michael was black, because he couldn't see him. So on one occasion when Esmond let slip a really racist remark, some sort of typically conservative, stuffy English comment, Michael told him that he was black. But they carried on being good friends.

But the press conference was also attended by the director of the Film Institute at the time, Finn Aabye, and a PR woman, Lizzie Belleche. And Aabye turns to Lizzie and says: 'I can only really respect the black bloke, because he's paid for his own ticket here!' Which was an interesting thing to say considering all the journeys he'd made round the world at the expense of the Film Institute, without achieving much at all for Danish film.

The Element of Crime did arouse a fair bit of attention. The German producer, Bernd Eichinger of Neue Constantin Film, got in touch with me and asked us to stop off at Munich on the way home. This meant that we had to change our train tickets and was going to cost about 500 kroner, which we didn't have. So we went to Finn Aabye and asked if we could borrow the money for the trip, but he categorically refused. 'The Film Institute isn't a loan company.' So we asked Lizzie Belleche and got the same answer. It was interesting, considering that we were on our way to a meeting with a producer who went on to be quite important for Danish film. But that was their attitude towards us. Quite appalling, no matter what they might have thought about us and our film. That's something I shan't forget in a hurry.

Somehow we managed to scrape together the money, I can't remember how. In Munich we were picked up at the station by a huge Mercedes, a 600cc or whatever it's called. And Eichinger offered me a contract immediately. It would have meant a monthly salary, evidently a fairly large amount. But I wouldn't be allowed to make any film unless Eichinger was completely behind the project and giving it his support. It was the sort of contract that stopped Orson Welles making films for years. His producers could never agree on any of his projects. I declined the offer, but said that naturally I wanted to earn enough money to buy a Mercedes like his. At which point he threw his car keys on the table. A nice gesture!

Later on we were invited to see a video trailer of their film *Das Boot*, by Wolfgang Petersen, in the directors' room at the top of the enormous tower housing the film company. The film was a pretty good action film and was about to be released on video. It was a really juicy trailer, with new pop music and magnificent shots of the submarine coming to the surface. It looked incredibly powerful. Then the lights came back on and everyone turned to me, smiling broadly. 'Well, what do you think?' I hesitated at first, not knowing what to say. Then I said, 'I've just got one question. Why did Germany lose the war?' In their eagerness to make an American-style action film, with a swastika-festooned U-boat at its centre, they seemed to have forgotten one troublesome fact. It was worse than Leni Riefenstahl's propagandist pictures. Quite unbelievable.

Nothing came of the idea of collaborating. We've spoken about it at intervals since then. Eichinger wants to film various cartoon strips. That's not really my thing. But he's worked extremely well with Bille August.

After The Element of Crime *you worked on a project for quite a while, but which never got filmed.*

Yes, it was a big project, *The Grand Mal*, which we didn't manage to get production support for, although we'd spent a long time working on it. The film needed nine million kroner, which was a lot of money back then. The head of the Danish Film Institute at the time, Claus Kastholm Jensen, could only offer us five million for the project, because that was the most they were allowed to give. So I said: 'Fine, if you give us grants of five million each for two films, first I'll do a little film for one million, then *The Grand Mal* for nine million.' We actually came to an agreement.

What an idiot I was! First of all I filmed the one-million-kroner film, *Epidemic*. Then there was no money for *The Grand Mal*. I should have made them the other way round, make the expensive one first and the cheap one afterwards. I'd also lost enthusiasm for *The Grand Mal* by then. It's not unusual, when you've been working on a project for a number of years, to lose your interest in it. I also experienced that a bit with *Breaking the Waves*, which I started working on four years before we began filming. Luckily the script had been lying there for most of that time. I rewrote it before we started filming, so it almost felt like a new project.

In retrospect it's probably just as well that *The Grand Mal* never got made, even if I still think it had quite a few good ideas.

Can you say something about the plot of the film?

The title of the film, *The Grand Mal*, was an expression a bit like '*le petit mal*', the little death, in other words the idea that during orgasm you can faint away briefly. It's also a medical term. The film would have been set in Berlin. And it would probably have been very Orson Welles-inspired in character and atmosphere. A

85

lot of the story takes place in a huge casino, and the casino is run by an old, autocratic man who is also involved in criminal activities. At some point the owner of the casino dies in a fire. Or rather, we think he dies. There's a good scene where the young hero comes into the office of the casino. He's the owner's son-in-law, I think I called him Mesmer or something like that. It's night, and the whole scene is very film noir. The office is right next to the Berlin Wall, which was still standing at the time. Suddenly the phone rings, and our hero answers it. On the line is the casino-owner. 'Oh, I thought you were dead,' our man says. 'I'm calling you from the other side,' comes the answer. And then we see the old man standing in a window on the other side of the wall.

It was a very complicated plot, with rival gangs and some sort of mafia war. And I think I made the hero a brain surgeon. He's supposed to carry out an operation to sever the links between the two sides of the brain. It was loaded with symbolism. The action takes place in Berlin, which had just undergone a similar operation when the wall was pulled down. The film was probably overwrought. I did use some of the visual ideas later on in *Europa*. One scene from *The Grand Mal* appeared in *Europa*, the one where they're carrying round the coffin.

Have you used anything else from this project in any of your later films?

The only obvious one is the car chase in *The Kingdom*, which is a remnant of *The Grand Mal*. There were quite a few dangerous car chases like that in it.

Are you sorry that the film never got made?

Well, life isn't really long enough to waste four years on a project that never gets made.

MANIFESTO 2

Everything seems fine. Young men are living in stable relationships with a new generation of films. The birth-control methods which are assumed to have contained the epidemic have only served to make birth control more effective: no unexpected creations, no illegitimate children – the genes are intact. These young men's relationships resemble the endless stream of Grand Balls in a bygone age. There are also those who live together in rooms with no furniture. But their love is growth without soul, replication without any bite. Their 'wildness' lacks discipline and their 'discipline' lacks wildness.

LONG LIVE THE BAGATELLE!

The bagatelle is humble and all-encompassing. It reveals creativity without making a secret of eternity. Its frame is limited but magnanimous, and therefore leaves space for life. EPIDEMIC manifests itself in a well-grounded and serious relationship with these young men, as a bagatelle – because among bagatelles, the masterpieces are easy to count.

Published 17 May 1987 to coincide with the première of Epidemic *at the Cannes Film Festival.*

5

Epidemic

SYNOPSIS

Lars von Trier and the author Niels Vørsel are working on the script to a film with the name The Inspector and the Whore. *Their work is almost ready to be presented to the film consultant at the Danish Film Institute, Claes Kastholm Hansen, but they are horrified to discover that the entire script has been erased from their word-processor. The film consultant has been invited to dinner on Saturday, and they have five days to complete a new script.*

Von Trier and Vørsel begin work on a new story, about a young doctor who works in a future no-man's-land which has been infected by a deadly disease, the plague. The idealistic young doctor sets off on a private crusade to try to cure the victims, unaware that he is transmitting the disease on his journey . . .

A hypnotist and a young woman also come to dinner, and under hypnosis the young woman experiences and relates terrible scenes from the fictional story created by the two script-writers.

* * *

You're a fairly private person, not always very accessible. But you don't seem to mind appearing in your own films every now and again, like in Epidemic, *and* Europa, *where you have an important part as the young Jew. You also appeared – in Dreyer's old jacket – after every episode of* The Kingdom *to offer advice and opinions.*

Epidemic is based entirely on the idea of Niels Vørsel and I playing ourselves in a story about the trials and tribulations of a director and a script-writer in trying to get a film made. So it's more of a private film, you could say. But generally I'm of the opinion that it's important for the creator of a work to show who he is. I've always been very interested in the film-makers who are behind the films I really like. That's why I've read books like *Bergman on Bergman*, because I wanted to get to know the man behind the work. Then, of course, there's the question of whether or not you get to know them better. Maybe you get to know fuck-all, but the man and the work are still intertwined. David Bowie, for instance, is interesting because he is who he is *and* because he composes the music that he does. Similarly, Dreyer was extremely interesting, despite being shy and withdrawn. But that persona has to be seen in relation to his work, the same as with a director like Fassbinder.

I've appeared in the contexts you mention, but at the same time I have to admit that I've got very tired of myself in contexts where I'm supposed to be accessible as some sort of media-figure. I wrote a little announcement to the 'world press' saying that I couldn't and wouldn't be available for interviews in connection with *Breaking the Waves*. I was suffering, rather unexpectedly, from extreme shyness and a sort of self-questioning where I thought it was more important to keep working on my projects than acting as some sort of living advertisement for my films.

After The Element of Crime *and the prize at Cannes you made* Epidemic, *a small, low-budget film costing about one and a half million kroner.*

Yes, the idea was that Niels and I should make it on our own. We were going to do the filming and carry the main roles ourselves. Yes, we were going to do everything! It was great! Just setting the cameras going, walking into shot, and seeing what we could come up with. We filmed in 16mm, in black and white. As I've said, it was great fun.

It's a fun film to watch, too.

Yes, we thought so too. But at the première there weren't many people who saw the humour in it. There weren't that many at the première at all actually, and not that many people saw it afterwards either. But we've showed the film to a few people recently, after *The Kingdom* had been on television, and *now* they all laugh, all the way through. It's strange, and it's made me reflect on what you can let yourself do as a member of an audience. The film can also be seen as some sort of prelude to *The Kingdom*.

Maybe a lot of people were afraid to laugh after they'd seen The Element of Crime . . .

But *The Element of Crime* also contains quite a bit of humour. We often had trouble keeping from laughing when we wrote the script. But in the transformation from script to completed film the humour changed from being fairly superficial to more abstract.

The Element of Crime *can be seen as dystopian, a film with a strong sense of decay, and that atmosphere seemed to muffle the comic episodes.*

There's a similar atmosphere in *Epidemic*, even if the film is lighter in tone than *The Element of Crime*. But it was actually the most difficult film I've done. It was a huge task to do everything myself. Niels and I sweated blood over the technical side of it. We dragged the cameras about, all the lamps, and loaded the film as well as dealing with the sound recording.

Did you learn about film technology at film school – how to use a camera, record sound and so on?

I learned that in my time as an amateur film-maker. But all the scenes of the film within the film were shot by Dreyer's old photographer, Henning Bendtsen.

How did you come to meet him?

He'd been a guest lecturer at the film school, talking about Dreyer and showing films. His black-and-white photography was incredibly beautiful.

The very first episodes of the film within the film – where the main character, the young, idealistic Doctor Mesmer, played by you, is walking about in a basement talking to the other doctors – is a technical tour de force. It's a long, unbroken scene that goes on for seven or eight minutes and has some quite complex scenography.

10 Lars von Trier and Michael Simpson in *Epidemic*.

Yes, we were trying to imitate Dreyer's *Gertrud* a bit. We shot the scene with a battered old 35mm camera. But it's an interesting scene in terms of content as well: bureaucracy and politics in a future society. My mother thought it was very interesting, me bringing up political ideas. That scene is mainly about the eventual form of the government after the anticipated spread of the disease. The government would have to consist of doctors, and they're discussing which doctors ought to take over the various departments. The Department for Culture would obviously have to be closed down! And they offer Mesmer the post of Minister without Portfolio, but only if he gives up the idea of trying to stop the epidemic.

Mesmer's role in the story is very ironic, the idealistic hero trying to cure the disease while at the same time being the one who's spreading infection through the country.

Yes, it's a fairly classic plot that's a bit reminiscent of Polanski's *Dance of the Vampires*, where the hero again is responsible for spreading infection.

Moving on to the framing story, with you and Niels Vørsel and your wives, how much of that was written down and how much was improvised at the time?

The situations weren't improvised, but quite a lot of the dialogue was formulated on the spot. For instance, the episode with Udo Kier, when he's talking about being born during a bombing raid, and about his mother and her death: part of what he said is based on his own life, some is from other people and a bit was made up by Niels and me. There was actually some written dialogue for that scene.

It was interesting to see how that scene was singled out for praise by the critics. A critic like Morten Piil in *Information*, who thought the film was awful, was appalled at how sarcastic and cynical Herr von Trier and Herr Vørsel were towards Udo Kier and his gripping and moving narrative.

So this is a completely acted scene that we wrote for the actor. The scene wasn't even shot in Cologne, which the film makes out. It was shot in my apartment in Copenhagen. In a later scene we took Udo Kier to a lake in a park, where he talks about everyone who died of the phosphorous bombs. That scene was filmed in Brondsholt, because we couldn't afford to go to Cologne and shoot the scene there. But Udo played the scene in a wonderfully sensitive and moving way, walking about and pointing out various streets and talking about which houses had been hit by bombs, and so on.

Before we began filming, at a very early stage, we asked Danmarks Radio if they were interested in buying the film to show on television. They said they were, and were even prepared to buy the film without seeing it. But I didn't think they should do that, so we went back to them when the film was finished. A programming committee of five people saw *Epidemic*, including Morten Piil. After the screening they explained that they'd never been so unanimous about a film. *Epidemic* was the worst film they had ever seen, they said. It was completely incomprehensible, its content was meaningless, and technically it was too deficient to be shown on television.

It's an interesting point of view, but more interesting was the fact that Morten Piil, as well as sitting on that committee, also reviewed the film – twice, both equally negative and spiteful. There were a lot of people who got upset about this project, which made me think quite a bit. The staff on the newspaper, *Information* – which is supposed to be intellectual and left-wing – in particular showed themselves to be extremely suspicious of my earlier films. Only after *The Kingdom* and *Breaking the Waves* did they change their opinion of me and what I do.

Wasn't it also the case that a lot of people in the Danish press were angry at you even while the film was being shot? Epidemic *was a very secret project, and you refused to let journalists have any information about the film.*

I don't know about that . . . I'd been in London a short while before and had come across the notion of the 'closed set'. So we decided to shoot the film behind closed doors, which wasn't exactly difficult, seeing as most of the film was shot in Niels Vørsel's apartment.

But by then the fax machine had made its breakthrough, and we and our production company, Element-film, were sending out constant press announcements via fax. We sent out messages like 'Element-film has consolidated.' We weren't really sure what the word meant, but the newspapers grabbed it and published it as news. It was ridiculously funny. But, above all, this led to a certain amount of suspicion about the project in the press, the same sort of suspicion that *The Element of Crime* had attracted earlier on. Despite the film being selected for the Cannes Film Festival – the first Danish film in competition for many, many years – it was regarded with deep suspicion.

Epidemic also made it to Cannes. It wasn't shown in competition, but in a sidebar series of screenings. The Danish journalists exhibited a certain amount of *schadenfreude*. They regarded the film as a fiasco.

Have you ever felt a victim of good old-fashioned jealousy? 'Don't imagine that you're anything special'?

I don't know . . . I think it was good that I didn't go to Cannes when *Breaking the Waves* was shown there. That time, the press were far more positive. I think it's probably a good idea for me not to appear in connection with my films.

But your relations with the press changed radically with The Kingdom. *That was something that everyone could feel involved in.*

Yes, I think they thought I was meeting the audience halfway on that one, so the critics allowed themselves to approach me. But I remember an interview with Danish television's film editor, Ole Michelsen, in Cannes, in connection with *Epidemic*. We did the interview before the press conference for the film, and one question he asked was: 'How come you can't talk to people?' And I replied that I didn't have a problem with it at all. 'But to me it seems that you have poor communication with your audience,' he replied. Then there was the press conference, where Gabriel Axel sat in, translating my answers into French. It took a long time, an hour or so, and occasionally of course you have to say that you don't have an answer to a particular question. And now and then you say 'Err . . .' or 'Hmm . . .' Ole Michelsen was there with his team, filming the whole press conference. They also filmed people leaving the room.

And what was the result of the television interview? Yep, first you hear someone ask a question, and me saying: 'Err . . . '. And you see some people leave the room. Then another question, and I say: 'I can't answer that.' And you see more people leave. Then comes Michelsen's question: 'How come you can't talk to people?' The whole interview was very tendentious and manipulative. That's something television is really good at, and it seems to happen a lot.

In the press release for Epidemic *you present the three films that were going to make up your trilogy about Europe, although you hadn't yet made* Europa. *You characterize the three films in the following way:* The Element of Crime – *Substance: non-organic,* Epidemic – *Substance: organic, and* Europa – *Substance: conceptual. Is there anything you'd like to say about that?*

That's a horrible question! They were probably just words that Niels Vørsel and I put together in the hope that they might be vaguely inspirational. No, there's a danger that I'm going to get into some sort of fabrication here. It's probably something Niels ought to answer. Shall I give him a call?

(Lars rings and gets hold of Niels Vørsel at once. But he hasn't got an immediate answer. He asks if he can get back to us. Time passes. The following arrives by fax:)

'As far as I remember regarding that definition, which was originally composed in English, is that we hesitated between different words, before settling on the term "substance". Another word we considered was "matter".

'I also remember (and this may in part be due to retrospective rationalisation) that the terms "non-organic", "organic" and "conceptual" were going to be connected to one of the common threads of the trilogy: hypnotism. In *The Element of Crime* the hypnosis theme is present as an obvious element, as theatre, make-believe. In *Epidemic* it becomes a real, documented, organic expression. And in *Europa* – which wasn't even written when this press release was composed – the thought/idea was that the audience would be hypnotised.

'That ought to explain the choice of "substance" over "matter".'

Epidemic *is divided into five chapters, with the chapter headings being the five days during which the action of the film takes place. This has the effect of making it look as though you were trying to anchor the film in some sort of reality. Even if the story is fictional, it gives the impression of being realistic. This happens in a similar way in Hitchcock's* Psycho, *which has titles indicating place (Phoenix, Arizona), date and an exact time for the drama that follows. And here, too, fiction gives the impression of being based on reality.*

Yes, I agree with you there. That was the thinking behind putting those titles into *Epidemic*. I had similar thoughts about *Breaking the Waves*. One reason for us setting the story in the past, in that case the 1970s, was that we wanted to underline the seriousness of the story. If you set a story in another time, it automatically gains more authority. I remember the introduction of *Psycho* very well. The information about what time it was has absolutely no bearing on the story, apart from the idea that we are supposed to think of it as based on reality.

It's odd because it doesn't happen later in the film. You might think that for the sake of continuity as much as realism, Hitchcock would have carried on with the indications of place and time.

But it could only work with the first scene of the film. The typeface giving the information is so tight and controlled that it fits the business environment where *Psycho* starts perfectly. Later, at the Bates motel, we're outside of time. It's still a peculiar tactic, which serves to underline the strength of the story.

(The conversation is interrupted for a while. The telephone rings for the third time in quick succession, and Lars answers it.)

I'm sure Woody Allen had a secretary who took care of phone calls while you were talking to each other in New York. Deep concentration. 'Hold my calls!' I'm never that serious, for some reason. Cosier. Which is why you're going to get a story about *Epidemic . . .*

We were going to do some filming in Germany, Niels and I and a photographer, Kristoffer Nyholm, who's also a director, a very nice bloke I've worked with quite a lot. And we rented a huge Mercedes and drove down to Germany, to Cologne. In the centre of Cologne we couldn't find a place to park, so we drove on to the pavement and left the car there. There were loads of other cars parked on the pavement.

For the scene we needed a pair of nail scissors and a cauliflower, so Niels ran off to buy them. Niels was good at running. Niels and I had very short hair at the time, but Kristoffer had a great head of dark hair and a full beard. He looks fairly Mediterranean, like a gypsy or an Arab. And he goes to the boot of the car to get the 'accumulator belt' [*a belt equipped with large pockets, where a cameraman can keep filters and other equipment*] and puts it on. I was going to be in the scene, so I sat in the car, trying out different pairs of sunglasses.

Niels comes back and sits in the car, with Kristoffer standing on the pavement. Then a young policeman comes over to me. He doesn't say anything, but gestures to me to wind down the window. With a rather shaky hand he shows me his identity card. And I say, 'I'm sorry, I appreciate that we can't park on the pavement. Is there a problem?' 'No,' he replies, 'just keep very calm.' And suddenly I see seven or eight young men in civilian clothing come running towards us with guns in their hands. One of them holds a pistol to my head, and Niels gets hit by another. And Kristoffer was forced to lie down on the bonnet. So there's all these policemen standing there, looking terrified. They were all very young, and they all made sure they had a clear view of the car in case they had to use their guns. I remember reading the day before about how the police had shot a young Yugoslavian because he hadn't stopped when he was asked.

It turned out that we were parked outside the biggest bank in Cologne, right under their video camera. And the Red Army Faction always used big Mercedes when they carried out their attacks. And there I was trying on sunglasses, with Niels running back and forth, and Kristoffer's camera belt looked a bit like a holster. So they must have been glued to the screen watching us and wondering what the hell we were up to. The whole thing was like a parody of a hold-up in a Fassbinder film! But we had to sit there for an hour while they checked out our story. There wasn't anyone who believed us: three Danes making a film in Germany! But in the end they let us drive off – without any sort of apology.

Were you frightened?

Not at all, but I was furious. I was beside myself with rage. It was so absurd. At one point I looked around me on the street. We were on one of the main roads in the centre of Cologne. And I saw that the police had blocked off the street at both ends of the block. We'd also tried to get hold of Niels' brother, who was living in Cologne at the time. But he wasn't home. And suddenly there he was, walking along the street and going past without noticing us. He was too busy watching the police. He'd never seen so many police in one place. I don't know what would have happened if he'd noticed Niels and come up to the car. The slightest unexpected development could have led to anything with those policemen. Kristoffer kept a tight grip on the camera the whole time. He didn't know if he could turn it on or not, so he didn't. If he had we'd have got some great footage!

To return to Epidemic, *and to the well-formulated frame story about you and Niels and the film consultant at the Danish Film Institute, Claes Kastholm Hansen: you and Niels are supposed to give him a completed script, entitled 'The Inspector and the Whore', which has disappeared from the word-processor.*

That much was true. A script of ours did disappear like that. It was a version of *The Grand Mal*. The script that we talk about in *Epidemic* is more like *The Element of Crime*. We discuss what we can do. We can remember the central section and can write that out again. We can probably remember enough of the introduction to rewrite it. But the ending has gone completely. Neither of us can reconstruct it; it was far too complicated. I think Niels says at the beginning of the film: 'How the hell did we start this script?'

Then Claus calls from the USA. That scene was actually filmed in the States, in Atlantic City, by Alexander Groscynski, a cameraman who usually works with Jon Bang Carlsen. We recorded a long scene first, which failed completely because I'd borrowed a camera from Jens Jørgen Thorsen, and was probably some old bit of rubbish. It was a Bolex with three lenses. The problem was that when we wanted to use the wide-angle lens, the other two lenses got into the shot.

The idea of *Epidemic* was that the film consultant, Claus, would be part of the final meal in the film. But he had begun to draw back and didn't want to be part of it. It took quite a few bottles of red wine before we managed to persuade him to join in. But he has quite a few good lines in the film. Especially one, after he's read our script, or rather our sketch for a script (it was only about twelve sides long). And he says, 'At best, it's pathetic.' It took a lot of alcohol to get him with us.

Was he nervous of taking part?

Yes, very nervous. Or rather, unwilling. But he became more willing eventually, which was great.

In the first part of the film, during the first day in the film, you've got an episode at the National Archive, entitled 'Denmark's Memory'.

Niels had worked at the National Archive. That was probably how that bit came about. But I think it's a terribly boring scene. It was a bit half-hearted. The text that the man in the archive has to read about the plague is endless. But on the other side I did get to try out effective lighting in the National Archive. That was one of the sequences I shot, and I was playing with the lighting a bit. That was fun; I hadn't tried doing any lighting before.

In Epidemic *you shift constantly between the actual plot and memory, which is something fairly characteristic of your work. That narrative technique, or narrative structure, was also present in* The Element of Crime.

You're right there. It's more a question of taste than anything – a desire to make the story more mysterious by letting it take place on different levels. Memory, in that sense, is an interesting level. I remember, for instance, films like Alain Resnais' *Providence*, which takes place on a lot of different levels. Perhaps the film has lost some of its power of attraction now, but I remember being impressed by it when I first saw it. It still has a positive impact, and John Gielgud and Dirk Bogarde are both extremely good in it.

You repeat different elements and motifs in your films, motifs which sometimes have an almost hypnotic effect.

Yes, that's true. I can't really answer that, because I don't always do things with a particular purpose in mind. You get an idea, but film is also highly technical. If you were going to paint instead, you have the choice of using a wide brush or a narrow brush, or of scraping the paint, like Munch did, or else you can glaze it, and so on. You can compare that to whether you use flashbacks or 'memory shots' in films, or if you want to stick to a linear narrative instead. You can choose to devote more attention to the locations and the props, or to the actors in the film. You're constantly confronted with choices about the construction of a picture, a complete image.

It's difficult to answer. It would be easier if I worked in just one genre, where everything I did was intended, first and foremost, to scare the audience. In that case it would be easy to choose images and techniques that you know have the capacity to scare people. But the films I've made haven't, as far as I'm aware, had so simple an intention. So it's difficult to give a plain answer as to why the films look the way that they do.

Of course. And the open structure that you give your films allows us to interpret them as we want to.

Yes. Or not to interpret them at all! There's always that option.

During the second day of the film, you and Niels Vørsel carry out an amusing demonstration. You paint a line on a wall, then divide it into sections and give the sections different titles.

That was done as a wink to the cinema dramaturges. It was something that's used all the time at film schools. It's a useful method if you want to structure a film.

Do you think the dramaturgical structures and methods that are taught at film schools can help people create good scripts and films?

I don't think you can create good films merely by slavishly following the methods that are taught. But of course they contain mechanisms and tricks that can work and which can be useful. It's important, for instance, to know which order you're going to introduce your characters in, or how you build a chain of events. That's extremely important if you want to maintain any sort of tension. And I don't just mean for a thriller, but also the sort of tension you get between two people in a drama. It might be a love story, where one partner in a relationship has met someone else and is thinking of leaving their partner. Tension exists in that case in when he or she is thinking of telling their partner the news. Or not telling them. Or draw the process out by disguising what's happening with chocolates and flowers. The dramaturgy is the same as in a detective film. It's still a question of *when* and *how* something is going to happen. In that sort of situation, dramaturgical theories can be useful.

This is something I've learned more and more about. Especially making *The Kingdom*. When and how you insert ideas and ingredients. The whole of American cinematic dramaturgy, which is the basis of all of these theories, is based upon the idea of making everything as dramatic as possible. Emotionally charged – whether it's about buying a box of chocolates or talking to a prospective buyer for your house, anything that can lead up to the inevitable revelation of infidelity and its consequences for those concerned. The more diversions the main characters make, the more tension is created in the audience before the final confrontation and the reactions it's going to provoke. Banal situations, which are nevertheless charged with meaning.

These theories also have their dangers. There was a period in Sweden, in the early to mid-1980s, when producers, and even the consultants at the Film Institute, were completely obsessed with the American dramaturgical model.

A lot of American films follow that model to the letter. I remember when I saw Nora Ephron's *Sleepless in Seattle*, I could predict minute by minute what was going to happen next. When the little boy was going to disappear, and how and when they were going to get him back. Every forward movement in the plot is constructed according to the template. It was incredibly trying because it was so predictable, and therefore incredibly boring. It's more fun to try to bring tension to your film in a rather more refined way, and maybe turn the screw one turn too far.

Looking at the production situation in Denmark, it seems as though people here have been considerably more open to new ideas and experiments than in other places. You were given the chance to make The Element of Crime *and several other films that, in comparison to past productions, were relatively avant-garde or extreme.*

That's true. I think we've had pretty good film laws here in Denmark – very good, from my point of view. I can't imagine being able to make the films I've made in any country other than Denmark. Maybe I could have made them in the Soviet Union before things changed. Tarkovsky could only have made his films in the Soviet Union. But the system here has been perfect for me.

Returning to the scene in Epidemic *with the line on the wall, you write the word 'Drama' two thirds of the way along the horizontal axis and say: 'This is where people will get bored and leave the cinema. We have to have some sort of drama here.' Is that your own discovery, or are you following the American model?*

It's probably in line with the American model. It's usually about two thirds of the way through that they put the turning point, the fulcrum of the plot. That's where the decisive final phase of the film starts. That scene in *Epidemic* was quite fun. We did it in one take. And we ruined one of the walls of Niels' apartment.

Didn't you have enough money to redecorate Niels' apartment? I know the film was shot on a tight budget, but . . .

I'm not sure that we did. The cost of producing *Epidemic* was about a million Danish kroner, and I think we went over that by about 10,000 kroner. The film was so cheap that the director of the Film Institute, Finn Aabye, was so suspicious of the project that we were given our production grant in several small instalments. I think he was concerned that we might put the money in the bank and get the interest on it, something that was forbidden in that situation. If the film had cost twelve million it would probably have been different. A feature film for a million, that's not only unusual but highly suspicious in the eyes of film bureaucrats.

At one point in Epidemic *you say that 'a film ought to be like a stone in your shoe'.*

That's probably because at some point I realized we were making a film that was like a stone in your shoe! So we might as well try to turn that into a virtue. But I probably do think that films ought to be like stones in your shoe. That's not so bad. It would be boring if you made something that people couldn't feel at all.

Then there's a long sequence of you in the bath . . .

Yes . . . where I'm lying there talking about wine. Well, I don't say very much, but we get a visit from a wine expert. And he talks about wine. He was very drunk when we filmed that scene. I can't remember how much wine he'd drunk before we started filming. He was also the sponsor for the whisky we were drinking, and of course it was great seeing all these crates of whisky being carried into Niels' apartment.

But you seem to get on well with water . . .

Right. And as you can see, we've got a jacuzzi in the house. Lying in the bath is something I enjoy a lot.

The third day has the title 'Germany' and begins with a list of German cities, just like Liberation Pictures.

Yes, and you can also note that we wrote them on a little type-writer, a Hermes Baby. And a Hermes Baby has a prominent role in Max Frisch's novel *Homo Faber*, which is one of Niels Vørsel's favourite books. The book was later filmed by Volker Schlöndorff, but the odd thing is that there's no typewriter of that sort in the film, so Niels thought it was fairly worthless.

But in that scene you talk about the central character in the film you're planning, 'the worthy Mesmer'. He's on his way through a plague-ridden Europe, and he ought to meet someone, a theologist, you suggest, which would give you the possibility of ridiculing religion and education, and introduce a bit of humour into all the tragedy. What's your attitude to religion?

I was brought up in a strictly atheist family. Atheism was practically a religion for my parents. So the subject was more or less forbidden at home. I still got interested in religion though. And I have a faith. I converted to Catholicism when I first got married. My former wife, Cæcilia, was Catholic, and my daughters have been christened Catholics. And that's the faith I practise. I pray several times a day.

But now I'm divorced, which is against the rules of the Catholic church. You can separate but you can't remarry if you can't get your previous marriage declared invalid. That's one advantage of having the Pope as God's representative on earth. God, and the concept of God, acquire a more human dimension as a result. Italian society is to a large extent built up on these favours and reciprocal services. I think Catholicism is a very human religion.

You became a Catholic in conjunction with your marriage. But the need for a faith, a religion, must have been there inside you before that?

Of course – the need was there. And I've always had a longing to submit to external authority. But at the same time it's been difficult, because my upbringing was based upon the idea of not setting my faith in these authorities. Thanks to my upbringing I can appreciate the importance of religious freedom. My father, for instance, was a firm opponent of missionary work, because he thought it was a hideous invasion of people's privacy. He always got incredibly annoyed when Jehovah's Witnesses knocked on the door. He also hated collections. At the same time, he worked in the Department of Social Affairs, whose main task was to take care of people and their needs. But he believed that this was the responsibility of politicians, not charities.

You don't only appear in the film as yourself. You also play the main role in the film within the film, Dr Mesmer. What are your thoughts about acting?

I'm not very good at it. I'd like to be a decent actor, but that would take a lot of time. It's a fairly nerve-wracking activity as well, throwing yourself into something you haven't any experience of.

Yet you've still given yourself small parts in several films, like the night porter in The Element of Crime *and the young Jew in* Europa.

They've all been roles of a fairly curious nature, not very sympathetic. Just like Polanski. He preferred to play villains or something similar. And you have to allow yourself a bit of exhibitionism.

You've already spoken about Udo Kier, an actor who's come to appear in most of your films. Did you know him before Epidemic? *And what is it about him as an actor that you like?*

I met Udo Kier at a film festival in Mannheim, where we were showing *The Element of Crime* and where Udo also had a film he'd directed, in which he also had two roles, one as a man, one as a woman. I think it was called *The Last Train to Harrisberg*. Of course, I'd already seen him in a number of Fassbinder films. We got talking during the festival, and Udo said he'd like to be part of one of my forthcoming films. I was already planning *Medea*, and the French actor who was originally going to play Jason, Niels Arestrup, had decided not to do it. So I asked Udo, and he wanted to do it. I asked him if he could ride, which of course he said he could, because he wanted the part. Then he went and took his one and only riding lesson! He was extremely brave. His first scene in *Medea* was pretty daring. He had to ride into a house, pick up a woman and ride out again – the sort of thing that you normally get a stuntman to do. But Udo jumped on to the horse and performed the scene over and over without the slightest difficulty, and without falling off once.

He often seems to embody evil in your films.

Yes, if you've got the sort of face he's got it's quite easy to suffer from that sort of typecasting.

The fifth day, and in the fifth episode of Epidemic *you and Niels invite the film consultant to dinner so that you can present your project. You also invite a hypnotist and his medium.*

He was a very well-known hypnotist, and he'd just got out of prison after serving one and a half years, or something like that. He had been convicted of abusing about fifteen women, whom he'd attacked after hypnotizing them. The verdict may have been influenced by his manner. He appeared very arrogant and unsympathetic, even in front of the jury. So in a way he had sentenced himself in advance. But he was very talented, and he could take hypnosis a long way.

At that time neither Niels nor I knew him very well, and we'd never taken part in a séance. He brought three girls with him, all of them good mediums. After a trial recording with all three, we chose the girl who ended up in the film. After fifteen seconds she was in a trance, and I remember Niels and I looking at each other, suspecting that it was a set-up. It was about as unlikely as it could have been. But just a few minutes later she was crying so inconsolably that her blouse was soaked. I've seen a lot of actresses who could cry to order, but I've never seen anything like that.

From that experience I got the idea of trying to hypnotize the actors. It's an interesting idea, because you're always working with their finite talent as actors. But if they happen to be very talented actors, and you can pair that with the liberation of hypnosis, you could create something remarkable. Werner Herzog has worked with hypnosis a fair bit, but in those instances the participants have been in a trance. I think that with hypnosis you could get an actor to behave completely normally.

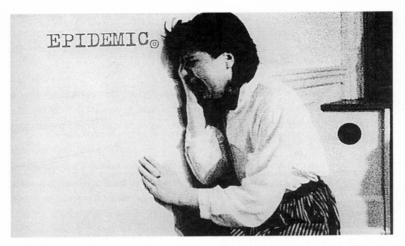

EPIDEMIC©

11 Gitte Lind, the medium. 'She was crying so inconsolably that her blouse was soaked.'

And how would that happen, do you think?

Well, you'd discuss the role and go through the character's lines and then let the hypnotist take over. The main thing is allowing yourself to become the other person. And I think hypnosis could help with that.

But what we see in Epidemic, *when the medium talks about the effects of the plague and reacts to them with uncomfortable intensity, that's real, not acted?*

Exactly. The girl who plays the medium was extremely nervous before the scene. So we suggested that we should do one take when she wasn't under hypnosis. But she refused to do that. So she did the scene under hypnosis. And she was incredibly convincing.

Had you told her the story of the film within the film first?

No, she was given an extract of a book about the great plague of London. And she was told that she was being transported to that time and that situation. In the film you get the impression that she is relating events in the planned film. The hypnotist's line, 'Go into the film. Go into *Epidemic*' was dubbed on later.

107

The line is similar to the narrator's voice in Europa, *encouraging us to sink into the film.*

Right. There's nothing new under the sun . . .

In the film within the film you have Henning Bendtsen, Dreyer's former collaborator, as the cameraman. And you carried on working with him on Europa. *Can you say something about your collaboration?*

It was an interesting collaboration. Henning had certain qualities or secrets that he thought the director shouldn't know about. For example, he always used a soft filter when he took close-ups of the female actors. I had nothing against that. I was just used to the idea from film school that if you were going to use a filter, then it shouldn't be discreet, but that you should use it to get a real filtered effect. That was something we got from Fassbinder and his cameraman, Xaver Schwarzenberger, who were never sparing with their effects.

I remember filming screen tests for the actors in *Europa*, and especially Barbara Sukowa, who had the female lead. Henning put her in front of the camera, and I said: 'Aren't you going to use any lighting?' He replied, 'Of course,' and went off and found a very low-wattage lamp. And he moved it round her face. 'Thanks, now I'm happy,' he said. 'Now I know what I need to know.' That fascinated me. He read her face, then he knew how he was going to film it.

What was his lighting like otherwise?

I really wanted the lighting to look like what he did in Dreyer's *Ordet* or *Gertrud*. He worked with a lot of small light sources and spotlights, which highlighted and divided the set into light and shadow. I once had the idea of making a film about *Gertrud*, where I would contact as many of the people who had been involved in the film as I could. But no one was interested in producing it at the time. Dreyer's a director that only film historians seem to be interested in. The Danish film industry doesn't pay him much attention at all. But for me, as you know, he's meant an enormous amount.

You've said – not without a certain pride – that many Danish crit-
ics pronounced Epidemic *the worst Danish film of all time after its*
première in 1987. In November 1997 it was re-released in Den-
mark. What was the critics' opinion of the film then? Had they
changed their minds at all?

I think so. A little bit, at any rate. I haven't read the reviews. I keep
thinking of Klaus Rifbjerg, the writer who once, many years ago,
reviewed Bergman's *Winter Light* and gave it a terrible review.
Shortly afterwards he wrote a new review, where he said that he'd
misjudged the film, that his initial response was hasty, and that
Winter Light was an important work of art. That's the only time
I've known anyone to behave like that. But it would have to take
someone of Rifbjerg's calibre to be man enough to do it.

6

Medea

SYNOPSIS

Medea is based on Euripides' classical drama, here performed in a slightly archaic but timeless setting. Medea has been abandoned by her husband, Jason, who wants to marry Glauce, daughter of Creon, King of Corinth. King Aegeus offers Medea and her children sanctuary. After the wedding, Glauce refuses to sleep with Jason unless he can persuade Medea to leave the country. Creon visits Medea and orders her to leave. Medea summons Jason, and pretends to agree to his terms. She gives Glauce a bridal crown impregnated with poison. Glauce pricks herself on one of the crown's thorns and dies, as does Creon. Medea hangs both her sons. Jason has now lost everything. Medea leaves the country on King Aegeus's ship.

* * *

You filmed Dreyer's script of Medea, *a film that he never managed to make himself. Do you see this as a tribute or an act of gratitude, or was it because the subject fascinated you?*

The subject didn't fascinate me at all! I've never been interested in classical drama. I was more interested that it was something Dreyer had been involved with.

I'd been commissioned by the television theatre department, and had suggested a version of *Romeo and Juliet*. The newly appointed head of television theatre, Birgitte Price, wasn't very interested in that. But they still wanted me to do something for them. Birgitte Price had herself produced *Medea* for the theatre, the classical version by Euripides, with Kirsten Olesen in the title role. Now she had plans to transfer it to television, but using Dreyer's script. But she wasn't sure about doing it herself, and asked me if I'd like to do it. Otherwise she would probably do it. And I didn't want to let her take care of Dreyer's script! In some way I felt connected to him and his way of seeing *Medea*. So I used his script and lines as a starting point, but changed it so that it took place in a Nordic setting. I'm not sure, but I think Dreyer had planned to film the introduction in Greece. There's a note at the beginning of the script that suggests he wanted to open the film in an amphitheatre. Unfortunately Dreyer never got to make his film. He had a whole load of projects that never got made.

But I wasn't very keen on the film itself. I was most interested in the landscape shots. For the first time I tried to get out into nature and film. It was fun, and Jutland provided a lot of beautiful locations. Before that most of my exterior scenes had been shot at night, where you create your own location with the help of lighting. But here we mostly filmed during the day. There's a bit of a Kurosawa atmosphere here and there in the exterior scenes, I think.

Working with Kirsten Olesen wasn't so good. But I did get Udo Kier as Jason. Originally I was meant to have a French actor in the role, Niels Arestrup, whom I met in Paris and who was unusually unpleasant. He said he was very keen to be involved. But as soon as I left the room I could feel his scornful grin. He'd been lying to my face. He didn't want to be in the film at all. We found that out ten days before we were due to start filming. A lot of Frenchmen are pigs, and I've been involved with several actors who've behaved just like Arestrup.

Why did you want Niels Arestrup in the part? Had you seen him in earlier films?

I can't remember, but he had a Danish background and could still speak a bit of Danish. But that didn't help much. I saw him later in István Szabó's *Meeting Venus* and wasn't entirely convinced of his talent. But he's a very successful theatre actor.

So I called Udo, whom I'd worked with before on *Epidemic*, and asked if he could ride a horse. He joined us, and his participation gave the role a completely different character.

Baard Owe also had an important role. As did Preben Lerdorff-Rye.

Two of Dreyer's old actors . . .

Exactly. We had one scene where Baard Owe had to ride a horse. It was going to be filmed in long-shot. First Udo was going to ride right across the screen, then, on the other side of a river, we see several riders going past Baard Owe. Then Kirsten Olesen comes into shot on our side of the river and has a long dialogue with Baard Owe. At the end we pan from them out across the landscape, where we see a couple of children running, and the camera stops on Preben Lerdorff-Rye, who says: 'Medea, the children have been sent home from school.'

Then the problems began. To begin with, Udo couldn't ride through the shot on our side of the river, so we put him on a ladder carried by two men. They ran along carrying the ladder and Udo, and it looked like he was riding past on a horse. There was trouble on the other side as well, because Baard Owe's horse kept sinking into the mud. But he managed to deal with that. He was evidently an experienced rider. Then there was the dialogue with Kirsten, which went well. But we had to take account of the weather and some sheep that were supposed to be in a certain place. And then those bloody brats . . .

After a lot of preparations, we were finally ready to film the scene at some point during the afternoon. Everything was perfect right up to the panoramic shot that stopped on Preben Lerdorff-Rye. 'I can't remember what I'm meant to say,' he muttered. It wasn't really surprising that he couldn't remember his line after waiting so long.

We shot the scene again and again, and each time I cut Preben's lines a bit more. Towards the end of the day, while the sun was still up but was slowly disappearing, we shot the scene one final time. By then I'd cut his lines to one single word: 'Medea!' It worked in the end. Everything went perfectly and we panned to Preben, while we sat by the monitor with our fingers crossed. 'Now, Preben, now! Let's hear it!' And he said the immortal words: 'What's her bloody name again?' That was pretty memorable – he'd managed to forget the name on the front of the script.

But he was very nice. He'd been a timber merchant earlier in his life. He'd kept that up as well as acting. He also had a few mottoes, such as never having met a director who had said anything that he had found useful. He'd spent his life in film, but I don't think he'd ever listened to anyone. But he was excellent in Dreyer's *The Word*, for instance. Really good.

One advantage of working like that was that we could always reshoot scenes we weren't happy with. We spent a long time recording in Jutland, and when the weather was OK we could just go out and start filming again. The worst part was those bloody Viking ships. We had to get a couple of horses on board, but they got scared when they had to leave *terra firma*. They got nervous if there was any wind at all and the ships rocked. So we had to swap them for smaller horses. We ended up with horses so small that you could hardly see them over the side of the ship. It's odd that the Vikings got about as much as they did if their horses were as nervous as ours.

We had a very good time on location, and I was working with good people. A lot of people had warned me about working with Danmarks Radio. They said the people there were impossible to work with, but it turned out to be the exact opposite. They were incredibly enthusiastic. The producer, Bo Leck Fischer, was very pleasant and talented. And I remember the film team with great joy. It's been sad to see how Danmarks Radio has changed and developed since then. The team spirit seems to have vanished. But it was still there when we made *Medea*.

You open the film with two quotes, saying that this is a personal interpretation and a tribute to the master: 'This film is based on a script by Carl Th. Dreyer and Preben Thomsen from Euripides' drama MEDEA. Carl Th. Dreyer never managed to film his script. This is not an attempt to reconstruct a Dreyer film, but an interpretation of the script, in respect and appreciation, and as such is a tribute to the master.'

Yes, that was the intention, but I don't know how much of a tribute it was in the end.

The film has no title sequence. It just says, 'Medea. Lars von Trier'.

You would introduce some of your later films like that as well, with your name and the title. You want people to get into the film at once . . .

Yes, I've thought about that a lot, how to get into a film. There are a lot of good examples in film history of title sequences that really work, like Hitchcock's *Psycho* for instance, where the titles contribute to the creation of an atmosphere. But I haven't found anyone who could do anything similar to any of my films, and I haven't had any good ideas myself.

The titles act as a sort of trademark.

I don't know if that's a good thing. At film school I once tried to make a long title introduction, a sort of prelude. I've tended to think that it's better to see the fiction first, then get the key to it, see who helped create the fiction. Obviously you could do it the other way round. But when you see a lot of actors' names, you're transported back to reality again and the fiction is subordinate to the names.

As soon as you sit down in a cinema there's a sense of expectation. The first scene of a film is extremely important. It embarrasses me and makes me impatient to see a mass of names on parade before the film has even started. It's better to leave the cinema with the credits rolling at the end.

I agree that the first scene of a film is extremely important, because that's where you set up the plot or the atmosphere. The first image in Medea *shows Kirsten Olesen lying on the shore with the tide coming in and starting to wash over her.*

I don't think that image works.

Why not?

I don't think it was a good solution. The image is a bit dull, and there's no continuity in the camerawork. The idea was for her to hold her breath as the water rose. Then she would get up, then sink into the water again. The idea was absurd. But I imagined that she was holding in all her anger and rage by holding her breath. That enormous rage she feels and carries within her. And that had

nothing to do with Dreyer. It was a purely Trieresque invention –
a prelude.

*But the image has connotations of timelessness – that we're going
to be presented with a timeless story. She's lying there, washed by
the tide, in a wild, deserted, barren landscape.*

Interesting. I hadn't thought of that. But it's clear that we were
introducing the landscape, where the tides are very important.
That's something that fascinated me about the coast of Jutland, the
big differences in the tides. Half the time the shore is completely
dry, and the other half full of water. We found a lot of wonderful
locations, like the one where the horse is racing about. We did a lot
of filming from a helicopter. It was a wonderful location.

The choice of landscape feels very important in Medea. *I think you
found a landscape which, like* Breaking the Waves, *becomes a sort
of emotional extension of the story you're telling.*

I hadn't thought of it like that, but *Medea* is a sort of landscape
film in the same way as *Breaking the Waves*, although in the latter
we inserted several landscape shots which mirror the story fairly
closely. I don't know how I got the idea of filming there, because
I'd never been to the west of Jutland before. I think someone at
Danmarks Radio suggested I take a look at it . . . No, I know! Birgitte Price wanted to make the film in the bunkers along the coast
of west Jutland. I thought it was a terrible idea. I'd never be able to
sit in a bunker and make a film. But during our research someone
said that there were other places – apart from bunkers – that were
exciting and visually suggestive. We also did a lot of filming on
Malø, which you could walk to at low tide.

The cave at the beginning of the film, was that a real place as well?

Yes, it's an old limestone cave close to where we were filming, a
wonderful place.

*Your representations of Kirsten Olesen in the film are very remi-
niscent of Dreyer's way of filming women. At the beginning of the
film you show several close-ups of her hands, and at the end you*

have a lot of close-ups of her face. Her clothes and the little hat she's wearing are reminiscent of both The Passion of Joan of Arc *and* Day of Wrath. *Was that a conscious decision?*

It must have been. The film was supposed to be a bit Dreyerish. I felt very connected to his aesthetic. But a lot of the film is too insubstantial. And we had that model of the Viking castle where Medea lived. I can't stand that sort of thing. It looked terrible. The problem was that the budget didn't let us film the whole thing on location. We came up with several Fellini-style solutions instead. We had Jason and Glauce celebrate their wedding in a tent on a small sandhill. We later set the tent up in the studio and shot the scene there. As soon as we had a set where I felt in control, everything went exactly as it should.

That scene is very sensual. It's also visually ingenious and inventive, with the swaying sheets hung up in the tent, where the shadows of people and dogs sway back and forth.

I'm pretty sick of that scene and the way we did it. It's funny, but there's too much aesthetic there, and not enough result. The woman playing Glauce was a ballet dancer who wasn't very good at expressing herself. It was all a bit sterile. There's no guts in the scene. Dreyer's films aren't very sensual either. They're more virginal. That came through in his script as well, and it all ended up being horribly virginal. We tried loads of different solutions, with back projection and chroma-key, like the scene where they meet each other on the beach with the sand blowing. Here and there I think the film works. The scene where Medea hands over the poisoned crown, for instance.

One very fine scene, in my opinion, is where Medea talks about how empty her life is, and you see the children sleeping in the background. They're filmed in back projection, and as she speaks they get closer and more in focus.

Well, it's OK I suppose . . . I don't feel very happy with the film. I think that's because of all that Viking crap that I never really got a grip on. No matter what you do with things like this, the result is always a sort of fancy-dress party. It's bloody difficult to get it to look at all sensible. I don't think we've really got enough distance to all this Viking business. But when you look at what Kurosawa does with similar things, it looks impressive. Like *The Seven Samurai*. But if you look at the film more closely, you can see that the helmets they're wearing are terribly badly made. Maybe Kurosawa thought his film was insubstantial. But both time and geographic distance have eroded that, so you go along with it.

I don't really notice the historical displacement in Medea. *As I said, I see the film not as a psychological drama set at a certain time, more as a timeless drama about fate.*

That's how I chose to interpret the script, because Dreyer's text didn't really allow for a psychological interpretation. Dreyer's films can't really be classified as psychological dramas. They're not really on that level. The difficulty is that he simplifies and concentrates the dialogue so much. There's nothing there that suggests everyday speech. They're like little captions thrown in here and there. Dreyer was more interested in creating an extremely beautiful and impressive stylization. There's no question of any realistic, psychological acting. The characters are almost icons. It's probably better to describe his films as visual art rather than cinema.

You diverge from Dreyer's script in a way that makes your version considerably more raw, both more primitive and violent. I'm thinking here of the scene where Medea kills her children. It's pretty unpleasant in your version. The mother hangs her children, and her eldest son even helps her kill the younger one. He says, 'I know what you're going to do to us.' He's prepared to let himself be sacrificed.

Yes. Dreyer wanted to give them poison. He thought it was too violent to have them knifed, which is what happens in the classical drama. He thought that was too bloody. He just wanted them to die in their sleep. I chose to make it more dramatic. I think there's more edge to my version as a whole. I thought it was better to hang the children. And more consequential. Either you kill them or you don't. The action ought to be presented as it is. There's no reason to tidy it up and make it look more innocent than it is.

Medea *was made by an unusual method. You filmed it on video ...*

Then we projected the completed film on a screen and filmed it on video again. That was to get away from that video look, which I wasn't keen on.

The colours in the film are very washed out. Was that a result of filming it that way, or did you tone down the colours when you were processing the film as well?

We toned down the colours in the first version in the laboratory, then ran the refilmed version through the lab a second time. We kept toning down the colours more and more. I was very pleased with the first version the developer presented. But then it got a bit less sure because it turned out that he was colour-blind! And we never got the same result again. No, he was actually very good. He lost his job shortly after that. He'd managed to hide the fact that he was colour-blind for all those years.

You broke completely with the tradition of television drama by filming so much of the film in very wide full shots. The landscape dominates the screen in a way that's very unusual in television.

I didn't really think about the fact that it was going to be screened on television when I made it. I've never been very concerned with what's suitable or not where television is concerned, that television is supposed to be a close-up medium, and so on. There's not really that much difference between film and television. If you're sitting in the fourteenth row of a cinema or two metres away from a television set, the experience is the same. The only difference is that your concentration is more vulnerable with television. You can be disturbed by noises in the house or other things going on around you. But you can't really take that into account when you're making a film. You just try to make it as good as possible, then your audience or viewer has to make use of it as best they can. If you start to take account of loads of different factors, your film just ends up as a product.

The reception Medea *got in Denmark was critical, to say the least. Most Danish television critics gave it the thumbs down, and their criticism wasn't just negative, but very hostile.*

Yes, Bettina Heltberg's review in *Politiken* was even quoted on the front page, under the title 'Washed out *Medea*'. I'd never seen a television review on the front page before, so the film really got it in the neck. The only person who defended the film was Christian Braad Thomsen, and strangely enough he was incredibly positive. But he's a bit like that. If he goes for something, he does it without reservation.

What do you think it was that made the television critics so furious?

The problem was that the people reviewing television theatre are neither television critics nor film critics, but theatre critics. They knew *Medea* from the theatre, and they would watch a television theatre production using the principles they would normally apply to a theatrical performance. Nowadays, of course, it's called television drama and not television theatre. But I thought the idea of television theatre was a good one. The idea of filming performances. They didn't have to be filmed on-stage: they might just as well be in a television studio. Bo Widerberg, for instance, did excellent versions of some Tennessee Williams plays.

But *Medea* wasn't television theatre, of course. It was a film that had been recorded on video. And these theatre critics thought that I'd slaughtered one of their classics. Maybe I had. I don't know much about theatre. I just tried to use the material I had to the best effect.

The critics also came to the screening with certain preconceptions and prejudices. Bettina Hellberg arrived quarter of an hour late for the screening at Danmarks Radio, and she sat there laughing out loud at scenes that were meant to be taken very seriously. Her behaviour was pretty appalling.

And that must have affected some of the other critics?

It must have done. You shouldn't be allowed to review something you turn up quarter of an hour late for. It's incredibly arrogant, for God's sake! The old bag should have stayed away.

But you were surprised that Christian Braad Thomsen defended the film?

Yes, I never understood that. I thought that Christian, with his rather Spartan attitude, would have appreciated a film like *Epidemic* more. But he couldn't stand that. He thought it was terrible. But he really liked *Medea*, and was even keener on *Breaking the Waves*. He's read the images and found in them the basic conflicts of drama. Because the story I've tried to tell is there inscribed in the images.

Did you read Euripides' play before you started filming?

Yes, I managed that at least. But I don't like reading plays. Or film scripts. You have to be so alert to pick up what's going on. The whole reason for the drama can be hidden in a couple of words. You have to read very carefully, because otherwise you can miss the whole point.

At one point Medea says, 'There's no greater sorrow than love.' That could almost be the motto of the film.

'There's no greater sorrow than love . . .' Yes, they have enough problems, those two. Dreyer must get the credit for that line. He was the one who distilled Euripides into his version of the play. And I tried to interpret his version as best I could. It's the only time I've filmed something I haven't written. And maybe that was the problem. One solution in cases like that is to follow the text exactly and merely illustrate it. But I have trouble doing that. For me, work also has to involve stimulation and enjoyment. A line like 'There's no greater sorrow than love' is pretty suggestive in itself. But it's not very cinematic, and that means you have to create a cinematic interpretation of it. It's just words. I was trying to create a style, an atmosphere – tableaux, in the spirit of Dreyer. But a few simple words can entice me so much that I think, 'Right, I've got to make a film about that!'

Medea doesn't say much to me these days. It's got some nice scenes, but only on a superficial level. *Medea* was possibly a precursor to *Breaking the Waves* in some of its usage of melodramatic form.

MANIFESTO 3 – I CONFESS!

Everything seems fine: the film director Lars von Trier is a scientist and an artist and a human being. Yet all the same I say that I am a human being, AND an artist, AND a film director.

I am crying as I write this, because I have been so arrogant in my attitude: who am I to think that I can master things and show people the right path? Who am I to think that I can scornfully dismiss other people's life and work? My shame keeps getting worse, because my apology – that I was seduced by the pride of science – falls to the ground like a lie! Certainly it's true that I have tried to intoxicate myself in a cloud of sophistries about the goals of art and the artist's duties, that I have worked out ingenious theories about the anatomy and nature of film, yet – and I am admitting this quite openly – I have never succeeded in suppressing my inner passions with this feeble veil of mist: MY FLESHLY DESIRES!!

Our relationship to film can be described in so many ways, and is explained in myriad different ways: We have to make films with a pedagogical purpose, we can desire to use film as a ship that can carry us off on a voyage of discovery to unknown lands, or we can claim that we want to use film to influence our audience and get it to laugh or cry – and pay. All this can sound perfectly OK, but I still don't think much of it.

There is only ONE excuse for suffering and making other people suffer the hell that the genesis of a film involves: the gratification of the fleshly desires that arise in a fraction of a second, when the cinema's loudspeakers and projector, in tandem, and inexplicably, allow the illusion of movement and light to find their way like an electron leaving its path and thereby generating the light needed to create ONE SINGLE THING: a miraculous blast of LIFE! THIS is the only reward a film-maker gets, the only thing he hopes and longs for. This physical experience when the magic of film takes place and works its way through the body, to a trembling ejaculation . . . NOTHING ELSE! There, now it's written down, which feels good. So forget all the excuses: 'childish fascination' and 'all-encompassing humility', because this is my confession, in black and white: LARS VON TRIER, THE TRUE ONANIST OF THE SILVER SCREEN.

And yet, in *Europa*, the third part of the trilogy, there isn't the least trace of derivative manoeuvring. At last, purity and clarity are achieved! Here there is nothing to hide reality under a suffocating layer of 'art' . . . no trick is too mean, no technique too tawdry, no effect too tasteless.

JUST GIVE ME ONE SINGLE TEAR OR ONE SINGLE DROP OF SWEAT AND I WOULD WILLINGLY EXCHANGE IT FOR ALL THE 'ART' IN THE WORLD.

At last. May God alone judge me for my alchemical attempts to create life from celluloid. But one thing is certain: life outside the cinema can never find its equal, because it is His creation, and therefore divine.

Published 29 December 1990 in conjunction with the première of Europa.

7

Europa

SYNOPSIS

Germany, year zero, shortly after the end of the war in 1945. The young Leo Kessler, who moved with his parents to the USA at the start of the war, returns to the country of his birth. He visits his uncle, who works as a sleeping-car attendant for the railway company, Zentropa. Leo is offered a probationary position as a conductor, and is to be trained by his uncle. During one journey Leo meets Katarina Hartmann, the daughter of Zentropa's owner, Max Hartmann. They fall in love.

Hartmann is under threat from the so-called Werewolves, a Nazi terrorist group who are attacking the occupying powers with bombs and armed attacks. A close friend of Hartmann's, the American Colonel Harris, is working on whitewashing Hartmann's collaboration with the Nazis during the war, and he coerces a young Jew to confirm that Hartmann helped and supported him. Despite this, Hartmann commits suicide shortly afterwards. After her father's funeral, Katarina marries Leo.

One of the Werewolves' leaders, Siggy, tricks Leo into taking two young boys on to the train, where they shoot a newly appointed mayor. When Leo finds out that Katarina has been kidnapped, and that her brother Larry has been shot, he is blackmailed into carrying out one final attack for Siggy – placing a bomb on the train, which is planned to go off when the train passes over a large bridge. Leo carries out the attack, but changes his mind at the last minute. At the same time, he is undergoing a parody of an examination to become a sleeping-car attendant. Leo betrays the Werewolves to the authorities and finds out that Katarina is one of them. He thinks that he has averted the catastrophe,

but the bomb explodes. The train crashes into a river and Leo
drowns.

* * *

Europa *seems to have been a film you spent a long time planning.*
The project was named in connection with Epidemic. *Epidemic*
was made in 1987, but in the brochure for that one it says that you
were going to make a film called Europa *in 1990. That seems*
pretty far-sighted . . .

It was. We'd worked out that we were going to do something that
we called the 'Europe Trilogy'. We thought that was a good name.
And in the trilogy there ought to be a film called *Europa*. Niels
Vørsel was very keen on Kafka's *America*, which is about Europeans
arriving in America. Here we have an American visiting Europe.

But *Europa* was very difficult to get finance for – like all my
films, I suppose, apart from *Epidemic* and *The Idiots*. It's always
taken two, three years before we could start production.

But was it just the idea of a film that you had when you made
Epidemic, *or had you and Niels Vørsel already written the script to*
Europa?

No, probably just the idea, and the title, which we already had.

There have been loads of films about the Second World War and
the period immediately following it. A lot of American and British
films, obviously, but also German, Italian . . . and the wave of
Polish films from the end of the 1950s and the early 1960s. Even in
Denmark there have been films about the war and the Danish
resistance movement. How come you wanted to make a film about
Germany after *the war?*

Because there aren't many films dealing with that period. The defeat
is interesting to deal with, the mechanisms that develop in the after-
math of a defeat. I was inspired to make *Europa* by several other
films, most notably Visconti's *The Damned*, which I thought was a
fantastic film. The idea of the family and how it functions and the
internal relationships and conflicts all stem from that, really.

I also thought it would be interesting to make my main character a sleeping-car attendant, building up his personality around a real job. Niels Vørsel had worked on the German railways, not as a sleeping-car attendant, but as a conductor, so he had inside knowledge of the industry. We had a lot of fun going through all the rules and regulations of the job, and they're correctly cited in the film. A lot of research went into *Europa*. I used to play with a model train set when I was little, so I was fascinated with this world surrounding the sleeping-car attendant. Also this business of a topsy-turvy conception of time, that he had to work at night and sleep during the day in some strange place, then start all over again.

There are a lot of people living very tough lives. It must be difficult to maintain a normal family life, for instance. They live a peculiar life. Some of them are terribly depressed, and they like telling you stories about their terrible existence. Some are incredibly grumpy. The idea of a conductor locking himself in his compartment and getting totally drunk, which happens in the film, actually happened to me on a journey from Paris. He was a young German, bald. Conductors like that are often a bit sloppy, but he was incredibly punctilious. He asked for my ticket and passport and if I wanted breakfast. He was extremely correct and gave a very proper impression. Often you get a bit nervous handing over your passport to a stranger, but with him I didn't feel the least bit concerned.

When he had been through the whole carriage and taken all our orders, he locked himself in his little compartment, and we didn't see any sign of him for the rest of the night. Not until we came to some little town in northern Germany, when two other conductors had to break the door in. And there he was, completely drunk, and they had to carry him out. It was an interesting experience. They have access to quite a bit of drink, although the idea is probably that they give it to the passengers . . .

The Swedish sleeping-car attendants I've come across have been some of the most officious and unfriendly I've ever met, real jobsworths. I remember one trip from Stockholm, when I hadn't managed to get a first-class compartment – a compartment with only two berths for Bente and me. So I bought three tickets for a second-class compartment. We'd be able to be on our own without anyone coming in to take the third berth. Stellan Skarsgård had come with us to the train and helped me speak to the conductor, because we wanted to fold up the middle bunk so that we only had two bunks. But that didn't work, not for Stellan or me. The conductor refused. It was against the rules. I explained that we had paid for all three places, but that didn't make any difference. He couldn't do it. So when we were in the compartment I took out my penknife and cut the strap of the middle bunk. Four and a half seconds and it was done!

That sounds just like Ernst-Hugo Järegård's character in Europa . . .

Yes, exactly! Trains – above all, night trains – offer a lot of interesting and exotic situations. Several peculiar things happened on our trips to Poland in connection with *Europa*. The first time I went to Warsaw we missed the connection in Berlin. We were late arriving, I think. Warsaw is one of the stops on the Berlin–Moscow route, and when we tried to get on the Moscow train it turned out to be full. We went right through the train to the last sleeping car, which looked a total wreck, but still seemed to have a few vacant spaces. So we asked the conductor if there was a spare compartment. He apologized and said that there wasn't, but when we pressed a few dollars into his hand he opened the carriage for us, and it turned out to be completely empty.

We found out later that the carriage was owned by two brothers, and that they had bribed the railway staff to connect it to the train. The brothers used it as a sort of travelling brothel, where passengers who had brought prostitutes on to the train could go along to the last carriage where they could have a quick one. Couples kept turning up during the night. It was bloody cold in there, though. The two brothers hadn't sorted out any heating at all. There was coal in the corridor, so there must have been a stove somewhere. But it didn't help much. It was an incredible experience – an illustration of true liberalization at work.

During our research for *Europa* we looked at Hitler's and Goebbels' private carriages, with their bullet-proof glass and three bathtubs. They all had their own private carriages. It was good fun to research, a sort of boys' adventure – all this business with trains and railways and so on. Like life-size model railways . . .

Trains and journeys are also very cinematic. There are loads of films that are set on trains, of course.

Right, and the railway track looks a lot like a reel of film.

Like the opening sequence of Europa . . .

Exactly.

Europa *is largely about power structures, something you went on to cover in* The Kingdom *and* Breaking the Waves. *Here it's economic power, in* The Kingdom *the doctors' power, and in* Breaking the Waves *religious power. What are your thoughts on the concept of power?*

Well . . . (*A deep sigh.*) I haven't really thought about it. I can't say that I consciously set out to deal with it as a subject, because I don't think like that. And that's odd, because I used to belong to the DKU [*the Danish Communist Youth movement*]. Peter Aalbæk Jensen was also a member. But I've never had any ambitions towards political analysis or analysis of the concept and consequences of power – none at all. What interested me most in *Europa* was how this sort of unformed, shapeless central character ended up in this inflamed situation. *Europa*, as we've said, is the third part of a trilogy, and the film really tells the same story as *The Element of Crime* and *Epidemic*: how an idealist with the best intentions ends up in a catastrophic and intractable situation, and how he's the one who unleashes the catastrophe. There! That's the story.

Katarina Hartmann in *Europa* also illustrates an interesting theory, when she suggests that it's the people who haven't made up their mind, the neutrals, who are the real villains. Looked at in that light, you can see most humanists as villains, because of course, they maintain a neutral position. For them, there's no such thing as pure goodness or evil, whereas people who fight see good in their own cause and evil in their opponents'.

The subject is also discussed in the scene with the priest, where he's talking to Katarina and Leo. The priest says that God is on the side of the combatant in war, and Leo points out that there are two combatants – two adversaries. But the priest still has an answer. He says that God is with those who really want Him to hear them.

Yes, God supports those who believe in their actions, regardless of which side they're on. He's a democratic God, you could say. But Leo can't really understand that.

Erik Mørk was very good as the priest. He managed to speak German very well too, unlike several of the Danish actors.

I'd like to get back to this business of power . . .

Thanks a lot!

Well, I don't want to leave it just yet, because even if Europa *can't be seen as a political film, it still illustrates, in an interesting and intricate way, the connection between different power structures, how economic power allies itself to military and religious power. In that sense the film does have a sort of political content.*

Well of course it bloody does! If the film has got any political content then it's that it adopts an almost anti-American attitude. The story takes place in the American zone, and we get to watch the intrigues that take place there. The film makes quite a lot of insinuations in that direction.

But the film also deals with post-war Germany and the financial corruption, or collaboration, between the Nazis and capitalists during the war, which later led to the fantastic blossoming of the German economy.

Yes, we did a lot of research into that, and spoke to a lot of historians. It turned out that a lot of German businesses were in American hands right through the war. There's an interesting story about the Coca-Cola Company. Before the war the Germans produced Coca-Cola in Germany under licence. But during the war they didn't dare continue making it. They couldn't really drink Coca-Cola while taking cover from American bombs. So they created their own Coca-Cola and called it Fanta. And after the war the Americans bought the brand from the Germans and turned it into an orange drink. You can almost tell from the name that Fanta has German origins.

Can you say a bit more about the research you and Niels Vørsel undertook before you began writing the script for Europa?

Well, we contacted a Danish historian who specialized in German history. Then we did some more research about trains and railway lines. We also kept an eye out for absurd details. But the story is a mixture of fact and complete fantasy. The characters and their internal relationships came first.

Somewhere at the beginning of the film someone working for Zentropa tells Leo: 'Your task is almost mythological.'

That's right! It's the director of the sleeping-car division who says that, and he's the one who at one point says that he met the wife of the legendary inventor of the sleeping car, the one and only Mr Pullman. The director always went around with a bag of sweets in his hand. To begin with we were going to give him chewing gum, but there wasn't any in Germany at the time. So he offers Leo a sweet and says: 'Crush it between your teeth, like it's the custom in your country!' We had fun with that. God, it's ages since I saw *Europa*.

Do you normally go back and watch your old films?

Occasionally. I haven't seen *Europa* for a long time. I saw *Epidemic* again about five years ago. Otherwise I don't really look at them.

Europa *has an almost mythological character right from the start, particularly the scene where they're pulling the locomotive out of the shed. The scene is reminiscent of the pictures of the construction of the pyramids, with slaves dragging enormous blocks of stone.*

Yes. The problem with that scene was that we didn't think they'd be able to pull the engine like that. It turned out to be far too easy. So we had to put the brakes on and add some more weight so that it didn't look too easy.

But why did you want that particular image?

I wanted to show that if there was anything they had a plentiful supply of at that time, it was labour. Even if a large proportion of the male population was dead, there were still a lot of people desperate for work. And there weren't many trains, because they had mostly been damaged or destroyed by the bombing. And it was nice to be able to get in the railway director's long eulogy about the mythological aspect of the business.

We tried to get a fairly humorous tone to the whole script, but the completed film never really showed that humorous lightness of touch. Not like *The Element of Crime*.

But the irony is still there, not least in the dialogue.

Yes, in the oral examination. That's a complete parody.

There's a lot of irony in the portrayal of the main character, Leo, the idealist in the film, not least in the scenes when he meets Katarina and the leader of the Werewolves, Siggy, played by Henning Jensen.

Yes, and Leo's forced to place the bomb on the train, of course. I like that whole sequence of images surrounding the bomb, particularly the shots of Leo lying in the grass looking up at the stars. Those scenes were inspired by Charles Laughton's *Night of the Hunter*, naturally. It was the only film Laughton directed, but it's a fantastic film. A masterpiece. And completely unexpected, particularly its originality and brilliance of form. There were a lot of other scenes that were inspired by Laughton, not least the underwater scenes at the end of *Europa*. The image of Shelley Winters in *Night of the Hunter*, sitting drowned in a car at the bottom of a river, with her hair floating about her into the weeds, gave me the idea for Leo's death in *Europa*.

When did you first see Laughton's film?

I don't remember, but it was a long time ago, and it's a film that stuck in my mind. It really is a unique film, with its theatrical stylization, and there are a lot of references to it in *Europa*. Also to Orson Welles' *The Lady from Shanghai*, with all its back projections.

You don't often see a film where form and style are as integrated as they are in Europa. *It must have been something that you – and Niels Vørsel – planned very carefully during your work on the script. Can you say something about that?*

I certainly had an idea of how I wanted to formulate the shots. But I can't say that I had any comprehensive visual idea. I had the idea of the back projections: that was the most important visual element. And it felt important to do it 'properly' like they used to, not with electronic trickery. I wanted to create different focuses in the shots, so that the actors could go in and out of different realities, like the scenes between Leo and Katarina where one of them is in colour and the other black and white. But my God, was it complicated! You've no idea . . .

There were two scripts for Europa: *a first one that you wrote with Niels Vørsel, then the shooting script that you wrote together with Tómas Gislason. As I understand it, the first one concentrated on the plot, whereas the second gives a more detailed description of the visual side of the film.*

Yes, the second was a visual script, more of a storyboard. And that's where it describes in more detail the connections between the different scenes. They were quite complicated at times. Occasionally we added a bit of text as well. 'Werewolf' and so on, when we superimposed Leo in front of the text.

Or the scene with the bomb, where Leo is racing against time and you see him running with a giant clock in the background.

Yes, we put a lot of emphasis on expressionistic shots like that.

And you mix black and white with colour. But colour only appears very sparingly in the film. Do you remember why you wanted certain scenes – or parts of scenes – to be in colour?

It was more an aesthetic principle. I wanted to film scenes where I could direct the colour. I added colour here and there to highlight certain things.

There are scenes where colour is used to great effect, like when Hartmann commits suicide in his bath and the blood flows out on

12 Jean-Marc Barr as Leo Kessler in one of *Europa*'s sophisticated back-projections.

to the floor. Then there are more everyday scenes of conversation between Leo and Katarina in the train, where you have one of them in colour and the other in black and white. Was there any special reasoning behind that?

I'm sure there was. The scenes were constructed in full shots and close-ups, and also extreme close-ups, and I used colour in these extreme close-ups. The colour gave a tighter, sharper sense to them. The images had to be more readable and give a stronger emotional effect. There was generally an emotional reason for colouring a particular object or person.

Europa could be classified as expressionistic, through its highly economical and studied visual style and narrative technique. I'm not just thinking of the shots that display some sort of visual trickery. Take a scene like the one at the start of the film, where Leo is trying on his uniform. Someone comes in with a big mirror, and suddenly you have three levels of activity in that shot: one with Leo in the mirror, the second his uncle watching him, and the third a person commenting on the scene.

134

There's also a scene where there's a close-up of a bullet that's fallen on to the floor of a train compartment. And behind it you see a limited back projection. The bullet is very close to the camera, but thanks to the back projection you get long focus in the whole shot. We couldn't have achieved that any other way.

Both those visual effects were planned in advance. The advantage of working with a storyboard was that I knew in advance what we could do and what we couldn't manage. There was never a case of trying to solve something on the spot.

An important person in this instance was Peter Aalbæk Jensen, the film's producer. You said earlier that Europa *was a financially risky project, which took a long time to get finance for.* Europa *was your first collaboration with Peter, something that has continued with your later films, and you've set up a production company together, Zentropa. Can you say something about your collaboration?*

We first met in connection with an advert that Peter was producing. He'd just finished the production course at the film school, and we got on well from the start. I asked him if he'd like to help produce *Europa*. As I said, it took a long time to get the finances sorted. Peter went round to all sorts of producers and financiers, and eventually the film ended up with Nordisk Film. But Peter was the film's producer. After *Europa* he said that he'd like to continue producing my films, but with a company of our own. So we set up Zentropa, named after the company in the film. One of the projects we planned together was *Breaking the Waves*, which also took a long time to get made.

Breaking the Waves *was already being planned when you finished* Europa?

Yes, at least in synopsis form. But while we were waiting for *Breaking the Waves* to happen, we produced a whole load of fairly feeble films and bought technical equipment which meant we would be able to produce films ourselves.

You put together a complicated and eccentric ensemble of actors for Europa. *How did you cast the film? Ernst-Hugo Järegård, for instance?*

Peter had seen Ernst-Hugo in a Swedish television series called *Skånska mord* [*Murders in Skåne*]. And I had seen him in other things on television, where he was a sort of dandy, a highly eccentric performer. We contacted him and he came down to Copenhagen. He was very persuasive. He performed a monologue from Strindberg in one of Nordisk Film's studios. And when he'd finished it, he looked at me enquiringly. I remember going out to the toilet, where I got a towel to wipe the table in front of him. He'd soaked it with saliva during the monologue! Ernst-Hugo asked me whether he ought to regard my gesture as positive or negative. 'Definitely positive,' I said.

What is it that you like most of all about Ernst-Hugo Järegård as an actor?

Well, to begin with, we're very similar. He's terrified of most things. He's an interesting and complex character. There's still a small child inside him, but at the same time he's extremely aware, very intelligent. And he expresses great aggression, in his being and his manner. He's so dynamic as a person, which gives him a tremendous edge as an actor. The thing I care for least with Ernst-Hugo is his technique. I've had to struggle with that.

He's definitely got 'star quality'. I've seen him on stage a few times, and I know of few actors who can occupy a stage and capture the audience like Ernst-Hugo can. He's also so easy to read. You can read emotions, experiences, thoughts in his face instantly. Sometimes this can be a bit problematic. Like in *The Kingdom*. If an actor is less expressive, we can interpret his feelings and thoughts in a given scene ourselves. And that was an advantage with a lot of the actors in *The Kingdom*. They could carry and keep secrets. In contrast to some of the other characters, Ernst-Hugo's role required him to give very precise delivery of his lines, purely because his face is so expressive.

The only thing that Ernst-Hugo can't do is play supporting roles. In *Europa*, there's a long scene where he's standing smoking a cigar in the background while Erik Mørk is delivering a monologue in the foreground. It was practically impossible to film when we first tried it. Ernst-Hugo was almost blowing smoke out of his ears out of sheer frustration. He managed to attract attention by a whole range of little tricks. So everyone looks at Ernst-Hugo, while poor Erik Mørk is struggling with his long monologue, which he actually did fantastically well. In the end I managed to subdue Ernst-Hugo somehow, but it was pretty bloody difficult. He can't bear just being on the sidelines.

And the other actors?

I asked Udo Kier if he wanted to be in the film, which he did. And Udo knew Barbara Sukowa and Eddie Constantine, who had both been in several Fassbinder films. I travelled to Switzerland to meet Barbara and persuade her to join us. She's a feminist and had a lot of political objections to the film.

Originally I was considering Gérard Depardieu for the role of Leo. Then the French producers suggested Jean-Marc Barr, and I looked at him in Luc Besson's *The Big Blue*. After seeing it I was hesitant. I thought he seemed too green for the part. But when we'd sorted out the rest of the cast, I realized that he'd be ideal for the part, because he'd be the only normal person in a collection of fairly bestial characters. All the others were like wild animals waiting to pounce on him. Jean-Marc contributed a sort of innocence and naïvety that I liked. He was also extremely pleasant and easy to work with.

Jean-Marc and Barbara Sukowa arrived a week or so before we started filming to go through the script. We had some unbelievable discussions! Barbara had quite a lot of objections and refused to back down. So after three days I thought I was going to have to put my foot down. I told myself that these three days were part of my work, and seen in that way, you could call them three working days. It was my duty as director to listen to her. But on a more human level I have to say that I've never experienced three more wasted days. She got completely furious and screamed and cried, while Jean-Marc looked on speechless. She also wanted Jean-Marc to leave the room, because she thought he was mad. She didn't want him to take part in the conversation.

But after that everything fell into place. Later on I found out that this is a technique Barbara often uses. She drives people to the brink of madness, before she manages to find a sort of equilibrium and balance. Then you can get on with the work without any problems at all.

13 *Europa*: The young Jew (Lars von Trier) whitewashes Max Hartmann
(Jørgen Reenberg) from any collaboration with the Nazis during the war.
Witnesses include Colonel Harris (Eddie Constantine), the family's priest
(Erik Mørk), Max's two children, Larry (Udo Kier) and Katarina (Barbara
Sukowa), and Leo (Jean-Marc Barr).

*Did the actors have any problems with the techniques you used in
the film? The back projections and the long and technically complex shots?*

Obviously it was difficult for them to go in and out in front of back
projections which sometimes represented the actor they were playing opposite, because they were performing dialogue with someone who wasn't there. That was part of the aesthetic concept of the
film. But it certainly wasn't easy for the actors.

And you gave yourself the part of the young Jew . . .

Yes, 'Schmuck of Ages' . . .

Why did you take that part?

I wanted to identify myself as part of the family I thought I belonged to. As I mentioned before, I've always had a certain weakness for all things Jewish. At the same time, it's a portrait of a wretched, faithless Jew who turns up to give false testimony. These 'Reinheitsschein' or whatever they were called actually did exist in Germany after the war. They were commonly known as 'Persilschein', because they were proof that people had been whitewashed. It was a sort of psychological confession with a bit of Catholicism thrown in. The questionnaire had been put together by American psychologists. As long as you hadn't been a member of the SS or something like that, you could emerge from one of these confessions as a worthy citizen again. But it meant being acknowledged by either a member of the resistance or a Jew.

It was obviously in the Americans' interests that the Germans they needed for the continuation of trade and other financial business were regarded as honourable and respectable people.

Yes, that's what we imply in the film.

The fact that you took the part yourself seems to imply that you think it's fun to step out of the shadows and perform ...

No, not really. It was more out of curiosity. In some way I suppose I thought that I belonged in this film, that I ought to be in it somewhere. *Europa* was like my family, the whole film.

Europa *often expresses a certain romanticism in its imagery, particularly in the scenes between Leo and Katarina. They're sometimes reminiscent of Fassbinder, or maybe a director like Douglas Sirk. I'm thinking of the night scene with Leo and Katarina on a bridge, with the snow falling down on them. But there are also other scenes where the expression of feeling is reminiscent of Sirk's elevated realism.*

I've had a certain interest in Sirk, but I've always thought of him as a director on the periphery. His films are largely melodramas, but they never get sentimental. You never sit and cry during a Douglas Sirk film. His work is so stylized that you never get that close to the characters and their interactions. Fassbinder was fascinated by Sirk.

The scene on the bridge in Europa *is in itself romantic, but it's filmed in a way that means that we never have to get out our handkerchiefs.*

That's right, because of the distance imposed by the stylization. I wouldn't have minded if the audience had got their handkerchiefs out, but the scene needed that stylization to fit in with the form and style of the rest of the film. Still, I think it's quite a beautiful scene.

The stylization in the film also creates a strong sense of claustrophobia . . .

That was one of the main reasons for doing it like that. It makes it hard to get your bearings. Figuratively speaking, you're shut in a dark cellar somewhere in Germany throughout the film. I also think that the film manages to capture that feeling of homelessness or rootlessness you get when you travel in a sleeping car. In a hotel room you can make it feel like you're in a domestic setting, but you can never do that in a compartment on a train.

There's also a sense of melancholy in this sort of impermanent lifestyle. I remember that when Niels Vørsel and I were researching *The Grand Mal* in Berlin we took a trip on the underground. The city was still divided at that time. A few of the stations were shut up, but you could still see the signs from before the Second World War. There were a few yellowish lamps left. It was incredibly melancholic. It felt like we were on a ghost train in a funfair. It was a weird experience.

Then the Wall came down while we were filming *Europa*, and I happened to be in Berlin two days after it happened. That was pretty interesting. Up until then, East Germany had always seemed to be the most depressing place on the planet.

I was once at a film festival in Berlin, and I turned up wearing a very thin suit. I was travelling home the same night and had rented a small BMW. Suddenly a whole load of snow fell, and the car got stuck. The first time this happened was in West Berlin, but I managed to get the car going again and carried on along the transit road through East Berlin and East Germany. I suddenly came upon a police roadblock and braked sharply. But the road was icy, so the car spun and ended up in a large snowdrift. The police came over and gave me a fine, because my manoeuvre was regarded as very dangerous. It was a pretty hefty fine, but they were so 'amenable' that I was able to pay in West German Marks.

So there I was in this snowstorm in my thin suit. I had no chance of getting the car free again on my own. So I asked if there was an emergency telephone I could use. Of course, that would be fine. But it wasn't something these policemen would recommend, because it would take at least three days before a truck got out to me. 'What should I do?' I asked. 'Can I get to a farm near by and shelter there?' 'Of course,' they said, but if I did that they'd have to arrest me, because I only had a transit visa. My dilemma wasn't their problem – fortunately for them. So I sat in the car and waited, while all the Mercedes rushed past on the autobahn.

It was snowing heavily and was getting darker. In the end I went to the police and asked if they had a snow shovel. Yes, they happened to have a little spade that I could borrow. So I lay there in my thin suit for about an hour digging the car out of the snowdrift. I was frozen solid, and I also had to try to push the car out of the snowdrift on my own. With no help. No, that's not quite true. One of the policemen agreed to help me, if I was prepared to sign a statement that a Lada was a better car than a BMW! But I refused. All of a sudden I was struck by a sort of pride, not national but western.

There's another story about *Europa*. Actually, there are loads of stories about that film . . .

We were filming in Poland, in Wroclaw and around Szczecin, and the time we spent there was awful. The work was tough and the surrounding area was poor, and it was difficult to get food. When we finished shooting, Peter Aalbæk was there as well, and we set off for home. We were going to drive back through East Germany. I was driving a camper van, and Peter was driving a car with a caravan on the back. We had all the props for the film in there. We had a voucher listing everything we'd brought into the country and would be taking out again. We got to the border with East Germany, and everything was fine. But four miles from the border I looked in the mirror and saw Peter's car go into a spin, and the caravan went into a ditch. The connection had come apart.

We were due to catch the ferry home fairly soon, a couple of hours later maybe. In the middle of this deserted motorway, we began madly pulling the props out of the caravan and throwing them into my camper van. The props included two coffins with corpses. We hadn't got enough room for the coffins, so we threw them into the ditch. There were also twenty machine guns. If an East German police patrol had come past, they wouldn't have believed their eyes. When we'd finished loading up, we drove like idiots and reached the ferry just in time. And I said to Peter: 'Sod the voucher, let's just drive on.' And he said, 'Are you mad? We could get put away for years for trying to take weapons out of East Germany.' But we put a blanket over them and went through customs. And they hardly looked in the back, although they must have seen that there were things under the blanket. Peter was so nervous that he started over-revving his engine. But the customs people came and helped us to get on board!

Did you film all the exterior shots in Poland?

Yes, everything. It was pretty tough going. It was extremely cold, and there were clouds of smog over the countryside. The first day of shooting, we had three of the producers there: Peter and the producer from Nordisk Film, and the French producer. After three hours at −18°C they went into the camper van and went to sleep. Then they went home, although they'd planned to stay in Poland for the whole shoot. They obviously didn't think it was much fun there either.

How long were you in Poland?

About two months, then shooting the interior shots in Denmark took about the same again. We filmed most of the backgrounds of the film in Poland, a lot of the material we used later in the back projections. We also had loads of extras there. Everything was terribly cheap there. We had a meal before filming to bribe the Polish officials: starters, main course, dessert and everything. It cost about 35 kroner per head.

On Europa *you worked with two very experienced old Danish film-makers, the cameraman Henning Bendtsen and the scenographer Henning Bahs. What did you think of working together, and how do you think they saw you as a director?*

I think they enjoyed working together. I think Henning Bendtsen regarded *Europa* as a big, important piece of work. It was difficult to film, not least because so much of the story takes place at night, which meant a lot of complicated lighting. Henning wasn't in Poland with us. We worked with a Polish cameraman there, someone who's worked with Wajda and Kieślowski, Edward Klosinski. We often ended up arguing. He wasn't used to sticking so closely to a storyboard as we were doing. He wanted to find his own locations and compose his own shots. He was fairly critical towards us and wasn't happy with the way we worked.

I worked very closely with Henning Bahs, who had put together some very expressive scenography. He also had a lot of experience. One of the main things he did was construct a railway carriage that was mounted on springs so that it would shake in a realistic way. The camera was hung from the ceiling of the carriage and was independent of the shaking. It was a very smart construction.

It sounds like you were often a hostage to events in Poland and East Germany. You could say that Leo in Europa *is hostage to the plot.*

I can identify strongly with the humanist in the story, which is what Leo is, of course. And I feel a lot of sympathy towards humanists and all the humiliations they have to suffer. At the same time, I don't think it's unreasonable that they have to suffer the things that they have to go through.

Why not?

Because humanism is based on a fairly naïve concept. I still think humanism is a good basis for possible co-operation here on Earth. But there's a lot of fiction in humanism. The idea that people will take the trouble to co-operate and work for the good of their fellow man is deeply naïve. That's probably what *Europa* was trying to express.

The film ends with Leo's death scene. He drowns after unwittingly contributing to the attack on the train and the bombing of the bridge. It's simultaneously a very grim and poetic scene. You don't often see a character's death throes on film. The history of film may

143

be littered with death scenes, but they're either very violent and quick, or romantic and drawn out.

The narrator's voice also provides a commentary on his death, predicting it and verifying it. That was to tie in with the theme of hypnosis that the voice projects at the start of the film. We were very fortunate with that scene, because Jean-Marc was able to hold his breath for an extremely long time. He'd had a lot of training for *The Big Blue*. We shot the scene in a swimming pool, and I could watch the progress with diving equipment. It was fun making *Europa* with all the constructions and special effects that it required, but I don't know if it's as much fun to watch. I'm pretty fed up of it, to be honest.

Why? Because you can see through the construction too well?

I think it was too polished. It lacks what I would call 'natural mistakes', the sort of thing that's more obvious in *Breaking the Waves*. They're very difficult to put together. *Europa* is far too insipid and vacuous in that respect.

8

The Kingdom

SYNOPSIS

The Kingdom Hospital in Copenhagen is the scene of a succession of strange and inexplicable events. Senior Consultant Moesgaard, head of neurosurgery, has his hands full, mostly with his Swedish import, the neurosurgeon Stig G. Helmer, who has just carried out a less than successful brain operation on a little girl, Mona, and who is now doing all he can to defend himself and destroy the evidence, a narcotics report that the maternal anaesthetist Rigmor Mortensen has produced. Rigmor is very attracted to the Swedish doctor, and is fascinated by voodoo and Haiti. Professor Bondo is obsessed by his studies into cancer, and junior doctor Krogshøj is upset. His partner, Judith, is pregnant as a result of an earlier relationship, and her circumference is rapidly expanding.

Much attention is paid to Fru Drusse, a perpetually recurring patient, and her attempts to solve the mystery surrounding a little girl, Mary, who has been haunting the hospital lift. Mary died in 1919, the victim of an experiment carried out by her father, Dr Aage Krüger. At the same time, Operation Morning Breeze, Dr Moesgaard's well-intentioned attempt to improve communication with patients, has caught the critical eye of the Health Minister. Stig Helmer abandons Rigmor and travels to Haiti on his own, while Judith gives birth to a boy bearing the unmistakable features of Dr Krüger.

* * *

With The Kingdom, *you began experimenting with a more open, freer form of film, something you would develop in* Breaking the

Waves. *How did you arrive at this way of working? And what do you think are its advantages over the stricter, more formally conscious way that you worked before? (This is obviously also a formally conscious way of working, even if it looks as if you don't care about form.)*

Mainly it means that I can work a lot faster. This way of filming is also much more intuitive. I think that's quite an important quality. The speed, and the more intensive contact with everyone else, both in front of and behind the camera, have meant that I enjoy my work more. I can probably say that it gave me pleasure in my work again.

The idea of the form came from Tómas Gislason, who suggested I watch the American television series *Homicide*, created by Barry Levinson. The series had been a revelation to him. The first episodes of the series were extremely interesting in terms of form. The form has been modified somewhat since then. The episodes became more comfortable, without the violent shifts produced in the editing and the earlier disregard for the unwritten rules governing direction. I think the producers thought the programme had become too out of control.

It was liberating to see those first episodes of *Homicide*, and they were the main inspiration for *The Kingdom* and its style. I consciously changed the actors' position on the set between each take, so that they came to perform the same lines from different positions in the room. When I came to edit the scenes, you got the impression that I had far more filmed material than was actually the case. I went on to use that technique in *Breaking the Waves*, where it was even more effective, because it was recorded in CinemaScope. But the technique itself gives the film a rare authenticity and authority.

How did you get the idea for the plot – or plots – of The Kingdom?

Well, we had that bloody production company, Zentropa, and for that to work, we had to make films. We were in touch with Danmarks Radio, who had asked me if I was interested in doing a small television series for them. I said that I wasn't interested in it out of principle. I don't do small things. If I'm going to do something, then it has to be big and on a grand scale! (*Laughter.*)

I'd wanted to do a ghost story for a long time. Not a horror film, but a story with ghosts. I always liked double exposures, with transparent figures wandering around on the screen. You don't need any other special effects, just tricks done right in front of the camera. Then I came to think of a French television series, *Bellefegour, the Phantom of the Louvre*, which I had seen as a child. It was about a ghost who lived in the Louvre. It was extremely frightening and I used to watch it with my heart in my mouth. It was probably the first television series I ever saw.

The advantage of setting a story like that in the Louvre was that the museum was so labyrinthine and difficult to get a grip on. So I started wondering if I could think of a similar setting. And I ended up with a hospital, with all its wards and corridors and underground passageways. Then I started thinking about Rigshospitalet (the Kingdom Hospital) in Copenhagen. I found out from a doctor who worked there that the hospital was called 'Riget' (The Kingdom) by the people who worked there. I thought it was a pretty blasphemous nickname, but perfect as the title of a film.

It turned out to be a good cocktail, because the hospital setting also has a lot of inherent value as the setting for a soap opera. People die and babies are born. Doctors in white coats casting glances at beautiful nurses above their surgical masks. And all the aspects surrounding medical science as well.

You wrote The Kingdom *together with Niels Vørsel. But occasionally you write the scripts to your films on your own. In which circumstances do you prefer writing together with someone – usually Niels – and when do you prefer to write alone?*

It depends what you think you're good at, what limitations you think you have. Niels is good at satire and more intricate plot constructions. But emotional and sentimental stories are definitely not for Herr Vørsel. So I've ended up doing them myself.

How did you organize the huge number of characters and events contained in The Kingdom?

We came up with something that I think was pretty smart. We took a person we both knew as the model for a fictional character in the film. In that way we could easily characterize him or her and work out his or her story. Both Niels and I knew these people, so we never needed to discuss much about them.

Fru Drusse, on the other hand, is inspired by a character in a novel by Hans Scherfig, called *Idealister* (*The Idealists*). There she's a half-mad vegetarian who writes recipes for a health magazine. Niels is a great admirer of Scherfig, and I also enjoy reading him.

We wrote the first four episodes pretty quickly. And we drew up a mass of different schemes of their activities and internal relationships. In *The Kingdom* 2 the gallery of characters and intrigues expanded, and the whole thing got a bit boring. (*Lars yawns.*)

What became more boring? Work on the script or the film itself?

The film. It was fun writing the second part, but not as much fun to film. I'd never done the same thing a second time before. It isn't very inspiring – not for me anyway. The problem with continuing the story is that all the characters are already there – and the actors suddenly have completely different opinions about their characters. Now they had been able to look at the first part and see their performances critically. I have nothing against actors having ideas of their own, but it's boring when you realize you're stuck in a set pattern.

Now we've got to write a third, concluding part. But I think we're going to have to come up with a new and different strategy for this one. I think the concluding episode is going to have a completely different character.

Can you say anything else about how you constructed the fairly complicated plots and set up the conflicts between the different characters?

We wrote the script according to the classic model. Neither Niels nor I had written a television series before, so we worked according to what I would characterize as dramaturgically correct methods. I'm no expert on dramaturgy, but every time we left an event, or an element of plot, we did it with a question mark leading on to the next character. The best bit was weaving the stories together and leading them in different directions. We're going to have a hell of a job with the third part. We've got umpteen different threads

148

all woven together and we've got to untangle them somehow. It would probably be easiest to put a bomb under the hospital and blow it up.

How did you cast the various roles? You haven't just got some of Denmark's most popular actors, but also some of the most renowned and experienced names within Danish film and theatre.

The most important thing when we chose them was whether or not they had been in *Matador* [*one of the best-loved and longest-running series on Danish television*]. But most Danish actors have been in it. And then there was Ernst-Hugo Järegård, whom I'd already worked with on *Europa*. He was an obvious choice.

Did you have Ernst-Hugo Järegård in mind when you wrote The Kingdom?

Yes, I did. I later found out that the name of his character, Stig Helmer, is the same as Lasse Åberg's character in a series of Swedish comedy films. I hadn't got a clue about that when I gave the Swedish consultant his name. The name was inspired by a character in books I read as a child, the 'Jan' series. The hero of those books was called Jan Helmer, and his father was a police chief – not a very nice one. So I always thought of Stig Helmer as Jan's father. And his first name? Maybe that's because I know Stig Larsson.

His name is Stig G. Helmer. And there's a worn-out joke that no one knows what the 'G.' stands for, but it definitely isn't Good.

I assume that the research for The Kingdom *must have been extensive.*

It was mostly Niels who went round hospitals meeting doctors. I didn't have a lot to do with it.

You must have had quite a lot to fall back on, with your hypochondria and consequently your extensive knowledge of different illnesses and symptoms.

Of course! But I try to avoid hospitals.

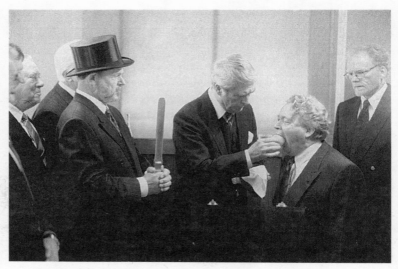

14 *The Kingdom*: Ernst-Hugo Järegård as Dr Stig Helmer is initiated into 'The Sons of the Kingdom'. Holger Juul Hansen, as Senior Consultant Moesgaard, puts a lemon in Dr Helmer's mouth.

But The Kingdom *still gave you the chance to deal with some of your imagined illnesses?*

God, yes! In *The Kingdom* 2 we give Stig Helmer some of my hypochondria, so he examines his own faeces. I've started doing that as well. Doesn't Bergman do that too? Didn't he have his own private toilet at Filmstaden, the studios in Stockholm, which no one else could use? I read an article about toilets in a British magazine. They'd looked at toilets around the world. And the only country where they have toilets where the shit lies there like it's being presented on a tray is France. There, you leave your shit on a little ledge before flushing it away. Now there's a country that really likes to admire what it produces . . .

Ernst-Hugo Järegård seems to be something of a father figure to you.

You could say that. No, on second thoughts, because I don't feel there's any great age gap between us, so I wouldn't want to call him a father figure. But we spoke regularly. We had very good contact. Ernst-Hugo was a very good friend. I probably regard Bergman as more of a father figure. So it's entirely logical that we don't talk. I did film studies at university, and almost an entire term was spent studying Bergman. That's why he occupies such a large space in my film memory. I've seen all Bergman's films, even the adverts he made for soap. And it's good that he hasn't given up yet. *Larmar och gör sig till* (*In the Presence of a Clown*) is a remarkable film. I think Bergman is the only director in the world who could get away with suddenly sending a white clown into the plot in a sort of dreamlike light and still make it work. At any rate, we as the audience immediately accept what happens.

Above all I admire Bergman as a scriptwriter. He really knows how to write dialogue. I can't really say whether he's good at directing people. But all the actors who've worked with Bergman seem to have appreciated him in that role. He probably acts as a father figure in those circumstances. It's as though a power structure is established, one which the actors perceive as positive. The acting isn't particularly natural, but mostly very theatrical: you can tell that both Bergman and his actors have a background in theatre. I recently saw *Scenes from a Marriage* again, which is said to be very realistic. But the film is terribly theatrical. Which is fine. I just became more aware of it when I saw it again.

It's odd that the film and the television series became so popular. I spent a lot of time in Sweden for a while and was living in Stockholm. I had quite a few Swedish friends there, and they thought Bergman was extremely childish. You could probably say that most artists are. But Bergman's psychology holds itself at a popular level, which might explain the success of the film and of his other films. It's not a criticism, just a something I'd noticed. Here I can see parallels between Bergman and a Danish author called Leif Panduro. Panduro wrote a series of very good scripts for television dramas, with a mixture of psychology and middle-class anxieties, a bit like Bergman. There were six or seven of his dramas recorded in the 1970s and '80s. They were incredibly popular and everyone used to talk about them. They had quite a lot in common with Bergman. They were middle-class dramas in comfortable surroundings where keeping quiet and having secrets were the most obvious dramatic ingredients. That sort of television drama doesn't get made any more. Now you have to kill people to get attention.

You mentioned power in connection with Bergman and his actors. Have you ever felt yourself to be in a position of power over your actors?

My relationship to my actors has changed a lot. I think it's been a pretty interesting process of development. I've got a lot better at involving the actors in a collaboration. This culminated in *The Idiots*, even if – contrary to what you might think – the film followed the script very closely. But, to return to Bergman one last time, I think that a so-called demon director can only work in very close collaboration with his actors. You can be an unpleasant director if you maintain your distance, like Hitchcock. I can imagine that. Steven Spielberg is said to be a bit like that, from what I understand from Stellan Skarsgård, who worked with him on *Amistad*. He hardly said a thing to the actors. Woody Allen is said not to have much contact with his actors when he's directing. A director who leaves his actors to their fate is, in my opinion, more demonic and unpleasant than a so-called demon director like Bergman. Hitchcock is supposed to have been pretty cruel and to have made fun of the actresses in his films.

But exploiting actors . . . You could probably say that I've done that, when I've made actors stand and act in cold water, which seemed to happen all the time in my first films. But that's superficial exploitation. If you really want to exploit actors, it has to happen in close collaboration, which for my part seems to be happening more and more. Exploit, as a word, has so many negative connotations, but in essence it's something positive. You could say you're exploiting them if you're trying to bring out their special talents.

You've travelled a long way since The Element of Crime *in terms of your attitude to your actors.*

To begin with I wasn't at all interested in the actors. In my first films the actors are more like chess pieces to be moved round a board. They had to stand in one corner and say a few lines, then move a couple of steps and say some more lines – no more than that. They just had to do the bare minimum. It was something of a reaction against what was regarded as correct behaviour in Danish film at the time. You were supposed to have a close relationship with your actors and discuss psychology and love them and so on.

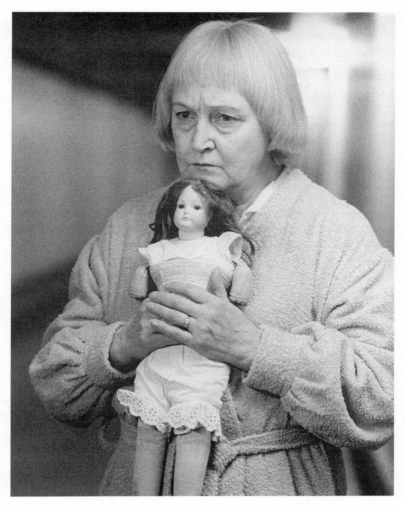

15 *The Kingdom*: Kirsten Rolffes as the telepathic Fru Drusse.

I might have fallen into that pattern now, though. It's interesting, and it gives more. My development has gone from control to . . . I don't want to presume it's the opposite, exactly. But I've relinquished that sort of control and exchanged it for something you could almost describe as a game of chance.

153

So it wasn't the case that you were scared of actors when you started making films? There are directors who are more than hesitant about entering into a dialogue with their actors.

I don't think so. It was just that everything else, the technical side of things, was more important at the time. I just wasn't interested in actors. I didn't want their opinions about things. I ended up arguing with several of them because of that.

After you've chosen the actors for a film, do you discuss much with them before you start filming?

In my old age I've come to the conclusion that the most important thing is that the actors really want to be part of the film. I've worked with a lot of actors who really couldn't be bothered. And the results are predictably poor. So I never try to get a star that I might somehow be able to persuade, the sort of actor who demands that you rewrite the part to suit him or her, and who you have to flatter to get them to take part. No thanks, fuck that! Better not to bother. The important thing is that they *want* to take part. That's the absolute prerequisite. That's why it turned out so well with Emily Watson in *Breaking the Waves*. To begin with we asked Helena Bonham-Carter, who didn't want to be involved when it came down to it. If I'd made the film with her, with her not believing in the project, it would never have been any good. The same with *The Idiots* – most of the actors in that had never made a film before. But they threw themselves into the project and that's why they're so bloody good. You enter into a sort of relationship with your actors, a marriage almost. And when someone doesn't want to be together with you, then the relationship breaks down.

Did you feel that willingness when you made The Kingdom?

Yes, that's why it was fun to do. We wrote the script without having any idea of how we were going to make it. I've generally always had an idea of the style of a project right from the start. Then I discovered, with Tómas Gislason's help – as I've already mentioned – a new form for the film. And through that I found a new way of behaving towards the actors.

154

In that respect The Kingdom *seems to have been something of a liberation for you. Can you say anything more about how you managed to free yourself up with the actors?*

To begin with it was obvious to me that this film required me to get something different out of the actors. I succeeded in doing that by distancing myself completely from the stylization that I was so attached to before. And that meant giving my actors more freedom. I developed the basic idea that I got from *Homicide*. For example, I asked the actors to adopt new motivations, and new positions, when we did a new take on a scene, which led to interesting results when we came to edit together the different takes. It was brilliant fun! In *The Idiots* we went a step further. We were able to film shots that were forty to forty-five minutes long, which we later edited down to two minutes. We ended up with a completely new but very interesting set of rules. But basically it comes down to giving actors optimal possibilities. And that's obviously something they like.

But might it not be risky shooting a scene again and letting the actors adopt new motivations? An actor invests a lot of time and energy on preparing a character before filming starts. Isn't there a risk of conflict if you ask them to diverge from their character in a given situation?

There weren't such big variations in their performances as I'm perhaps suggesting. It was never the case that they couldn't justify their character's behaviour and reactions in any given scene. But a lot could still happen. We don't always react the same way in different situations. A lot can happen within a specific framework. But we set it up as a game, as a theatre-school game. Thanks to these variations we were able to make a number of psychological leaps when we edited the scenes. And I think they were pretty interesting. Since *The Kingdom*, editing has become more important to me. In my earliest films editing was almost a formality to be endured once recording was finished. We had already decided on the finished product in the storyboard we had drawn. Editing on Avid is also fantastic. It happens so quickly, and offers a wealth of possibilities.

Certainly, speed is one advantage. But it also means you can easily try different variations. You can pick and choose between different scenes. Everything is there in the computer. But I still miss the old editing tables, with the reels of film and soundtrack. The tactile sense of feeling the film and holding the frames up to the light. That feeling of workmanship.

I know what you mean, but sometimes you could clip that bloody working copy so many times that it hardly held together. Then you had to order a new copy to work with. But of course it was nice to feel what you were working on with your fingers.

What did the actors think of this new way of filming?

I remember filming the first scene involving Ernst-Hugo Järegård. He started saying his lines, then the camera suddenly panned away from him. And he stopped in the middle of a sentence. 'Sorry,' he said, 'but the camera just disappeared.' 'Yes, that's how we're going to work on this film, Ernst-Hugo,' I explained. 'Are we!' He'd never been involved in anything like that, where the camera wasn't on him when he was speaking. But he soon got used to it. And he thoroughly enjoyed himself. But that first take was a bit tough. He'd prepared his monologue so carefully, and now he didn't get to say it all in shot!

And the other actors, who must have been more used to a more conventional method of filming?

The technique was adapted to suit a group. Naturally some individual actors could use the technique better than others. Even those with more traditional training and experience soon adapted to the new method. The flexibility and adaptability it offered also fitted in with the whole acting situation of the time. Take two actresses like Katrin Cartlidge in *Breaking the Waves* or Paprika Steen in *The Idiots*, who've been trained in this improvisation technique. They're perfect for this way of working. Paprika Steen, who plays the estate agent in *The Idiots*, is a very good example. She was only with us for one day, but she immediately grasped the style and technique, and she performed her role with marvellous presence and precision.

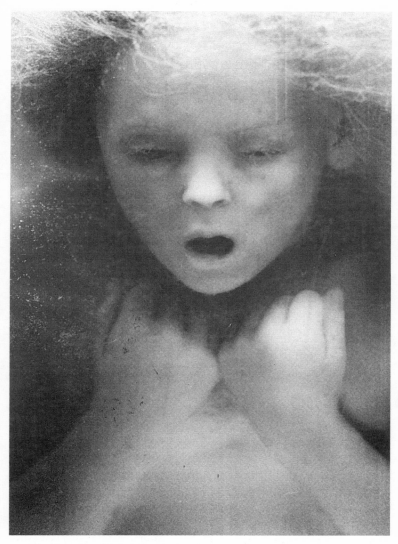

16 *The Kingdom*: Little Mary in the glass container.

There's a horror story built into The Kingdom: *that of the little girl who's haunting the hospital, the daughter of a demonic doctor, Krüger, and the victim of one of his experiments.*

Yes, but I didn't think that story worked very well. It's been very difficult to balance, particularly in *The Kingdom 2*. When satire takes over it's hard to make the horror elements convincing. *The Kingdom 3* will have to be a lot more evil. The film will have to reclaim some of its danger. It was great fun letting go and writing *The Kingdom 2*, but now we're going to have to pull in the reins a lot in the conclusion. *The Kingdom 3* has got to be seriously dangerous.

With your films you've contributed to building up a Danish production company, Zentropa. For what would you like to use the resources that Zentropa now possesses – both for yourself and for other people?

I don't really know . . . It's suddenly grown into quite a sizeable company. I'd mainly like to see it functioning as a lively and creative environment. The producer, Peter Aalbæk Jensen, has already set up a whole series of production activities. Through my own connections with the company I hope I'll be able to have a bit of fun and experiment with the new media techniques that the future offers. And naturally it's nice to feel the support of a company like that, and to know that I'm going to have complete control of whatever I want to do in the future.

MANIFESTO – DOGME 95

DOGME 95 is a collection of film directors founded in Copenhagen in the spring of 1995. DOGME 95 has the expressed goal of countering 'certain tendencies' in the cinema today. DOGME 95 is a rescue action!

Slogans of individualism and freedom created works for a while, but no real changes. The wave was up for grabs, like the directors themselves. The wave was never stronger than the men behind it. The anti-bourgeois cinema itself became bourgeois, because the foundation upon which its theories were based was the bourgeois perception of art. The *auteur* concept was bourgeois romanticism from the very start and thereby . . . false!

To DOGME 95 cinema is not individual!

Today a technological storm is raging, the result of which will be the ultimate democratization of the cinema. For the first time, anyone can make movies. But the more accessible the medium becomes, the more important the avant-garde. It is no accident that the phrase 'avant-garde' has military connotations. Discipline is the answer . . . we must put our films into uniform, because the individual film will be decadent by definition!

DOGME 95 counters the individual film by the principle of presenting an indisputable set of rules known as THE VOW OF CHASTITY.

In 1960 enough was enough! The movie had been cosmeticized to death, they said; yet since then the use of cosmetics has exploded. The 'supreme' task of the decadent film-makers is to fool the audience. Is that what we are so proud of? Is that what the '100 years' of cinema have brought us? Illusions via which emotions can be communicated? By the individual artist's free choice of trickery? Predictability (dramaturgy) has become the golden calf around which we dance. Having the characters' inner lives justify the plot is too complicated, and not 'high art'. As never before, the superficial action and the superficial movie are receiving all the praise. The result is barren. An illusion of pathos and an illusion of love.

To DOGME 95 the movie is not illusion!

Today a technological storm is raging of which the result is the elevation of cosmetics to God. By using new technology anyone at any time can wash the last grains of truth away in the deadly embrace of sensation. The illusions are everything the movie can hide behind.

DOGME 95 counters the film of illusion by the presentation of an indisputable set of rules known as THE VOW OF CHASTITY.

The Vow of Chastity

I swear to submit to the following set of rules drawn up and confirmed by DOGME 95:

1 Shooting must be done on location. Props and sets must not be brought in (if a particular prop is necessary for the story, a location must be chosen where this prop is to be found).
2 The sound must never be produced apart from the images, or vice versa. (Music must not be used unless it occurs where the scene is being shot.)
3 The camera must be hand-held. Any movement or immobility attainable in the hand is permitted. (The film must not take place where the camera is standing; shooting must take place where the film takes place.)
4 The film must be in colour. Special lighting is not acceptable. (If there is too little light for exposure the scene must be cut or a single lamp must be attached to the camera.)
5 Optical work and filters are forbidden.
6 The film must not contain superficial action. (Murders, weapons, etc. must not occur.)
7 Temporal and geographical alienation are forbidden. (That is to say that the film takes place here and now.)
8 Genre movies are not acceptable.
9 The film format must be Academy 35mm.
10 The director must not be credited.

Furthermore, I swear as a director to refrain from personal taste! I am no longer an artist. I swear to refrain from creating a 'work', as

I regard the instant as more important than the whole. My supreme goal is to force the truth out of my characters and setting. I swear to do so by all the means available and at the cost of any good taste and any aesthetic considerations.

Thus I make my VOW OF CHASTITY.

Published in Copenhagen, 13 March 1995
Signed by Lars von Trier and Thomas Vinterberg

9

Breaking the Waves

SYNOPSIS

The early 1970s. The innocent Bess McNeill lives with her mother and Dodo, the recently bereaved widow of her brother, in a small, strictly religious community on the west coast of Scotland. Bess is regarded by most people as an overgrown child, with the ability of childish faith to communicate directly with God. She marries the older and more experienced Jan, who works on an oil rig out at sea. The marriage is regarded critically by many in the Puritan society. The sexually inexperienced Bess is overwhelmed by the secrets and pleasures that the more experienced Jan introduces her to. For a short and happy time the newly-weds live out their love for each other.

When Jan has to return to his oil rig for a new shift, Bess is distraught. Long telephone calls do nothing to calm her. She prays to God that Jan should come back. Her prayers are soon answered, but not as she wanted. Jan comes home paralysed and afflicted by life-threatening head injuries after an explosion on the platform. Jan realizes that he will never be able to sleep with Bess again, and he asks, or rather commands, Bess to take a lover. Bess rejects his demand, but when she comes to realize that this might renew Jan's will to live, she throws herself into increasingly promiscuous behaviour. When she thinks that she can see some signs of improvement in Jan's condition, she subjects herself to ever more degrading situations, despite criticism from her family and the church. She believes that a miracle will give Jan back to her. For the sake of his and their love she is willing to put her life at risk.

* * *

163

Breaking the Waves took five years and 42 million kroner to make. Where did the original idea for the film come from?

I prefer working with extreme ideas, and I wanted to make a film about 'goodness'. When I was little, I had a children's book called *Guldhjerte* (*Goldheart*), which I had very clear and happy memories of. It was a picture book about a little girl who goes into the forest with some slices of bread and other stuff in her pockets. But at the end of the book, when she's got through the forest, she's standing there naked and with nothing left. And the last line in the book was: '"But at least I'm okay," said Goldheart.' It seemed to express the ultimate extremity of the martyr's role. I read the book several times, in spite of the fact that my father thought it was absolute rubbish. The story of *Breaking the Waves* probably comes from that. Goldheart is Bess in the film. I also wanted to make a film with a religious theme, a film about miracles. And at the same time I wanted to make a completely naturalistic film.

The story of the film changed a lot over the years. To begin with, I wanted to shoot the film on the west coast of Jutland, then in Norway, then Ostende in Belgium, then Ireland, and in the end Scotland. It's probably no coincidence that a lot of the film is set on the Isle of Skye, where a lot of painters and writers went during the Romantic period in Britain in the 1800s. I worked a lot on the script of *Breaking the Waves* over the years. I've been a bit like Dreyer, cutting bits out, condensing and refining it. But then just before we started filming, I lost my enthusiasm for the piece. It had taken so long to get the film made that I was tired of it. I'd already moved on from it.

I can understand that. It can be difficult holding on to the same idea for so long. All the time you're getting new ideas for films and other projects.

Yes, and there's a risk of adding new material to the project to freshen it up, which isn't always a good idea. You run the risk of losing what you originally had, forgetting what it was you wanted to depict to begin with. But it did take a long time to get financial support for the film.

17 *Breaking the Waves*: Stellan Skarsgård and Emily Watson as the young couple Jan and Bess.

That's odd, because it feels as if Breaking the Waves *ought to have been more commercially attractive than your earlier films.*

Yes. There's a funny story about that. We got financial support for the script from something that I think is called the 'European Script Fund'. There were lecturers who read script proposals, and they were getting a lot of criticism. So to protect their position, they constructed a computer programme out of about ten projects that had been suggested to them. The idea was that the computer could work out the artistic and commercial relevance of a project. And *Breaking the Waves* got top marks! That was fun. It must have had all the right ingredients: a sailor, a mermaid, a romantic landscape – all the stuff the computer loved!

Did you get the idea for the film's very particular technique, with hand-held camera and the CinemaScope format, at the same time as the idea for the story?

No, that came from my experiences on *The Kingdom*. In this film there are some of the same clichéd elements as in *The Kingdom*, which is why I thought it was important to give the film as realistic a treatment as possible. A more documentary style. If I had made *Breaking the Waves* with conventional techniques, I think it would have been unbearable.

I think it's important to decide upon a specific style for a story if the project is going to be at all practical. Normally you choose a style for a film that's going to emphasize the story. But we did the opposite. We chose a style that contradicts the story, giving it the least possible emphasis.

Yes, if you'd chosen to give Breaking the Waves *the 'Merchant– Ivory treatment' it would probably have been regarded as far too romantic or melodramatic.*

The film would have been far too sickly. It would have been unbearable. What we did was take a style and lay it like a filter over the story. It's like decoding a television signal when you pay to see a film. Here we encoded the film, and the audience has to decode it. The raw, documentary style that I imposed on the film, which actually dissolves and contradicts it, means that we can accept the story as it is. That's my theory, at any rate. It's all a bit theoretical. Then we manipulated the images electronically. We transferred the film to video, and worked on the colour, before transferring it back to film again.

Like Medea, *which you shot on video, then transferred to film before copying it to video again.*

No, that was a much more basic process, where we filmed direct from the television monitor. In *The Kingdom* the transfer process was a bit more advanced. And here it was even more refined. It's interesting to transfer Panavision to video and then back to film again. Maybe it makes it a bit too attractive . . . In between there are some completely digitally produced panoramic shots that introduce the different sections in the film.

They're also a bit reminiscent of a classic English novel, with chapter titles and headings that indicate the chapters' content.

I collaborated on these images with a Danish artist, Per Kirkeby, who has developed a form based on romantic painting. He's an expert in his field, and the results are very interesting. There are so many ways of expressing romantic painting. There are the pictures that people hang on their walls, then there's the more genuine article in galleries. Our pictures might have become a bit more abstract than I planned at the start.

In 1995 you published a manifesto, Dogme 95, with the aim of 'countering certain tendencies in the cinema today'. The manifesto attacked illusory cinema and promoted naturalistic cinema with a series of rules, like filming everything on location, using hand-held cameras without any special lighting, and with directly recorded sound. The last rule is that the director mustn't be credited. Apart from the film's large budget, Breaking the Waves *largely follows the manifesto.*

Yes, which was fortunate, really . . . But the manifesto goes a step further, which was important to me personally when I planned to make a film according to the rules. As you can see, *Breaking the Waves* doesn't follow the rules exactly. I wasn't able to resist tinkering with the film's colour and technical appearance. Maybe I shouldn't have done, if I was going to be faithful to my own theory. But I felt a need to restrict myself, and that was the spirit in which the manifesto was created.

You also break the rule about the film being uncredited. Breaking the Waves *is undoubtedly 'a film by Lars von Trier'. A French author, Paul Valéry, said that 'the decline of art begins with a signature'. In other words, a work will be judged in relation to its creator. Do you see this as positive or negative?*

I see it as positive. I haven't got any problems with that. When I was younger, I was fascinated by David Bowie, for instance. He'd managed to construct a complete mythology around himself. It was as important as his music. If Bowie had composed music that didn't need his signature, maybe he could have learned to do something else. I don't really think it's important not to acknowledge a work's originator within the relationship between an artist and his audience. The important thing here is the process in which the work is created.

The manifesto is purely theoretical. But, at the same time, the theory is more important than the individual. That's what I wanted to express. Somehow or other the identity of the director will always get out. It will be obvious who has directed each Dogme film.

Of course, I think that most serious film-makers will be recognizable whether or not their signature is there in black and white.

Yes, I've always thought it was important that you can tell just by looking at a film whether or not I made it.

What do you think is unique about your signature? What is it in a film that means that we can see it's one of yours?

This will probably sound pretentious, but somehow I hope people will be able to see that every image contains a thought. It probably sounds arrogant, and it might not be true. But I think that every image and every edit is thought through. There's no coincidence at all.

Breaking the Waves *has a strong religious background. What made you include that in the film?*

Probably because I'm religious myself. I'm Catholic, but I don't pray to Catholicism for Catholicism's sake. I've felt a need for a sense of belonging to a community of faith, because my parents were committed atheists. I flirted with religion a lot as a young man. In your youth you're probably attracted to more extreme religions. Either you disappear to Tibet or you seek out the strictest faith available, with total abstinence and so on.

I think I've developed a more Dreyeresque view of it all now. Dreyer's view of religion was primarily humanist. He also tackles religion in all his films. Religion is attacked, but not God. That's what happens in *Breaking the Waves*.

In the film, religion is described as a power structure. The mechanics of power and its problematics is something you've tackled in several of your previous films.

My intention was never to criticize any particular faith, like the one in this Scottish setting. That doesn't interest me at all. It's too easy, and it's not something I want to get involved in. Cultivating a point of view that's easily accessible and generalized, it's like fishing in shallow water. In many ways I can understand people who are obsessed by spiritual issues, often in a very extreme way. It's just that if you're going to create a melodrama, you have to include certain obstacles. And religion struck me as being a suitable obstacle.

Bess's conversations with God have a directness and an intimacy that gives a human voice to the religious theme.

Bess is also an expression of that religion. Religion is her foundation, and she accepts its conditions without question. In the funeral scene at the beginning of the film, the priest condemns the deceased to eternal damnation in hell, which is something Bess finds completely natural. She has no scruples about that. But we, on the other hand, do. Bess is confronted with a lot of other power structures, like the power exerted by the hospital and the doctors. And she has to adopt a position using the inherent goodness that she possesses.

To a great extent the film takes the actors as its starting point. Do you think your attitude towards actors changed and developed in Breaking the Waves?

You could probably say that it did. But I also used a different technique in *Breaking the Waves*, a technique based upon a relationship of trust between director and actors, a classic technique really. I probably got closer to the actors in this film. But it's easy to suggest that I've finally learned that as well! In my earlier films it was more a conscious matter of not getting too close to that actors.

How did you come to cast Emily Watson in the role of Bess? She gives a fantastic performance, despite at the time being a novice when it comes to film.

One of the problems of financing this production was that we didn't have any big names in the leading roles. We realized that early on, when we couldn't find any big names who wanted to be involved. They were scared of the character of the film.

18 *Breaking the Waves*: Bess (Emily Watson) and her sister-in-law Dodo (Katrin Cartlidge).

Was that because of the sex scenes?

It was probably the story as a whole. It's a strange mix of religion and sex and obsession. The well-known actors we approached didn't want to lay their careers on the line, like Helena Bonham-Carter, who pulled out of the project at the very last minute. So it felt important to find actors who really wanted to be involved. And I think it shows, that the actors we chose in the end are wholeheartedly committed to the film.

We auditioned several actresses for the role of Bess. Then I looked at the video of the auditions together with Bente [*Lars' partner*], and she thought it was obvious that Emily Watson ought to get the part. I was also very taken by Emily's acting, but it was mainly her enthusiasm that convinced me. I remember that Emily was also the only one who came to the audition without any make-up and barefoot! Their was something Jesus-like about her that attracted me.

Emily had no previous film experience, which meant that she was more reliant on me as director. Our work together was extremely relaxed. The funny thing is that with Emily's scenes I chose to use the last take of each scene, fairly consistently. Whereas with Katrin Cartlidge, I almost always went for the first take. The difference was in their individual styles of acting. We improvised a lot, forgot all about continuity and gave the actors more freedom in their performances. As far as Katrin, a more experienced actress, was concerned, the intensity of her performance diminished for every new take. In Emily's case I gave more exact instructions, which meant that she refined her performance in each take.

And the other actors, how did you choose them?

I was considering Gérard Depardieu as the male lead, as I had for *Europa*. I met him in Paris, but he was far too overwhelmed with work and not particularly interested in the role. The character was more like Depardieu when I began writing the script. But it developed in a different direction, and Depardieu would have been too old for the part.

Later on, Stellan Skarsgård was the natural choice. He also had the physique that was right for the part. And he was excellent. He's also a very nice person. I shall probably always have him in mind, if there's a suitable part for him.

And Katrin Cartlidge? I know that the role of Dodo was originally intended for Barbara Sukowa.

That's right. That was because we'd worked together on *Europa*. But for various reasons it didn't work on this occasion. Katrin was someone I originally auditioned for the role of Bess, but she wasn't quite right for that – or rather the part didn't suit her. She was an incredibly talented actress, and extremely intelligent. But I offered her the role of Dodo, and she wanted to do it. They were a fantastic trio, Emily, Stellan and Katrin. And I think Jean-Marc gives one of his best performances in *Breaking the Waves*.

The way you edited the film is fairly unorthodox, and breaks all the rules. Did it take long to do?

No, the editing was very easy. We'd shot very long scenes and none of them was like any other. The actors were allowed to move in the scene if they wanted to, and never had to follow any precise plan.

When we edited the scenes, our only intention was to strengthen the intensity of the acting, without worrying about whether the picture was sharp or well-composed or if we were riding roughshod over the invisible sight axis. That resulted in great jumps in time within the scenes, which might not be perceived as jumps in time. They almost give a feeling of compression. I basically developed the things I learned from working on *The Kingdom*.

If you had to choose a single image from Breaking the Waves *that you think represents the film, which would you pick – and why?*

Well, you know very well, as a director, that one of the reasons you make films is that one image isn't enough. At the Cannes Film Festival we had a completely black poster, because we couldn't decide on a single image to represent the whole film. We had a poster with a plain black background. It had just the title and a few names. It looked a bit like a concert poster and was printed on some sort of velvety material, and I liked it a lot. So without wanting to be negative, I have to say that I can't pick any image that I think represents the whole film.

One image from the film that's often used, which you must have picked out from the hundreds that were taken, is a close-up of Emily Watson, looking directly into the camera and thereby out into the audience. Why did you choose that one?

This business of stills is often pretty haphazard. There isn't always a still-photographer around, and the stills don't always match the scene in the completed film. That close-up of Emily is where she first comes into direct contact with the audience. But I'm not that keen on the picture. If there's a point in the film where I think there's a certain artifice in Emily's acting, it's there. I remember the moment we shot that very well, and we had to try a whole load of different ways of getting that shot. Maybe because it's not a scene with any interplay of acting, it's more of a planned scene, which is subordinate to an idea.

Seeing Emily in the film always makes me glad, but that picture really isn't a favourite of mine.

But if you had to pick another picture of Emily . . .

That I liked? Then I'd probably pick the confrontation between Bess and the young doctor, Dr Richardson (Adrian Rawlins), at the end of the film. It was a scene we shot very early on, and it's a very emotionally rewarding, but very difficult, scene. That's somewhere I feel that Emily exhibits an almost sublime presence.

If I had to pick separate shots of Emily that I was particularly fond of, I'd probably pick shots from the short montage sequence, accompanied by music by T. Rex, where she's dancing about. They're playful scenes, a bit 'New Wave', and I like them a lot.

Breaking the Waves is full of dramatic events, and it expresses strong feelings and thoughts – love, passion, faith, betrayal – but it also pays a lot of attention to detail. The interior of Bess's home, for instance, with the pictures of the dogs and cats on the wall, or the hospital, where during one dramatic scene you can see a woman in the background sitting beside a hospital bed in the corridor consoling her husband. Can you say something about how that was done?

Breaking the Waves is a film where a lot of things happened by accident. The art director, Karl Juliusson, who I think did an excellent job, had decided how the different locations should look. But what we ended up seeing in shot was a complete coincidence – which happens, of course, when you work with a hand-held camera. There were loads of details in the décor that we never see in the film, and others that appear more clearly. But we did have a lot of fun with those dog pictures in Bess's home. They're pure kitsch, and we did wonder if it was a bit too much. But on the other hand they suit the situation. They strengthen the sense of authenticity.

As far as the scene in the hospital is concerned, and others like it, we were trying to create a credible location, most of which was later edited out. The things that all the extras are doing around the actual scene were mostly there to create a convincing atmosphere for the actors. The fact that the couple by the hospital bed ended up in shot was a complete coincidence, and not particularly important. The important thing was what was happening with the actors in the scene. In my earlier films I spent more time worrying about that sort of detail, and less on the actors. That's all changed now.

I think it's nice to get glimpses of details like that in the edge of the picture, because it gives a sense of there being a wider world outside the reality that we're concentrating on.

How did you choose the pictures for the chapter illustrations? Can you say something about some of these pictures and their background? One that has stuck with me in particular is the one illustrating the film's epilogue, the bridge over the stream.

Most of those panoramic shots were described in the script, but several of them changed quite a lot. I travelled round Scotland for a long time together with the photographer Robby Müller and Vibeke Windeløv, and we took loads of pictures, and even some film footage of the landscape. This was long before we started filming. At a later stage we contacted the painter Per Kirkeby, who worked on them and retouched them on his computer. What I particularly wanted was for Per – who's both an artist and a theorist – to find different ways of expressing the romantic landscape. I had the impression that this romanticism ought to betray a deeper banality, but Per's first suggestions were a long way from that idea. The finished result could be described as a diplomatic mixture of his and my ideas. What he did to the pictures made them considerably more interesting and ambiguous. Perhaps I was aiming more towards the grandiose.

The picture of the bridge was actually the first chapter illustration we did, and it was created before Per got involved. The bridge was on the Isle of Skye, but it was in the middle of a village. So we took the bridge out of context and put a mountain behind it and had a waterfall rushing beneath it. Per did some more work on it later. He put his special sense of lighting into the picture. The idea was to collect more intense light under the arch of the bridge in the centre of the picture. And there's no naturalistic light illuminating the distant landscape.

I'm very fond of that picture. You can read as much symbolism into it as you like. You can see the bridge as a link between life and death. And the water representing eternity. And so on. But I haven't really thought about it. Everyone can interpret any perceived symbolism as they like. But I think it's an expressive picture. And I think it works well with David Bowie's 'Life on Mars'.

I like some of those chapter illustrations better than others, especially the one of the bridge. But I'm also very fond of the one of the silhouetted city and the rainbow.

What did the landscape of Skye mean to you?

I just know that a lot of painters and writers associated with British Romanticism visited Skye. The landscape there is extremely romantic. It's nothing like Danish Romanticism. It's a lot more grandiose. I was particularly struck by the contrasts in the landscape. In the midst of a range of bleak mountains there would be crevasses with luscious vegetation.

When you visited us on location, we were filming on the hill above the place where we put the cemetery in the film. We actually wanted the cemetery higher up on the hill, but we couldn't manage that. We'd measured a plot and started constructing the cemetery when people came and protested and were almost prepared to start throwing stones at the team. So we had to move the cemetery down to a more sheltered position nearer the water. We managed to find a wonderful spot with exactly the same dimensions we were planning higher up.

The cemetery is still there. The man who owned the land wanted to sell the gravestones and other props to the BBC, but he hasn't managed to yet. So it's become a tourist attraction; people go and look at it and take picnics. But they wanted to clear it away. Because it is, after all, a cemetery – and almost all the production team is buried there! We had to put names on the gravestones, so the team used their own names on them.

You've often mentioned Dreyer as a source of inspiration. Do you think that's the case even on this film?

Yes, I can see that films like *The Passion of Joan of Arc* and *Gertrud* have probably been significant for *Breaking the Waves*. Dreyer's films are naturally more academic, more cultivated. What's new for me is having a woman at the centre of the story. And of course, all of Dreyer's films had women as their main characters – women who are suffering, as well. The film's original title was actually going to be *Amor Omnie* (*Love is in Everything*), the epitaph that Gertrud wanted on her grave in Dreyer's film. But

19 *Breaking the Waves*: Bess (Emily Watson) is ostracized from church and community.

when my producer heard the title, he exploded. He had trouble imagining that anyone would want to go and see a film called *Amor Omnie*.

At the end of Breaking the Waves, *in the scene where the wounded and expelled Bess comes into the church, she contradicts the church council's rule that women must remain silent in the congregation, and says: 'You can't love the Word. You can only love a person.' That's a line that could be interpreted as both an* hommage *and a response to Dreyer.*

That might be taking it a bit far, but it's actually one of the few lines that I rewrote on location. In the script there was something far more wordy and generally unformed. The idea of her outburst was to pick up something that the members of the congregation said and stood for – and to contradict it. The priest talks about loving the Word and the Law. That was the only thing you had to obey. That's what would make a person complete. But Bess twists the concepts and says that the only thing that can make a person complete is loving another person. This is really the formulation of the film's moral.

176

But the line was rewritten just before shooting. In the script it said that Bess should say: 'Dear God, thank you for the divine gift of love. Thank you for the love that makes a person a person. Dear God . . .' Emily Watson discussed the lines with me and said that she didn't understand them. And I can appreciate that, because they were pretty poor. And according to the script, no one in church had said anything before that. No, the revised script was much better. It's also better that she got into a debate with the priest. So what you could say about Bess is that she represents feminism against the extremely misogynist priesthood. And her sister-in-law, Dodo, does pretty much the same.

Yes, not least at the end, at Bess's funeral.

Yes, where Dodo rebels against the establishment, the male hierarchy.

One concept, one element that links most of your previous films is a sense of irony. There's not a lot of irony in Breaking the Waves.

When I was at film school they said that all good films were characterized by some form of humour. All films, apart from Dreyer's! A lot of his films are totally 'vacuum-cleaned' of humour. In a sense you could say that when you imbue your film with humour, you're establishing a certain distance from it. You create a distance. With this film I didn't want to distance myself from the emotions contained in the plot and the characters.

I think that this strong engagement with emotions was very important for me, because I grew up in a home – a culturally radical home – where strong emotions were forbidden. Those members of my family whom I've showed the film to have been very critical about it – both my brother and my uncle [Børge Høst, Danish director and producer of short films and documentaries], who's also involved in film. My brother thought the film was indifferent and dull, and my uncle saw it as a total mistake from beginning to end. But otherwise, with my earlier films, he's been extremely supportive. Perhaps *Breaking the Waves* is my teenage rebellion . . .

Breaking the Waves *was a success all over the world. It was awarded the Grand Prix du Jury at Cannes, and garnered numerous* awards at different festivals all over the world. *The critics were overwhelmingly positive and audiences flocked to it. After a while, though, there was a counter-reaction, both in Denmark and in Sweden, where the film was criticized by feminist commentators. They reacted against the portrait of Bess sacrificing everything, even her life, for her husband.* Breaking the Waves *was accused of misogyny and of shameless manipulation.*

I haven't come into direct contact with those accusations. Everyone is entitled to formulate their own opinion of the film, of course. The only thing I would say is that I'm surprised that it took so long for this particular strand of criticism to appear. I'd expected it sooner. Even at the synopsis stage, when we were trying to get financial support for the film, and later on, when we were casting the film, we were confronted by this sort of criticism. Most of the women who read the story reacted in the same way, and just as strongly.

But later on, the film managed to create its own authority. What was provocative in the script wasn't as provocative in the finished film. If you condense the film's story into a few words, obviously it looks provocative. In Denmark none of the film critics saw that as a problem. Even *Information*, which is a radical and academic daily paper, praised the film, which was remarkable given that they've always been extremely critical towards my work. But then they published the opinions of a group of fairly agitated feminists, a debate that I wasn't interested in joining in with. I understand that quite a bit of this was reproduced in Swedish criticism of the film.

One idea of the film was to try out this extremely provocative and completely incredible plot, and I thought that if we got the audience to accept it, if we could make it palatable to an audience, then we would have succeeded. But without manipulating the audience, which I never wanted to do. I think that *Breaking the Waves* is a beautiful story, but the reaction to it hasn't surprised me. And in that sense the film has worked again. It ought to be manna from heaven for people involved in the debate. Feminists and other people ought to be delighted to find a work that can instigate this sort of debate and lends itself to their arguments so readily.

A female American professor of art history, who started the debate in Sweden, summarized her criticism with the younger Alexander Dumas' advice to budding writers: 'Make your heroine suffer!'

But, for God's sake, most American films follow that advice . . .!

In one response to that, Maria Bergom-Larsson, who is both a radical feminist and a Christian, described the film as the story of a modern saint, and proposed the hymn of the Virgin, the Magnificat, as a motto for the film: 'He hath put down the mighty from their seats, and exalted them of low degree.'

It's a beautiful thought, one that I wholeheartedly agree with. Danish feminists, on the other hand, would hardly offer religious interpretations. A hymn is something that they would instantly attack. It's just something that would make them even more angry. Mind you, Danish feminists have probably become better behaved over the years. A decade ago they had more gumption. They'd probably have liked to see me castrated then.

10

Psychomobile #1: The World Clock

DESCRIPTION

The world clock consists of nineteen rooms, housing fifty-three actors. In each room there are four lamps, one red, one green, one yellow and one blue. A video camera is positioned above an ant hill in New Mexico. On a screen in the exhibition space you can watch the ants running around inside the ant hill. Beside it is a map of the nineteen rooms. On the video screen are nineteen squares, each one representing one of the rooms. When the ants have crossed one of the squares seven times, a different lamp in the corresponding room is lit. When the colour of the room changes, all the performers in that room have to change character and mood. Each of the actors taking part has been allocated different characteristics linked to the four colours. The actors can move freely between the rooms and perform improvised conversations and meetings, which take their character and colour from what the lamps – i.e. ultimately the ants – dictate.

* * *

LARS VON TRIER: The artists' association in Copenhagen suggested that I work on an installation in conjunction with Copenhagen being declared European Capital of Culture in 1996. I was more than willing, but when it came to it, I only had time to sketch out the concept of the installation. Then other people, Morten Arnfred and a scenographer and others, constructed the actual installation, or performance, or whatever it should be called, themselves.

This is a huge project, involving a lot of people. Can you tell me

*how you got the idea for the concept and for the basic conditions
of the 'happening' that developed from it?*

Other film-makers have also been called into artistic situations,
often in connection to installations of various kinds. I spent a long
time wondering what to do. I thought I ought to do something
involving people, characters in some sort of cinematic context,
something I could work with. If it wasn't going to become a theatrical performance – and that wasn't the idea – then I wanted to
create something where chance played a central part. Chance con-
trols our psyches. That's where the title came from, *Psychomobile*.
Mobiles were something that artists spent time creating in the
early 1960s, of course. Isn't there a huge mobile by Alexander
Calder outside the Museum of Modern Art in Stockholm? Mobiles
were an interesting and slightly old-fashioned phenomenon. I
thought it would be fun to merge the concept with a group of people. A work of art is often very close to an idea, so I thought it was
probably enough if I was responsible for the concept. And I contributed a description of the sets, and also the list of characters.
The project didn't need any real direction, because it was dependent upon an external impulse that coincided with total improvisation. The 'stories' that appeared didn't require the presence of a
director. So the work of art is the idea in this instance. The execution of the idea is a reproduction that can take many forms. I
wanted to hand the project over to Morten Arnfred and the others.

Have you seen the installation?

No.

Don't you want to?

Yes and no. Naturally I was curious about how it would work. The
whole performance is dependent on ants running about in an ant
hill in New Mexico, and I would have liked to see how that
worked from a technical point of view.

How did you get the idea of using ants?

We had to find something that was compatible with the actors. If
the lamps that indicated a change of emotion were lit too often, the

effect wouldn't have been much fun. Morten had the idea of the division of the video screen into different squares, and the condition that an ant had to pass a square seven times before the lighting was changed. But the idea of the ants was entirely my own.

Why ants in particular? And why New Mexico?

There was a good visual parallel between humans and ants, if you look at it globally. And I thought there was something mythological about New Mexico. It was a good place. I also thought it was exciting to have a link like this with New Mexico. It sets your imagination going. Obviously the psychomobile could be governed by loads of other things. A satellite picture of clouds could govern it, or anything else that's out of our control. Naturally we could have used a computer of some sort, but I preferred the idea of a 'superhuman' power.

But you were responsible for the types of room and the different characters you wanted to put into Psychomobile?

Yes, I described the rooms I wanted included, and described and named the different characters. But the most important thing was deciding the relationships between them. We had a huge plan, where you could refer the characters to each other. A lot of them had no relationship to most of the others to begin with. They got that as things progressed. But at the start each character had ten or so relationships with other characters; they were related to them or whatever. We divided them into close and distant relationships. So there was a reasonable framework for everyone involved from the outset.

But in the programme to Psychomobile *there are no clues about these relationships. There, only the actors are presented, with the name and age of their character. We in the audience have to work out everything else ourselves.*

The original idea was probably to make the plan available at the exhibition. But for whatever reason, that didn't happen.

You could see the installation as one big, simultaneous soap opera.

Of course, there's a large element of soap opera in it. But I think it could be a very entertaining one to follow.

It could. I remember getting attached to a couple of the characters and trying to follow them from room to room. One of the more entertaining was a young woman called Mimi, played by a Norwegian actress. She had a short, black leather skirt and was a drug addict. Her character was pretty provocative, and her performance was best observed in the room called 'The Gallery'. There, the actors were in an enclosed room and the audience could watch them through rectangular openings in the walls. We became pictures that they could look at. And this Mimi had a few choice things to say about these 'portraits' whose appearance was constantly changing. It got quite lively. Then I followed her to a couple more rooms before I lost her in the mass of spectators standing in the way.

The idea was that in certain places it would be very easy to get from one room to the next, but that in other places it should be more complicated, so that the viewer would have to switch their attention from one character or event to another. There was also an inaccessible room that the audience couldn't get to, that was only visible on a monitor.

Psychomobile might fulfil the curiosity that most people probably have, the desire to look into other people's lives and act like a Peeping Tom. I also like the interaction that the performance offered. The idea that you could choose to follow a character or a plot in one of the rooms if you wanted to, or how the relationships between the characters developed. The choice was yours.

Chance is an important factor, and it directs our lives to a great extent. We're always getting into situations where we have to make decisions that will have consequences for us. Here we're presented with a host of choices, and it's very entertaining to see how they have to be solved immediately.

Certainly chance is important, but there's also a superior, divine order represented by the ants. The ants direct the lives of the characters, which is quite fun.

You could describe *Psychomobile* as a completely new genre. It's a hybrid form of improvisational theatre and theatrical sport. I don't really want to call it a 'performance', because that's not what it is. It's just an example of what you can do with the patterns and characters and rooms and scheme of movement that we created. You could lay out the setting in 17,000 different ways. When you get past the novelty value of the mechanism and the systematics of it, it can be repeated in other places and in different ways. And you could probably start judging the quality of different installations. It would be fun if other people around the world started making psychomobiles.

In Psychomobile *you abdicated from all future control of an exhibition you set up. You often come back to your need to feel in control.*

In my life, like so many other people's lives, this business of control and a lack of context is very important. And it's largely what life is about. What you have control over and what you don't. That's something that this installation is about, at least in part. It's 'divine power' which is in control here.

What's your opinion of the control you have to assume and exert during a film shoot? There, of course, it isn't 'divine power' that's in control. Divine power is something the director himself has to possess.

I haven't got a problem with that. If you take Ernst-Hugo Järegård as an example, he's a very anxious person. So am I. I get very nervous and have trouble sleeping. So the other day, when I was speaking to Ernst-Hugo, I said: 'You can always console yourself by thinking that since we've spent every bloody night practising to die, we're going to be bloody good at it when it actually happens.' Then you get the chance to be really frightened.

What the hell, Ernst-Hugo is always frightened, except when the spotlight's on him, because then he's in control. He knows what he's doing there, enchanting a group of people who are just watching him. As soon as they look away, he gets frightened again. It's the same when he's alone in a room.

When I'm doing something I know I can do – it might be one of several things, film-making, for instance – I don't feel frightened.

There I'm in control. But I only feel that in those few instances, in work situations. On *Breaking the Waves* I had a particularly good time with the editing, because there you really are in control of the situation. And it was fun to do, it was bloody good fun. *Breaking the Waves* was the most enjoyable of all my films to edit – largely because I edited quite a lot of it myself. We did the editing on Avid, on computer, and it's much easier to explain what you want to do. You just bring up the scene you want to edit, and show what you want to do. Avid's a great invention, in my opinion.

Did you feel the same on your first film, this feeling of security and control and freedom from fear during recording? Or were you more scared to start with?

No, I've never really been scared in professional situations. But I'm always worried that I'm going to get ill or somehow be hindered from working. I'm scared of things I can't control. But I don't feel the slightest bit anxious about things I know I can control. Work is sheer pleasure. In that respect I can quote Bergman, who on one occasion said that he had probably never had as much fun as when, on one shoot, he was able to command a couple of dozen policemen through a megaphone and see that they obeyed his every command. That's when he realized what 'power' was. And when I made *Europa* I got to give orders to Red Army soldiers, which was pretty interesting . . .

At the same time it's nice to abdicate from power, or to share some of that power. It's an important insight. I did that with some of the actors on *Breaking the Waves*, for instance. My need for control was stronger on my first films. To an increasing extent, I've learned to relinquish some of that control. And with *Psychomobile* I've let go of it completely. I just provided the basic idea and a concept that has been developed by other people. You get an awful lot back if you dare to give that up. *Breaking the Waves* would never have been the film that it is if I hadn't relinquished some of my control over the actors. It isn't just that the technique we used led to greater freedom of movement; it's also that I was more prepared to accept the actors' own interpretations of their roles than I used to be.

You've also relinquished control in your collaboration with Morten Arnfred, who was your assistant director on The Kingdom *and* Breaking the Waves.

That's right. Things went well with Morten, but it still wasn't easy to give up some of that control. It's easier to give up a certain, clearly defined part of it. If you say, for instance, that you can take over here – I've done my bit, you're responsible for the next bit of the film. Having a co-director is a complicated way of working, in the sense that you aren't entirely sure of what you've let go of and what you're still in charge of.

It's like a marriage. You have to get to grips with a whole load of new things when you have a wife. She uses the dishcloth in a completely different way. But when you get married, it might be that you'd like to do something completely different with that dishcloth. Even though you have to force yourself to do it, because like everyone else, you're a creature of habit. But with Morten I've had to force myself both to relinquish some things and make certain demands to get the collaboration to work. He's also had to adapt in various ways.

Can you give any examples of that?

Well, it's mostly a question of taste. Morten and I don't have the same tastes. Everyone has different tastes and preferences, of course. We think differently, about what the crux of a scene is, for instance. Or about what's funny. Everyone has a different opinion of what's funny and what isn't. That's something you have to accept when you direct together. Morten and I have had very few disagreements in our work together. I think we've used one another in a good way. I hope that it's been inspirational for Morten as well. I think it has.

How come you chose to collaborate with Morten Arnfred?

It was partly complete chance. I was making an advert for an insurance company for French television, *La rue*. It was an extremely complex production. I hadn't written it myself. But the whole film was going to be one single long shot, going along a street in Paris, starting with a 1940s' atmosphere and ending with a contemporary feel, i.e. 1994. And we follow a few people through the years and along the street. It was a pretty sentimental, nostalgic trip.

The film was highly regarded and is still shown every now and then, from what I understand. I've been to Paris a couple of times and have met people from the Ministry of Culture. When I mention *The Element of Crime* or *Europa*, they pat my shoulder and say how nice they thought it was. But if I happen to mention that I made *La rue* as well, they get very excited. 'No! Did you do that?' Perhaps that says something about how they see their work.

It was in connection with that advert that I came into contact with Morten. I needed an assistant who was talented *and* disciplined, and had experience of film work. And Morten's certainly got that. He's both talented and disciplined.

We constructed the entire street in a factory outside Copenhagen. I hate travelling, so instead of going to Paris, we moved Paris to Denmark. We worked with so-called motion control. During the walk along the street the actors' appearance changes and they get older, get married, have children, the children grow up, and so on. With motion control we could pull the film back and for every five-year period change the set, the façades of the houses, through the use of overtones. And in the foreground the actors disappear behind a car or a lamppost or something else, then emerge on the other side with a different appearance and clothes. And they're accompanied by music that changes as well.

Had you seen any of Morten's films before then?

Yes, I think I'd seen his first film, *Mig og Charlie* (*Me and Charlie*). I haven't seen *Johnny Larsen*, but I have seen *Det er et yndigt land* (*It's a Wonderful Country*). That's not a film that I feel very attached to, I have to say.

Someone else you've worked with who must mean quite a lot to you is Vibeke Windeløv, who was co-producer of The Kingdom *and* Breaking the Waves, *as well as your later films.*

Yes, Vibeke is above all a wonderful facilitator. She's got the ability to put her arms around her poor director – both physically and metaphorically – and make him feel that he doesn't have to worry about anything. It's so obvious that it doesn't really need an explanation.

Vibeke reads the scripts, just like Peter Aalbæk Jensen. If they like them, I listen to them, but if they don't, I don't listen to their opinions at all. If they don't like my ideas, I just get more stubborn. It can take a while until they manage to get enough enthusiasm for a project. But it usually happens. Enthusiasm is something you can work on.

11

Change, Music Videos and Adverts

LARS VON TRIER: *Change* is a music video I made sometime in the early 1990s. A nice experiment. I think we had a list of fifty or a hundred different directions to get everything to work, directions governing when things should happen, when the background should change, when people should come in and out of shot, and how things should move on set.

How long did it take to make?

We had one day of shooting, but the preparatory work took longer. So a few days or so.

I can see how you made the film, but it's still pretty amazing how well timed it is. It must have been incredibly difficult to get everything to coincide the way that it does.

Yes, we were bloody lucky. And in a few places the timing was perfect. What was good about this was the practical and technical challenges it posed. Shooting it as a single fixed shot, which somehow works.

Change *shows a side of you that's quite revealing. This desire to experiment, to try different ways of doing things, to explore and test the limits of the medium you're using, whether it's film or television or video or whatever. You're fairly driven by that, aren't you?*

Yes, a great deal! I can't do anything unless I really want to. You can see that very plainly in *Change*. It was great fun to make. I think that's pretty evident. It was tough on the poor singer though. Because we shot the whole thing backwards, he had to learn to sing the song backwards. Just learning those strange words and sounds, and still keeping the rhythm. But he'd been a drummer before that, so he managed it pretty well.

In between your feature films you've made several music videos and adverts . . .

Yes, mainly for the money. I have to earn my living, to pay the standing expenses. But I have to admit, I've mostly only chosen the things I thought were most fun. That French advert I was commissioned to do, *La rue*, wasn't so much fun, but it did pay better. Compared to the money you get from a feature film, those French adverts are incredibly well paid. But I don't really like doing them. Just every now and then.

But haven't these jobs allowed you to experiment with the medium a bit more?

No, not really. But, with *Change*, I had the chance to decide things myself. And mess about a bit. But commissions are nearly always pretty fixed. In France and Germany, which I know most about, the ideas have already gone through storyboards in some advertising agency and been accepted by the customer. Then they go out and find someone who can do the work and make the film. The advertising agency don't want anything creative beyond what they've already come up with. The whole thing is their idea, and that's the idea they've managed to sell. So often it's a pretty ridiculous situation. You just have to turn up – then you get a load of money.

But La rue *seems to have been fairly experimental . . .*

Hmm, I don't know about that. It was the first time I'd tried motion control, which was interesting. I think the film ended up being quite poetic in spite of everything.

You made a series of very funny adverts for the newspaper Ekstra-bladet *with Ernst-Hugo Järegård . . .*

The good thing about them was that they only took a couple of hours to shoot. We made five films, which we got through one morning before lunch. They look a lot fresher as a result. We'd arranged much longer for the shoot. But we were finished so quickly that I asked Ernst-Hugo to say to the agency that sadly he couldn't manage doing any more so that they didn't get upset with us.

Did you write the scripts for them?

We started with a text that I'd prepared, but soon digressed from that, because Ernst-Hugo couldn't really do anything with it. So we changed a lot of it and improvised those monologues or outbursts about Denmark. 'What else shall I say?' Ernst-Hugo asked. 'Look out of the window,' I said – he was in an office looking out over Rådhuspladsen, the square by the City Hall – 'and say, "Ynk, ynk, ynk!" That's what you think of Denmark, isn't it?' So he turned round and looked out in three directions and said, 'Ynk!' and it was extremely effective. It's become part of the Danish language now. During some recent industrial action by nurses, they had big banners saying 'Ynk, ynk, ynk!' And it's been used in newspaper headlines as well.

I don't know if all the adverts were as much fun. But the idea was for Ernst-Hugo to have a go at the newspaper and voice his contempt for the country, which was fun.

And Ekstrabladet *liked the films?*

Yes, they were incredibly positive, even though the text was completely different to what they had originally approved. One of the original ideas was 'I love to hate *Ekstrabladet*'. But I said we'd never get Ernst-Hugo to say that. No, he'll just have to hate it all. He's not supposed to love anything.

And you get a picture of Ingmar Bergman into a corner as well.

You noticed that! Yes, he's a part of the archetypal idea of Sweden that Ernst-Hugo eulogizes. Bergman and Björn Borg and Dala horses.

12

The Kingdom 2

SYNOPSIS

At Kingdom Hospital in Copenhagen everything is as it was, yet somehow nothing is the same. Senior physician Stig Helmer has returned from Haiti, and is soon consumed by worries. Partly there is the legal investigation into his unsuccessful brain surgery on poor little Mona. And his beloved colleague Rigmor is trying to entice him into marrying her. He is also afflicted by serious hypochondria. Fru Drusse is fatally wounded by an ambulance just as she is leaving the hospital. In the waiting room to the Kingdom of Death she is called back to life to help in the fight between spirits and demons taking place in Kingdom Hospital. Judith Petersen's child, Lillebror (Little Brother), is growing incredibly quickly and is fighting for his life. Professor Bondo is also fighting for his life after becoming his own experiment by injecting himself with cancer cells. The triangular relationship between the medical students Mogge, Sanne and Christian seems to take up more time than their studies. And is there really no one behind the wheel of the apparently unmanned ambulance racing along the motorway? Considering all the intrigues and conflicts raging within The Kingdom, it's hardly surprising that Senior Consultant Moesgaard has had to seek psychiatric help.

* * *

After the first part of The Kingdom *and the great success of* Breaking the Waves, *one might have thought that you would have entrusted the continuation of* The Kingdom *to another director. What was it that made you want to do* The Kingdom 2 *yourself?*

Well, deep down . . . (*Long pause.*) It's difficult to say. But I'd written the story myself, together with Niels Vørsel, so . . . I can't really remember how we came to the decision. But the idea was always that I'd do it. I think it'll probably be the same with the last part of *The Kingdom* as well. I have to see it through, in a way. But at the same time, it's a bit dull doing something again, I have to admit. I've never done anything a second time before. But you could also say that I've changed my mind about that.

The Kingdom 2 is a lot lighter in tone than The Kingdom 1. *Is that because you know the characters in the story better now, and because you have an almost friendly relationship with them?*

I think it's more to do with the general attitude. I think dialogue that approaches comedy is fun. At the same time, I think it's fun that the pace is more forced. There are also a lot more comic scenes.

What was it that interested you in this sequel? Developing the plot or developing the characters?

That's a difficult question. But *The Kingdom 2* is much faster paced than the first part. The episodes are twice as fast compared to the first series. Whereas then we might have had five parallel story lines on the go at the same time, now we have eleven or twelve. So in that way you could say that the web that Niels and I have woven is twice as complicated. The separate stories are on a different level, a much more superficial level this time. And it has to move a lot faster if we're going to get anywhere near the end of the story. That's why we put a load of secondary threads that need tying up to one side.

So you've already got an idea of how to finish it and how to tie everything up?

Yes, I know how we're going to tie it all up. Obviously.

Regarding Dante's Divine Comedy, *you've said that he thought it was great fun writing 'Hell', but a lot harder to write 'Paradise'. Is it the same with* The Kingdom *for you? Is it easier and more fun to write for the wicked characters and their hell than the good characters and their light and optimism?*

Yes, it was like that before. Evil is so much easier to depict. It suggests a lot more visual interpretations, whereas goodness doesn't really offer any particularly good images at all. Visual goodness easily gets banal, in terms of imagery. You know, you light up people and have situations with sunlight. It's far too emotive and banal. I realized how easy it was to risk ending up in that situation in *Breaking the Waves*, where I really tried to avoid images like that. I used that sort of expression in the chapter titles, however, that excess of romanticism.

There are so many chords to play on when you're depicting evil. I'd have to qualify that by saying that I've never been interested in the psychology of evil, not in the slightest. I'm probably not really interested in evil *per se*, but in people's dark sides. People are what interests me, but to get inside a person it's not unlikely that you're going to have to look at evil from a psychological point of view. But I've only ever been indirectly interested in that.

You mention 'The Swedenborg Room' in the film. Are Swedenborg and his ideas something that interests you?

No, I don't really know much about him. We just wanted to give a name to the room, this anteroom to the Kingdom of Death. I think I'd heard some name for the room you go into before you're transported further. But we couldn't find out anything about it. So we came up with Swedenborg.

The Kingdom is actually a good illustration of Swedenborg's philosophical rationalism and mysticism.

Niels Vørsel probably knows something about his ideas. But, of course, Swedenborg would probably like having a room named after him, a carpeted room with two chairs and two doors and a picture of a landscape with a tiger and a snake and a few birds . . .

A lot of your films depict the struggle between two extremes: chaos and order, good and evil . . .

It's not something I think about consciously, but you tend to use

20 *The Kingdom* 2. It all begins to tell upon Judith (Birgitte Raaberg)

classic oppositional pairs in films like this. They're also something that characterizes workplaces like the Kingdom Hospital, with illnesses and nursing and so on . . .

In The Kingdom 2 *you created a character who personifies this conflict between good and evil – Lillebror. He seems to embody the conflict, both physically and psychologically.*

Yes, albeit in a slightly comic way. But I think that those scenes with Lillebror have space for philosophy and a bit more engagement.

Actually, speaking of that, I wanted to use the film's première to publicize my first real political manifesto, which was about a new law on fertility treatment here in Denmark. A very, very strange law appeared, forbidding lesbians from receiving fertility treatment. I thought that was outrageous, especially from a Social-Democratic government. If two women can't prove that there's a man in the relationship as well, it would be a criminal offence for them to have children together. Regardless of what I think of gays and lesbians – people can do what they like – I think that law was very easy to find holes in.

So I wrote to Danmarks Radio and said I wanted to arrange a

première to support a foundation helping childless lesbians. But they said no. So we didn't do it with the première, just one of the other screenings instead. It was a pretty good opportunity to do it, because of *The Kingdom* being set in a hospital. And you could set up a foundation that would somehow be illegal. That was an unusual thing for me to suggest, because I don't usually get involved in political issues like this. But I thought it was a remarkably retrograde step.

The Kingdom is set in the Kingdom Hospital in Copenhagen. What's your relationship with doctors and the medical profession?

Well, it's not great . . .

And your hypochondria?

That just gets worse and worse. Since we last met, in March, I've got through four or five different sorts of cancer which have completely paralyzed me. It's amazing how many different cancers you can worry about when hypochondria really sets in.

In The Kingdom 2 *you give Ernst-Hugo Järegård's character, Stig Helmer, a whole load of hypochondriac worries.*

Yes, so you could say that these episodes are a bit more satirical. There's satire on a lot of different levels. In the earlier episodes there were funny scenes, but the satire was a bit aimless.

There are several Swedes in the story. Not just Ernst-Hugo Järegård as the Swedish senior physician, Stig Helmer, but also Stellan Skarsgård as Stig Helmer's defence lawyer. And at the end there's another Swedish surprise. Is that because you feel that you can use these Swedish characters and actors to criticize and comment on Denmark and Danish concerns in a more effective way than if you were using Danish characters?

No, I only set up a Danish–Swedish conflict at the end, a conflict that we perhaps ought to think about a bit more. Because the Swedes are now thinking about shutting down Barsebäck [*a nuclear power station on the Swedish coast facing Copenhagen*], we can't fight about that any more.

But the decision hasn't been confirmed, and there's still an ongoing debate about it, so if you're lucky it will take a bit longer . . .

Yes, but we've still got a few Swedish cards up our sleeve . . . I think *The Kingdom 3* will probably be a fairly strongly spiced smörgåsbord. There'll be more humour in the next sequel, some pretty good satire.

I have to say that I haven't got much more to say about *The Kingdom 2*. It's something I've already moved on from.

13

The Idiots

SYNOPSIS

A group of people in their twenties and thirties have withdrawn from the world to challenge the norms and values of bourgeois society in various ways. They play the fool in different social settings – to test the tolerance levels of the defenders of convention, and perhaps also to test and challenge their own self-imposed limitations. The Idiots depicts how the rules of the game became a game of rules. Provocation becomes pure art.

A young woman, Karen, the last person to join the group, is our guide through the activities we are confronted with. In a central scene she questions the purpose of the collective's challenging behaviour. The self-appointed leader of the group, Stoffer, sets things straight for her. He says that they all have to look for and discover their 'inner idiot', i.e. a sort of existential base for their most genuine feelings. Being an idiot is a luxury, he explains. In a society that keeps on getting richer, while its inhabitants keep getting poorer and more unhappy, an idiot is a far-sighted person.

Karen continues to question the implications of the group's peculiar mission and also has to ask herself why she is continuing to share her life with the collective. When one day she lets go of her repression and lets her 'inner idiot' have free rein, she gets her answer. She can happily hand herself over to the group, who receive her with warmth and tenderness.

* * *

In 1995 you and your fellow director Thomas Vinterberg published a manifesto, Dogme 95, which called for a completely new type of film

– and a whole new way of looking at film: the production of films with extremely low budgets, made according to very strict rules – as you called it, a film-maker's 'vow of chastity', which amongst other things meant that films had to be shot on location, with hand-held cameras, direct sound recording only, no music (unless it was fully integrated into the scene), and so on. And one final, important rule of chastity was that films mustn't be credited, so the creator's or direc-tor's name shouldn't appear in the opening or closing credits. Why did you and Thomas publish the manifesto at that point in time?

I can't really remember the exact reason. Actually, yes . . . Dogme 95 was published before the financing for *Breaking the Waves* was sorted out. I was very tired of waiting for decisions about whether we could make the film. And I'd just finished the first part of *The Kingdom*, and I felt that we had to try to start something com-pletely different.

So Dogme 95 wasn't a protest against the current state of Danish film and film production?

No, I stopped protesting about Danish film a long time ago. If you want to protest about something then the thing you're protesting about has to have a certain amount of authority. And if you believe that something lacks authority, there's no reason to protest against it. If there's anything in the film world that has authority, it's the American film industry with all its money and its incredible domi-nance on the global market. I'm not really into protesting; I'm fairly liberal on that point. I'd rather make suggestions instead, and that was our intention with Dogme 95. I actually sent a copy of our Dogme manifesto to Bergman and suggested that he make a Dogme film as well.

Did you get a reply?

No, of course not. But I see Bergman rather as my spiritual father. And he had problems with his father, of course. Nor has he had much response from his spiritual father, God. God never responded to Bergman, so it's entirely logical that Bergman doesn't respond to me. And it must be hard to get any response from the man who made *The Silence*!

But with Zentropa, the production company you own together with Peter Aalbæk Jensen, Dogme 95 became a reality. The Idiots *was subtitled Dogme #2.*

Yes, the first Dogme film, *Festen*, was made by Thomas Vinterberg, and after *The Idiots* came films by Søren Kragh-Jacobsen and Kristian Levring.

Were you pleased with the results?

Yes, the interesting thing is that all four films are so different in character, even though they all follow the rules of the manifesto. The idea was that we would engage several different film-makers on projects and see what we got. It's an experiment that's worked well, in my opinion, because the films are so different.

Can you explain how they differ?

Well . . . I'd prefer to talk about their similarities. The strange thing is that all of them are ensemble pieces. All four films are about a group of people, oddly enough. And that happened without us having any general discussion of our projects. But it's possible that the idea behind Dogme 95 tends to encourage that sort of story.

I could probably say that Thomas, being a bit younger than the rest of us, has a more youthful approach to his story.

But don't you think that you have a youthful approach to your story in The Idiots?

No, or if I do, it's a old man's sort of youthfulness. You know, that sort of built-in idea that everything was much better before. I hope that *The Idiots* is a modern film, but at the same time it's also a nostalgic film that expresses a yearning for the French New Wave and everything that happened in its wake. It's impossible to deny that Dogme 95 is largely inspired by the New Wave. It was a fantastic shot in the arm. Maybe we won't be able to do the same, but we might be able to provide some sort of preventive vaccine.

Both Thomas Vinterberg and I think this was the most fun we'd had with films so far. It was great fun working within this concept and according to the rules that we set ourselves. That sounds a bit evangelical. You know, 'following the Bible brings you such joy'!

21 *The Idiots* begin to get frisky in readiness for a 'gang-bang'

But it really was like that.

You're supposed to have written The Idiots *in four days . . .*

Yes, I did say that. I got the idea for the film as we were writing the script. I had the idea of a group of people who chose to behave like idiots – no more than that. Then this embryonic idea developed into a story over a long period of time. I went about thinking of all the opportunities the story offered. I started to fantasize about the different characters in the story, and eventually they began to react and live their own lives in my imagination. So when I eventually came to sit down and write the script, the story was more or less ready. So, yes, I did write it in four days.

In the documentary De udmygede *(*The Humiliated*) by Jesper Jargil, you say that the idea for the film comes from Rudolf Steiner and a suggestion of his that 'mongoloids are heaven-sent'.*

I don't know where the hell I got that Steiner quote from, but he had some theory that mongoloids were a gift to humanity, that they were like visitors from another planet or from heaven. I thought that was a lovely idea, seeing people who are different as a gift. The activities of the group in *The Idiots* were inspired by that idea. The last thing you'd expect would be to use that idea as a sort of therapy, based on finding yourself. Finding the child or the animal within. But you might also find something that would make other people happy, in the same way that mongoloids are a gift – not to themselves, but to the world.

At one point in the film someone says that 'idiots are the future'.

Yes, you can see them as a counterweight to the rationality surrounding us. Rationality is something I think is based in anxiety. If you're afraid of chaos, if you're afraid of living life, with all its conflicts and contradictions, then you grasp rationality as a defence. That's what happened to me with my background. In my family most things were looked at from a rational point of view.

I've always had a weakness for the irrational. Film work embraces a whole load of irrational qualities. *The Idiots* isn't merely a defence of Steiner's thesis. That's just one of the points of departure for the theories expressed by Stoffer, the leading figure in the group. The idea has been corrupted by him, you could say, in the same way that he tries to corrupt the other members of the group. You can draw parallels to politics or to people who, for various reasons, work in groups.

One important scene is when Karen asks Stoffer, 'Why do you do this?' As I understand it from Jesper Jargil's film, this was a scene that caused quite a few problems. First it was filmed inside the villa a couple of times, before you shot the final version during the trip to the forest.

The scene is important, and it was difficult to get it to work. I had my suspicions in advance, because I thought the scene was too explicit in the script. That was confirmed when we tried to shoot the scene indoors. Karen and Stoffer were sitting on the floor in one of the rooms, and neither of them had enough space to react to what they were saying and hearing. One problem was that Karen asked a couple of very down-to-earth questions, and Stoffer replied on a completely different level. In the end I had him give equally down-to-earth replies to her questions. And they weren't that bad, even if they weren't as precise as the first version. And I think moving the scene outside helped. It gave them much more freedom of movement. It was great to get out into that Fellini-style forest.

And Stoffer replies to Karen by saying it's about finding 'your inner idiot' . . .

The idea was that the idiot is just as nuanced an individual as a rational person. That there's a personality hidden beneath our permitted personalities which is just as unique and nuanced. It's an interesting idea, I think. And worth defending, as far as you can anyway.

Have you been in therapy yourself?

Yes, I've tried loads of different things.

When?

God! All the time, over the years. But it's like hypnosis. It's hard to get anything out of it if you're constantly trying to see through the techniques. And I have great trouble throwing myself into something if I can't see how it's done. I suppose I mean I have trouble letting go. It's that control thing again. So maybe the results weren't all they should have been.

But The Idiots *must have been a therapeutic experience. I watched one day of filming, and you seemed unusually relaxed in the company of your 'idiots' in front of the camera.*

Yes, it was certainly a very intense experience.

The finished film also gives an incredibly liberating impression.

I think so too. I think it was an important experience for everyone who worked on it. There was a feeling of psychodrama about the whole thing.

This business of film going beyond fiction at the moment of shooting is something I've aimed for in all my films. Even in *The Element of Crime*. What used to happen on the technical side is something I'm trying to transfer to a more psychological level.

Do you ever feel abandoned when a film shoot is finished?

Anxiety, you mean? Yes, I suppose I do. But at the moment my anxiety is entirely taken up with phobias about cancer. I'm suffering from umpteen different types of cancer. It hasn't happened like this before, when I could get panic attacks about all manner of things. Now it's very concrete. So I've started taking Frantex. It's a drug that's supposed to suppress anxiety a bit.

You have a new family now, you and Bente and the twins, and your two daughters from your first marriage. Doesn't that give you the security to hold these anxieties at bay?

It's almost the opposite. In my new relationship there's more space for anxiety.

In the diary you wrote during the shooting of The Idiots *you mention film as a game on several occasions. In one place you wrote that 'it's nice that it's my game we're playing'. And at another point you wrote: 'It's a tiny, little game that tiny, little Lars has set up.'*

That's an almost exact Bergman quotation! He said the same thing at some point, that he sees film as a game. Yet at the same time he wrote that he'd never had as much fun as the time he had twenty policemen in front of the camera. He was so intimidated by their authority, and now all of a sudden he was the authority figure. I really can't understand why Bergman keeps popping up . . .

But I remember when I used to make films as a child it was important that the whole thing was my game. And, of course, it was. It was my ideas and my games that I made my friends join in with. It gave me a sense of satisfaction, but it also gave me responsibility. You have to make the game work, after all.

It wasn't hard to persuade them to join in your game?

It probably was. But I usually managed it. And I got hurt if anyone didn't want to join in, in the same way that I felt hurt if an actor didn't want to be in *The Idiots*. Which happened, of course. They didn't want to join in my game.

How did you find your actors, your playmates, for the film? Most of them aren't very well known for their work in film, and several had never worked on films before.

No, that's probably true of most of them. The exception was Anne Louise Hassing, who played the lead in Niels Malmros's *Kärlekens smärta* (*The Pain of Love*). I thought that was a great film. Malmros's best film, and probably one of the inspirations for *Breaking the Waves*. But the other actors hadn't had much experience of film. Most of them were from the theatre, and I didn't know any of them beforehand. I think we auditioned about 150 actors. I had a very good casting director, Rie Hedegaard, who selected them. Then we had a number of large casting sessions, where a lot of actors performed at the same time. I wanted to see how they worked in a group situation like the one we were creating in the film. We had a director who did improvisation exercises with them, and these were recorded on video. From those videotapes I chose the actors for the film. Then we added a few other actors, like Erik Wedersøe and Paprika Steen, who have important supporting roles in the film. It was wonderful to work with all these young actors, who all felt such a strong desire to express themselves.

What did you think of the very close collaboration you had with everyone who worked on The Idiots?

It was very liberating. This technique is a dream come true for actors. We never had to set up any lights, and there were no lengthy technical preparations. We just set out some basic scenery and let the actors get on with it. We didn't have a big production team either. During the actual takes, it was really only me, doing the camerawork as well, plus a sound technician who followed them as they performed.

It was also a challenge for them to express themselves in a completely different way. They had to live their characters rather than act them. Perhaps it didn't turn out exactly as I imagined to begin with, but it was fun to try that way of working. I also got to test various experiments that I had wanted to try.

Such as?

Well, trying to get closer to the actors' anxieties and sorrow and internal conflicts. The sort of thing you dream of doing but never have time for. But here we had time. I could spend a whole day sitting down with a couple of the actors, talking to them about their childhood and upbringing and memories and experiences. It was incredibly exciting, but also difficult for the person taking on the role of therapist.

If I've understood correctly, this happened with one of the most central, tender and moving scenes in The Idiots, *the one where Karen confides in Susanne. They're sitting in a window recess, talking, and you get extremely close to them, both visually and emotionally. It must have taken several days to get that scene.*

Yes, it's the emotional heart of the film, if I can put it like that. It was very hard to get what I wanted. Bodil Jørgensen, who played Karen, finds it very easy to get access to her sorrow. She's been through personal tragedy, and has the capacity to access that and make use of it. And Anne Louise Hassing, who played Susanne, is extremely good at delivering her lines, very natural and relaxed. The problem was that when these two were supposed to talk to each other, it just didn't work. Anne Louise didn't manage to convince me that her character was seriously interested in Karen. The idea was that Susanne would command such an excess of understanding that she could absorb Karen's problems. She was supposed to be expressing sympathy. But on every take Anne Louise seemed to be strangely distant and, to my eyes, not really credible.

Then my therapeutic self suggested that if Anne Louise could see her own problems in Karen's then she would be able to express the sympathy that was lacking. You can't show sympathy for something you can't share. Sympathy requires imagination. And you can't take imagination for granted. My starting point was that, if we could get Anne Louise to experience or remember a similar sorrow to the one Karen tells her about in the film, about losing a child, then she would be able to perform the scene in a way that expressed the emotional weight it needed.

So we set up a purely therapeutic situation, where Anne Louise ended up sniffing about events in her childhood. In Jesper Jargil's documentary about the shooting of the film, there's a long

22 *The Idiots*: Bodil Jørgensen as Karen and Anne Louise Hassing as Susanne.

sequence where we see her wandering, red-eyed, through the rooms. It was very intense. And on the verge of sadism. That's how I see it, anyway.

The scene was very good in the end, very believable. It could have been a lot longer in the finished version. We cut it quite severely, because it could have become painful, and it would have weighed down Karen's character with too much sorrow. We had to finish the scene with a little smile, an assurance that Karen belonged to the group and that she could continue living as part of it. If I'd kept a longer version of the scene, Karen would have risked looking like a cry-baby.

For me the scene was credible, and that was important. I was very strict about that, even if Stellan Skarsgård has teased me by saying that a lot of the scenes aren't credible. It's typical of him to exploit my weaknesses like that! Stellan thought the scene where Stoffer runs naked through Søllerød had no logic or psychology to it. I can accept that, but I don't know if it's a bad scene in spite of that. I like the lack of psychological relevance there. I think the outburst is in line with Stoffer's character.

Do you think that in earlier films you were able to be as careful and consequential? I mean, did you have the chance to work on a scene until you were completely happy with it? Or did you have to make compromises that you later regretted?

That happened a lot. The great advantage of *The Idiots* was that we could keep going until we were happy. The film was shot on video, of course, so technical costs were very low. We also shot the script in order, which I'd never had the chance to do before.

What was the biggest advantage of that, do you think?

That we could see how it was working. You can do that with separate scenes during a normal shoot, but here we could follow the development of the characters in a more natural way. We knew how they had reached a certain point in the film and where they were in their own development, and the actors could adjust their performances accordingly. When you shoot a film by the conventional method, short sequences here and there from different places in the script, according to a shooting plan, you can get horrible surprises when you come to edit the film. You can find out that there's no psychological consistency. I've found out that if you shoot a film conventionally, like a big jigsaw puzzle, you often have to tone down the acting so that it doesn't get exaggerated and inconsistent. Here we could highlight clearer lines of development for the actors and let them react accordingly.

I think this is apparent from the diary I wrote during filming, which has been published, together with the script. I sat down every day after shooting and spoke into a little tape-recorder for fifteen to twenty minutes, recounting everything that had happened that day. Whether or not you like the result, it does give a unique insight into this way of working. It has no literary pretensions. I handed it all over to a journalist, Peter Øvig, who wrote it out and edited it so that it made some sort of sense. I haven't censored his work at all. I haven't even read it through.

I haven't seen a book like that before, but it's something I wish Bergman had written, day by day, for the whole length of a shoot. What Bibi said, and why and how he could get Bibi to act this way or that way. And why Bibi didn't want to do it that way, and why she was stupid, and so on. In the autobiographies he's written in his old age, the descriptions are more anecdotal and therefore more generalized. They're a bit like Buñuel's memoirs, *My Last Sigh*, which is great fun to read. A lot of it must be lies, but it doesn't matter. You can always elaborate your memories if it suits you.

From the diary it looks as though shooting didn't get off to a good start. You shot a scene at Amalienborg Palace that didn't make it into the film.

It was terrible! Absolutely impossible! It was strange, because we'd spent the fortnight before we began filming preparing and rehearsing. And everything was working really well. But then we had the camera there, and all of a sudden it was for real. And they were all struggling to give a performance. That was after I'd given a long speech to the cast before we started filming and stressed that the whole point of this film was *not* to perform. It was about forgetting most of what they knew about acting technique and performance. But the actors had been to drama school and had been taught that here was a story, and that a story needed to be told. In *The Idiots* they weren't supposed to be telling anything. They just had to exist and react in certain situations. Then, afterwards, I would construct the story and tell it. After rehearsing with them for a fortnight I thought we could let them loose. But they all started acting crazy in such an exaggerated way that the results were dreadful.

The thing that struck me most when I visited the shoot was the feeling of euphoria that everyone involved seemed to have been infected with. The work seemed characterized by a contagious lightness. It almost made me feel like joining in and getting involved.

It wasn't always like that, of course. What day were you there, do you remember?

It was the scene where Josephine's father comes to take her home.

Right, that was an example of everything working at its best. It was towards the end of the shoot, and the group had gelled and they were working together well. The only one who wasn't part of the group was Anders Hove, who played Josephine's father. As an actor he was a bit irritated at feeling excluded, and he was able to use that in his role. I was later criticized because he had a copy of the newspaper *Politiken* in his pocket. A lot of people thought that was far too obvious a cliché. But Anders Hove actually had it in his pocket when he arrived. Not as part of his character, but because he had been reading it on his way to the shoot. According to the Dogme rules, I wasn't allowed to give him any props. But when he suggested taking it out of his pocket, I told him not to bother.

The script for The Idiots *is pretty extensive. Did the freer attitude you had towards this style of shooting make it harder to stick to the original script?*

Naturally there were a few lines here and there that disappeared. I had a huge amount of material to work with, 130 hours' worth of footage. But every time we made changes between takes, we referred to the script, and mostly followed it fairly closely. The finished film follows the script very closely, which is interesting, because we weren't actually trying to.

It's well known that when you let actors improvise, you have to start with a fixed idea and direct the improvisation in a certain direction, otherwise it doesn't work. Nothing happens – apart from using up loads of film. You have to sow the seeds. You create characters out of dust and blow life into them. You have to have some sort of plan, a plan that you impose on the actors, whether they're conscious of it or not. Then they can carry on working on the characters that you've given them.

One thing that wasn't in the script is the interviews with the cast. How did you get that idea?

It was actually in the script that we would insert these interviews, but not where or when. So it was actually planned. Later on they went into the film, then got taken out again. I kept editing them in and out. The idea of the interviews has been used in a lot of films before this. I can't remember a case where I thought that these inserts worked. But the fact that they ended up in the finished film indicates that I thought they worked here. They were completely improvised. The actors answer for their characters, and at the same time they defend their characters. You can't write those sorts of answers beforehand, because they'd look false and constructed at once.

The breaks caused by the interviews have a kind of distancing effect. But they're also an affirmation. This whole idea of a few people running round playing at being idiots gained a whole other significance because of the interviews. If the members of the cast could sit down afterwards and talk about their experiences, then it must have meant something to them. And that validates the interviews, as well as giving impetus to the plot and the film as a whole.

Did you shoot the interviews after the end of filming?

Yes. They were done over three days, and I suppose we spent a couple of hours on each character. At one point we had the idea of doing a longer version of the film for television, because I've got more than enough material. But I don't think I have the energy to do that any more.

You shot a lot of the film yourself. How much were you responsible for?

About ninety per cent, I'd say.

And how did it feel?

It was great, really wonderful. It's the best way to make a film. Especially in this case, where the camera is inquisitive, invasive. I was only aware of what was going on in front of and around the camera. The camera movements that we ended up with are the result of my own curiosity. I, and my camera eye, could move from one situation and the people in that situation to something taking place outside my field of vision. I was a sort of listening camera. You end up with a sense of curiosity that I chose to retain in the editing.

Have you come across any disadvantages of filming in this way?

The film was originally going to be shot on 35mm. That's what it says in the Dogme regulations. But a 35mm camera was obviously too heavy and unwieldy to use in these circumstances. So 16mm

23 'It was great, really wonderful to do the filming myself!': Lars von Trier like a fish in water behind the video-camera for *The Idiots*.

was suggested, under the loose interpretation that the rules only meant that the film had to be distributed in 35mm. But in that case we might as well shoot it on video, then copy it on to 35mm film. That had the advantage that if you ended up editing an hour of film down to two minutes, it's a lot easier to maintain the same concentration of expression if it's shot on video. You can squeeze a lot of energy into those two minutes. And that's precisely what I think *The Idiots* has got. It crackles with energy. That was very important to me.

In your earlier films, like The Element of Crime *and* Europa, *aesthetics played an important role. You gave up on that entirely with* The Idiots, *after testing it and tinkering with it in films like* The Kingdom *and* Breaking the Waves. *What do you think of that development?*

The Idiots was a liberation from aesthetics. According to the rules, the film had to be shot in colour, but you weren't allowed to manipulate the colour in a laboratory, for instance. It felt good not to have to consider that at all. With my earlier films I spent a long time in the lab trying to get exactly the right colouring and temperature for the film. Now I wasn't allowed to do that, to change the lighting or the tone or the colour at all. I didn't have to make any decisions at all. That was extremely liberating.

Quite often we edited scenes with regard to the sound, the dialogue, without worrying about the images, a bit like making a documentary. That was also a very interesting aspect of it.

The free style you used to film The Idiots *has strong links to the French New Wave and the developments that took place in film during the early 1960s – New American Cinema, represented by John Cassavetes, Bo Widerberg in Sweden, new Polish and Czech cinema, and the British realists led by Ken Loach.*

I don't really think *The Idiots* matches my perception of that period. The film is more about my longing for that period, which I obviously wasn't able to experience and take part in. But it was an era that promoted freedom and liberation on every level. We went into that wholeheartedly. Those nude scenes were fairly liberating! They were extremely important. And fun!

You mean the actors in front of the camera weren't the only ones taking off their clothes?

Of course not! Behind the camera we stripped off as well. Me and Kristoffer Nyholm, who was filming as well and is a bit older than me. We loved it!

Another aspect of it is that you can keep control of your face; you know which side is best and which angle is most flattering. But you don't have the same control with tits and willies. You just don't have that control when you're naked. You have to give up your vanity, one hundred per cent. That's not a bad realization, and it's something you can make use of when you're making a film, even if the film in question doesn't require any nude scenes.

There was a Swedish director who proposed similar ideas, Vilgot Sjöman. There's a line in one of his films that could be a motto for the whole of his work: 'When you undress people, they're all the same.'

I don't know if nudity lets you see someone as they really are, but it does provide them with a useful tool. Relinquishing control, hiding who they are. Because no matter which theory of creation you believe in, you have to accept that man started his historical development without clothes. So if we want to try to get back to that starting point, you have to use nudity to get there.

In my naïvety I thought the actors would end up fucking. But they didn't. They probably would have done in the 1960s . . . Well, there are always improvements to be made! But three of the members of the group managed to get erections during shooting, which wasn't such an easy thing to do under the circumstances. So it wasn't a complete flop. But we had to seek professional help for penetration.

Did you gain any experiences that you'd like to develop and use again? Or do you see the film more as an interesting experiment?

I think it's probably something I'd like to come back to every now and then. Making a new Dogme film. I've never regarded any of my films as an experiment that I'd like to develop and use for something else. I do them for their own sake.

You've said that The Idiots *is your most important film, particularly with regard to your search for authenticity.*

Yes, authenticity! This is authenticity in the guise of comedy. And comedy isn't really something you associate with authenticity. But *The Idiots* had the same impact on me as *The Element of Crime*. *The Idiots* was an all-encompassing experience for me, which is how I felt about *The Element of Crime*, even though they're completely different in character. But they were both serious milestones for me.

The Idiots *was shown in competition at the Cannes Film Festival, along with* Festen. *You went to Cannes and took part in the festival. What did you think of the reception there, particularly with regard to both Dogme films and the Dogme manifesto?*

Obviously the Dogme manifesto was noticed, because both of the films were in the official programme. Everyone was talking about Dogme. Dogme's a good word, as well, in the same way that

Communism is a good word. A lot of people thought it was a load of rubbish, of course. But we managed to start a debate, which I think was a good thing. It's a long time since we had a debate about why we make films, about what they should contain and how they should look.

It's interesting that *Festen* was such an immediate success. After less than two months in Danish cinemas, 200,000 people have seen it. And after three weeks, *The Idiots* is doing pretty well. It's nice that both films have been fairly popular.

I also met Martin Scorsese, who was chairman of the jury in Cannes. He was very positive. What struck me most was that he was so short. I realized then that the film wasn't going to get a prize. I've never had any luck at Cannes with short directors or directors with an Italian background! First Polanski, then Coppola . . .

14

Dancer in the Dark

SYNOPSIS

It's the middle of the 1960s in a small industrial city in the state of Washington. Thirty-year-old Selma has emigrated here from Czechoslovakia with her son, who is now twelve. Selma works in a factory making kitchen equipment, but she also does as much work elsewhere as she can to save money for her son's future. She still finds time to rehearse a musical with the local amateur dramatic group. Selma's best friend, Kathy, is a constant source of support and encouragement. Selma also socializes with Bill and Linda, her neighbours in the trailer park where she lives. Bill has lost his job, but he is keeping this from his wife. Now he wants to borrow money from Selma, but she refuses. She can't touch her savings. One day Bill steals all her money. Selma can't and won't expose him. When she loses her job as well, she asks Bill for the money. He refuses to give it to her, claiming that it's his money. In desperation Selma shoots Bill. She is arrested and accused of murder and theft. She can't prove that the money was hers or that she was acting in self-defence. She now awaits the trial where her fate will be decided.

* * *

You had plans to make a musical for some time. Finally you made Dancer in the Dark.

Yes, to begin with I wanted to call the film *Taps*. But that's a protected title. So it was renamed *Dancer in the Dark*. It couldn't be called *Dancing in the Dark*, which was another idea, because that title was taken as well. The musical is the third part in my

'Goldheart' trilogy, following *Breaking the Waves* and *The Idiots*. First Bess and Karen, now Selma.

How come you ended up making another trilogy? First you had the trilogy about Europe, with The Element of Crime, Epidemic *and* Europa, *and now the 'Goldheart' trilogy.*

It's probably the fault of you Swedes! Bergman and his trilogies . . . But it's fairly practical as well. It's like being in a department store and buying three pairs of socks in one pack. That's how films are sold these days, in packs of three. If a distributor wants one good film, he has to buy two bad ones as well.

It also makes it easier for the critics as well. They can always devote a column to comparing the three films in the trilogy. They can write at length about the role of the heroine in each film. You don't think it gets a bit . . .

Boring?

No, just easier to compartmentalize the films? It's not unusual in other art forms, after all – painting, for instance, where artists go through different phases and styles in their art, or within music.

It's the idea of allowing yourself to repeat yourself, like Monet when he painted the same bloody thing all the time. He kept on and in the end they accepted him. He kept going, refining his art. Using the word 'trilogy' indicates that there's a theme that's shown in a new light in each film. Or that you're trying to expand on an idea. It turns into an excuse for concentrating on the same thing once more. Hopefully it won't be like this for the rest of my life.

When you were writing this third chapter in the 'Goldheart' trilogy, did you start with the female lead or with the story she's part of?

The female character came first. That was the case with *Breaking the Waves*, and to an even greater extent in the new film [*Dancer in the Dark*].

And Karen in The Idiots?

I think she just happened to be passing. On her way from one film to the other she stopped off in Søllerød.

There's also a recurrent theme in your films, of idealists who fall victim to their own beliefs and who, as a result, have to sacrifice themselves.

(*Laughter.*) Yes, that's probably a fair description. I don't know where it comes from. But it is noticeable. I can see that myself. And there's certainly a large chunk of naïve idealism in Selma.

We might also draw comparisons to Medea. *There you've got a heroine who sacrifices her children. In* Dancer in the Dark *the main character sacrifices herself for her child.*

Well, the difference isn't that great. I don't think Medea's life gets much better after the sacrifice she felt herself compelled to make. Not the way the story is interpreted in Dreyer's version, at any rate. After all, people are always sacrificing themselves completely in Dreyer's films – and in mine. It must be a particularly Danish characteristic!

So what can we say about sacrifice? I can't stop myself thinking at least ten times a day about how pointless life is. You make your entrance, then bow and disappear again. And I suppose you also have time to get a bit of food inside you while you're here. But someone who sacrifices himself or herself is at least giving their existence some sort of meaning – if you can see a meaning in doing something for others, for an idea, a belief. The characters in these films are struggling to bring meaning to their time on earth. It must feel easier to die if you're doing it for something you believe in.

Were you hoping to transform and recreate the musical genre with Dancer in the Dark?

I was trying to give it the same freshness that I think the Dogme films have, or *Breaking the Waves*, for that matter. But I prefer not to start with a form or a style any more. I'd rather start with the content of the story.

When I was writing the last draft of the script, I got a new idea about the relationship between Selma and her son, which is pretty

24 *Dancer in the Dark*: Björk as Selma

important to the story: the idea that they both suffer from an inherited disease that will eventually lead to blindness later in life. In order to stop this happening, Selma is saving money for her son. So when, towards the end, she is asked why she did what she did, she replies that it's because she wanted to hold a child in her arms so badly!

I got the idea for this from a cartoon – a completely impossible and terribly sentimental film. It's set in New York, where a policeman finds a doll in a rubbish bin. He gives it to an Italian woman that he's evidently quite fond of. She gives the doll to her daughter. At one point the girl drops the doll on the floor, and as she's trying to find it again she feels her way along the floor, and only then do you realize that she's blind. It's an extremely effective scene. As the film goes on the girl talks to the doll constantly – just like Bess in *Breaking the Waves*! She goes around the city with the doll, and it acts as her eyes. But the film ends with the girl able to see her mother for the first time in her life. It's a ridiculously sentimental but incredibly driven cartoon.

Blindness is a wonderful melodramatic tool. I also came to think of Douglas Sirk and *Magnificent Obsession*. That's a completely incredible story. Jane Wyman is blinded in a car accident caused by

Rock Hudson. He trains to become a doctor so that he can cure her. Then they get married, of course! God, that's pretty heavy stuff! I've tried not to use such coarse strokes in *Dancer in the Dark*.

The film is set in the mid-1960s. Was that to draw associations to the old American musicals?

No, if I'd wanted to do a pastiche, I'd have gone further back, at least to the 1950s, when several of the genre's highpoints were created. *An American in Paris, Singin' in the Rain* and *The Band Wagon*. That one was great, with Fred Astaire. And *Singin' in the Rain*, of course. I put a song from *The Sound of Music* in *Dancer in the Dark*, 'My Favourite Things'. It works well in the context it's in. It's fun hearing Björk's version of it. But the real era of the musical was already over by the time *The Sound of Music* was made, though now and then something still turned up, like *West Side Story*. And *Cabaret*, come to think of it.

Cabaret, of course, is a film that shows just how much you can do with a musical. It's interesting, not least because of its political content and message.

That's true, but now I've seen it so many times I've started to get tired of it. But I was completely blown away by it when it first came out. The problem with most musicals is that they're so horribly American. Not even *Cabaret* managed to escape that. That's probably why *West Side Story* is my absolute favourite, because it deals with such an archetypal American subject. *West Side Story* also seems to me to be the most successful musical on film in most respects, possibly also because it took the musical out into the streets more than most others did.

Out of the old film-studio productions, *Singin' in the Rain* is probably the one I'm most fond of, not least because of Gene Kelly. Fred Astaire was a tremendous dancer, but Gene Kelly was more than that; he was also a leading choreographer, imaginative and innovative, a bit like Bob Fosse later on. Incredibly clever! He was badly hit by the McCarthy blacklists and had more and more trouble finding work in Hollywood.

Gene Kelly is one of the things people think of when they think of America, but he was radical in a lot of ways. But he disappeared almost completely from the screen. Well, he turned up in Jacques Demy's *Les Demoiselles de Rochefort*, with Mademoiselle Deneuve . . .

You took tap-dancing lessons yourself when you were younger . . .

Yes. I tried to learn how to tap-dance. I've studied more recent techniques now. Tap-dancing has changed a lot over the years. It's partly been influenced by flamenco, and partly by what's become known as 'Riverdance'.

Were you any good at tap-dancing?

No, it's bloody difficult. But it was fun trying. It's really a very bizarre form of dance, especially in its American form. It's a form of artistry as well as dance. You can hardly call it classical dancing. In flamenco it's more integrated, more powerful. American tap-dancing is seen more as an offshoot of that, with its roots in black culture, barbershop dancing. It's a strange form of dance, which really doesn't belong in musicals.

Tap-dancing is often highly static and doesn't need a lot of choreography, like in some of the routines in Singin' in the Rain, *where Gene Kelly and Debbie Reynolds and Donald O'Connor stand in a row and tap-dance. There was one exception among the tap-dancers: Ann Miller. Do you remember her? She used to rush into scenes and race through a tap-routine that stole the scene. She was a real virtuoso.*

Yes, was she that dark-haired dancer with long legs? Who was always grinning like an idiot? Yes, she was great. But Gene Kelly also choreographed a lot of wonderful solo routines for himself. The scene with the newspaper getting stuck to his shoes in *Singin' in the Rain*, for instance. I also like the dance routines where everything becomes completely abstract. There are scenes like that in *Singin' in the Rain*, and even more so in *The Band Wagon*, where reality disappears and fantasy and dreams take over.

Dancer in the Dark *is set in Washington state in the USA in the mid-1960s. Why Washington?*

I'd never been there, but I chose Washington because they used to execute people by hanging them, and hanging is one element of the film. Yes, hanging can still happen, but the convict can choose a lethal injection if they want to. And I was also inspired by the American expression 'tap-dancing at the end of a rope'.

I got a video from the prison where these hangings take place. It's a very strict, macabre ritual. Amongst other things, the knot in the rope has to be tied in a special way. Whenever I've seen Westerns, I always thought the knot was tied in a special way to make it slide better. But here the knot's supposed to break the convict's neck.

Have you seen Nagisa Oshima's film Death by Hanging?

No, but I recently saw *In Cold Blood* by Richard Brooks, which is a very good but incredibly unpleasant film. Execution scenes work very well on film.

The fact that Selma comes from Czechoslovakia, was that because you wanted to give her an Eastern European background?

Yes. And I think Selma's a nice name. After all, I've got a daughter called Selma! The name has its origins in that part of the world. I also wanted an East European country as a contrast and counter-weight to the USA. It's all a bit *Joe Hill*. That's a good film as well. Do you remember the ending? With the bird flying past just as Joe Hill is about to be shot? If I remember rightly he doesn't see it. He's got a blindfold on. He just hears it. A nice touch.

Dancer in the Dark *includes a lot of Americana, the sort of thing we associate with the USA, and with American films especially: the courtroom scenes, for instance.*

Yes, that's a classic setting.

And the fact that Selma lives in a trailer park.

Yes, that's a typical American way of life. But I got the idea from an old film by Werner Herzog, *Stroszek*, with the actor from *The Enigma of Kaspar Hauser*, Bruno S. That's another film I like a lot. Herzog is a very original talent.

What do you think was the most positive thing about the making of Dancer in the Dark?

The most positive . . .? Well, when you refine the script to the extent that I did, or simplify it to the extent that it almost becomes a soap opera, then you get very good, clear scenes that are very good to work on with the cast. They contain fairly basic conflicts, because you've peeled away almost everything surrounding them. There's someone who's going to die, there are two people in love, and so on. The cast are also presented with portraits that are almost outlines, which ought to be more interesting for them than being given characters where everything's cut and dried. That's one reason why it was an enjoyable film to work on.

Dreyer used to use that way of working as well. He worked towards achieving ever greater simplification. But the difference was that he never let the actors make any additions or elaborations. That's the complete opposite of what I try to do. I want to give the actors the freedom to build on their own ideas. It's a bit like a children's game of cops and robbers, where the characters and conflict are clearly defined right from the start. So you can move on from there.

But was there a written script that you and the cast followed?

I followed the same principles that I've used in my more recent films. In the first takes we stick as closely to the written script as we can, then for each new take we get further and further away from it. It was incredibly interesting for me to work with Catherine Deneuve, for instance. She's wonderful at improvisation. Yet from what she said, she'd never done it before. She saw it as a challenge, and she was bloody good at it.

Catherine Deneuve said that she had found it inspiring to work with a director who was so open to all sorts of discussions with the cast.

I think I was, as far as I could be. But I was still surprised at how open-minded Catherine was about our not entirely conventional ways of working. One thing that might have been disconcerting was that I sometimes give instructions to actors in the middle of a

25 *Dancer in the Dark*: Selma (Björk) with her friend and factory co-worker Kathy (Catherine Deneuve). Deneuve contacted von Trier herself about the part.

take. I shot most of the film myself, and quite often I gave directions in the middle of a scene, like in *The Idiots*. But all of the cast accepted it without any problem.

Had you decided right from the start that you were going to film Dancer in the Dark *yourself?*

Yes, because I'd already filmed *The Idiots* myself, and I wanted to use the experience I had gained there. I wasn't entirely happy with the photography on *Breaking the Waves*, because we had a cameraman who was far too skilful on that. The images were far too beautiful, in my opinion. It's difficult for a professional to do a bad job!

Besides, it's a completely different experience when you're doing the filming yourself and letting your curiosity steer the camera. I think that's important. I use the zoom a lot in *Dancer in the Dark*, for instance. Quite suddenly, intuitively, on the spur of the moment. I can zoom in at precisely the moment that something unexpected happens in front of the camera. That's my improvisation, my contribution to the improvisation. And it's bloody good fun!

You filmed some extremely long scenes with the actors improvising in front of the camera, just as you did for The Idiots. *I saw a scene on the editing table that was maybe twenty minutes long, with all the main characters, Björk, Catherine Deneuve, Peter Stormare, David Morse and Cara Seymore, and Björk's son in the film, Vladan Kostig, a scene where he's trying out his new bicycle. In the finished film the scene lasts something like two minutes, and it looks like you returned the scene to what was originally in the script while you were editing it. Did you work like this throughout the film? You let the actors improvise, but the final result is still very close to the script?*

Dancer in the Dark has a fairly strange structure, or rather an extremely clear structure. To begin with you don't know what's happening. Gradually all these loose threads come together and then the drama continues in the traditional way. I like the first part of the film a lot, the bit that's more loosely structured. But even here events have to be kept within certain boundaries. So maybe it is like *The Idiots*, and maybe I have edited my way back to the script again. But at the same time I hope I've succeeded in retaining some of the gifts I was given while we were working. Such as one line Peter Stormare comes out with in the scene on the bridge you just mentioned: 'Russian women are the same. My father said Russian women are the same,' and everyone laughs. And then he says, 'I don't know what he meant though.' I think that's a funny, mysterious line.

Later in the scene Björk says to her son, 'I'm not that kind of mum.' And her son replies, completely improvised: 'Can't you be that kind of mum then?' That's a line I could never have written or come up with myself. So you get given a lot of unexpected treasures this way.

This rather haphazard way of introducing the characters means that you force us to become active viewers. We have to think about who these people are and about the relationships between them.

Hopefully the audience becomes more involved in the characters and their fate as a result. If you give the protagonists clear, unambiguous characteristics right from the start, and lay out the conditions for the drama, the story becomes one-dimensional. It's better to introduce your main character in situations that are completely different, of a more transitory nature, so that she becomes more human and understandable to the audience. Your palette has to have both light and dark colours when you're trying to paint a portrait. And this is very consciously done in *Dancer in the Dark*.

It seems that with this method – and in the song-and-dance scenes with one hundred fixed video cameras – you're trying to find the unexpected.

You could say that. The advantage of those hundred cameras is that we got everything we expected from the scene, but at the same time we also got a load of shots that were governed by chance, images with a random effect, captured by fate, which could be extremely expressive and telling.

How did you get the idea for the hundred cameras?

It was actually my old friend Tómas Gislason, the editor, whom I'd fallen out with a long time ago, who came up with the idea. We were sitting and chatting about how a musical ought to look. We were talking about all sorts of things. And we agreed that the modern musical's greatest strength should be the fact that it's trying to get away from everything artificial. I could compare it to filming a scene with a juggler. Either you hire a real juggler who knows his stuff, or you get an actor who stands and makes juggling movements in the air, then you copy in a number of balls technically. Both of these scenes can end up looking almost identical. But they still wouldn't feel the same. If someone's standing there juggling for real, we experience it in a completely different way to if we're watching someone pretending. It's the same with stuntmen. There's a big difference between a stuntman jumping from a great height, and throwing a doll instead.

That's why we decided that all Björk's musical numbers in the film should be live, that everything should be live transmission, a direct broadcast of a performance. Unfortunately that turned out to be impossible for various reasons. But the basic idea was that the singing should be live, and when we shot those scenes, that's what we set out to achieve.

The majority – and best – of the musical numbers in the classic film musicals were filmed using extremely mobile cameras. But at the moment I'm at a point in my life where I've had enough of elegant camera movements. But I'd always wanted to make a musical. If I was going to do it the classical way, I'd have used a camera crane and a dolly and sophisticated camera choreography, and song-and-dance numbers that had to be recorded in a studio. But that's just what I didn't want to do.

That's why it felt important to film those scenes in static shots. It 'underplays' the sense of musical. That's how I see it, anyway. I've also got a weakness for luxury. And luxury to me is not using a camera crane when it would be natural to do so. It's a pretty perverted luxury. So it felt very luxurious to set up one hundred cameras to capture one scene. But if we were going to try to give the impression of live transmission, then it had to be covered by as many cameras as possible. Whatever happened on stage, it would be documented. We weren't able to follow that exactly in every musical scene, which I think is a great shame. But in a couple of places we got as close to the idea as we possibly could have. *Dancer in the Dark* wasn't a Dogme film, so I didn't feel compelled to follow any fixed rules. But the intention was always to give an impression of live performance.

So only a couple of the cameras were manned by cameramen?

Yes, mostly to make sure we got close-ups of Björk. And they would have been tricky to get any other way in the large locations where we recorded the musical numbers. The main advantage of these song-and-dance numbers was the presence of Björk herself. Mind you, we could have done with a thousand cameras in those scenes! I said two thousand to Vibeke Windeløv, the producer, with the millennium in mind.

And then you would have got into the Guinness Book of Records *as well?*

Exactly.

Did you find it difficult editing the musical scenes?

Yes. What I always try to find in situations like this is some sort of generally applicable system. And I was in part forced to find that system after filming was finished. The scenes where the system was most thought out in advance are also the ones that I think work best. Like the song-and-dance number right after the murder. That was also the easiest to edit, because there we had hung up all the cameras rather like surveillance cameras. That gave a very particular atmosphere to the scene. Other scenes that weren't so well thought out from the start were a bit trickier to edit. But I've learned a lot from it.

So what was the general system as far as editing the musical scenes was concerned?

Well, the system was that there shouldn't be a system! Just that we should have so much comprehensive material on film that we could do whatever we wanted with it. The problem was that the separate images of the montage became too short, in my opinion. I would have preferred considerably longer shots. But you can't have that with this method of filming. The cameras were positioned in such a way that the images wouldn't hold for longer.

I wanted to be able to smother myself in close-ups of the people in the musical numbers. They're Selma's fantasies, after all, and she's populating them with the people around her. And they are themselves in these musical scenes; they act in accordance with their roles in the realistic part of the film. That's why I wanted to be able to show them in greater close-up – but these shots, of necessity, were far too short.

But thanks to the amount of filmed material and the wealth of images you were also able to fashion a sort of choreography from the editing, such as the first big song-and-dance number, in the factory.

That was probably the most problematic scene. I wanted to have machinery in the foreground all the way through, but that wasn't possible. And more real sound, but that was difficult to modulate, what with the singing and the music as well. I don't know if it benefited the film, but it might have done.

The musical number on the train was more planned out from the start. And that was also something of a mistake, because that wasn't the point of all those hundred cameras. Now you can see quite clearly that a large number of shots were consciously composed. Coincidence and chance aren't as important here. The advantage of the hundred cameras in the train scene is that we were able to film it in just two days. If we'd used traditional methods it would have taken us a month to complete.

So the system never worked as well as it should have. Maybe we should have had a thousand cameras. That would have been possible. Cameras aren't particularly expensive, and they're getting smaller and smaller and easier to hide around the set. We hid ours or, in certain cases, edited out the ones that ended up in shot.

Dancer in the Dark *was shot on video. What were the advantages and disadvantages of that?*

I can't see any real disadvantages: quite the opposite. *Dancer in the Dark* was shot on video, in Panavision format. The transfer to film worked really well, it really did! The images have got a very cinematic feel to them, even though you know that they came about through a transfer from video. Excellent quality! In a couple of years most films will probably be shot on video, and even now you can see the possibilities of that.

I'm still very fond of old video footage, like the clip of Neil Armstrong walking on the moon. The shot with that strange object along one side, something that looks a bit like a tripod. We sat up all night watching those bloody pictures over and over again. They look like they were shot in a studio. Of course, there are also rumours that they *were* filmed in a studio somewhere on earth.

But the method you chose for Dancer in the Dark *gave a mixture of stylization and strong realism.*

Yes, that was the basic idea of this film, a collision between man and abstraction, or . . . how can I put it? The human and the artificial, truth and untruth. Because the songs are born in Selma's head, and Selma is a humanist more than anything else. She values things that people generally don't see any value in any more: noises and human frailty. And this is all turned into music and dance – by thought.

26 Lars von Trier dons cans on location for *Dancer in the Dark*

How did you find the film's choreographer?

One of the first preconditions for the film was Björk herself. And
she was going to write music that would fit the idea of the film; in
other words, music that would express both Selma's humanity and
the inhumanity of the musical genre. I think she captured that brilliantly. The idea was to express something similar in the dancing.
I'd looked quite closely at something called 'stomp', which seems
to be popular at the moment. It's a style of dance where you use
anything you like to create a rhythm. First I was going to have an
older choreographer, an old hand who had worked in the old
musicals and who might enjoy helping to break the mould. But it
was hard to find someone like that, especially as I'm not really an
expert in the subject. So I started looking through a lot of music
videos. One of the few videos that had impressed me before and
that I thought was both attractive and challenging in terms of its
choreography was the video for Madonna's 'Vogue'. Vincent
Paterson was the choreographer on that. He's also choreographed
a couple of Michael Jackson videos. So I thought if we were going
to have one of those video people, it ought to be him. And he was

233

incredibly good. He tried to create choreography that matched what I thought about dancing. I was very impressed with him.

At one point in the film Selma says that she likes musicals because 'in musicals nothing dreadful ever happens'. You prove that wrong pretty categorically in Dancer in the Dark.

Yes, in some ways I suppose so. What I was trying to do was to give the musical a more dangerous function. Not in a stylistic way, though. I wanted to create a tighter atmosphere and arouse emotions that the musical genre usually holds at a distance. The classic musical is a sort of descendant of operetta. Opera, on the other hand, allows itself an entirely different register and range as far as emotions are concerned, and it was that sort of intensity I was after.

Even so, I think I probably made it easier for myself by making it clear that what we see are Selma's daydreams and fantasies. But I saw that as the only way of accepting the musical interludes in the film. Maybe it was naïve or cowardly. Because I think it ought to be possible to develop the film musical considerably in this respect, and be more adventurous. But that would require the development of film, and greater sophistication in the audience: back to the situation where you could sit and let the tears gush while some great interpreter of Wagner or Verdi is singing as hard as he or she can and practically falling forward into the prompt box. If we could reach that level of abstraction, then a whole new world would open up to us.

Is this one of the reasons why you opened your film with an overture?

I've always liked the grandiosity of overtures. Like in *2001* or *Lawrence of Arabia* or *West Side Story*. Opening the film in that classical, operatic way.

In cinemas that still have curtains, I wish they would play the overture with the curtain closed, and only open them when the film starts. One problem with that is that the curtains cover the speakers. But that could be solved somehow. I'd like to lull the audience into a particular atmosphere. That's something I've always tried to do – setting the mood before the film has properly got going.

Something else that's unusual in the film is that all the musical scenes occur in connection with extremely unsettling situations, and – for the central character – highly dramatic scenes.

That was consciously done. I wanted to introduce the musical numbers into crisis situations for the protagonist, or into scenes that could be regarded as turning points in the drama. This is true even of the first numbers, even if the situation there is less pointed than later on. I'm a novice at this, of course, but to me it seemed to make sense to position the musical numbers like this.

The first musical number, the one in the factory, comes a long way into the film, about three quarters of the way through.

That was the point, as I saw it. Well, in so far as there was a point. But I like that idea: you know that you're going to see a musical, but it takes a while before anyone bursts into song.

The musical numbers have a strictness that contrasts in a very dramatic way with the character of the rest of the film. We're suddenly thrown abruptly into the situation at the very first scene of the film, with the amateur dramatic group's rehearsal.

I like the abrupt shift from the rather reserved overture to a situation that is also about the creation of music, albeit on a more modest and less serious level.

Björk's performance is remarkable, and admirable considering her lack of previous acting experience.

Yes, her portrayal was practically created in spite of herself. She acted out of pure emotion, and that was naturally very painful for her. And for a lot of the rest of us as well . . . It's interesting, because I had never tried to work in that way with an actor before. When an actor is offered the part of a particular character in this particular medium, they usually express great joy in the work. A joy in the challenge that the role presents.

It's easy to compare Björk's role in Dancer in the Dark *with Emily Watson's in* Breaking the Waves . . .

Of course, but with the decisive difference that Emily acts her part whereas Björk feels hers. Which of them is best under the circumstances is difficult to say, but their working methods are entirely different.

Selma's daydreams, her musical fantasies, are reminiscent of Bess's conversations with God in Breaking the Waves. *Was that a conscious decision on your part?*

Well, it's true in so far as both situations involve a dialogue orchestrated by the lead character. You could probably say that they're directing their own dramas in their respective films. I'm not sure if it works in quite the way that I imagined it would. Things never turn out the way you imagine they would, which is perhaps just as well.

In connection with the première of The Idiots *you made your own singing début. You recorded a single with the cast of the film as backing singers.*

It was a spontaneous idea we had, that I and 'the idiots' – i.e. the cast of the film – would record something together. I've liked that song by Peter Skellern, 'You're a Lady', for a long time. So I thought that I could do that, and the others could do something else. It was a lot of fun. It's a good feeling, singing.

I took singing lessons for five weeks beforehand. My teacher said something good. She said that you have to lean into the music. You imagine that you're facing into the wind, and you lean into it. It makes you feel as if you're floating. You don't remain standing.

That's something I don't think Bergman has done. Made a record. But that feeling of being able to float in your art, I'm sure he's experienced that.

THE SELMA MANIFESTO

Selma comes from the east. She loves musicals. Her life is hard, but she can survive because she has a secret. When things get too much to bear she can pretend she's in a musical . . . just for a minute or two. All the *joy* that life can't give her is there. Joy isn't living . . . joy is there to make it bearable for us to live. The joy that she is able to conjure up from within is her spark of happiness.

Selma loves *The Sound of Music* and the other big song-and-dance films. Now she's got the chance to play the lead in an amateur version of *The Sound of Music* . . . At the same time she is about to fulfil her life's greatest goal. It looks like dream and reality are going to melt together for Selma.

So, popular music and famous musicals are what fills the spaces in her brain. But she isn't just a dreamer! *She is someone who loves all of life!* She can feel intensely about the miracles that every corner of her (fairly grim) life offers. And she can see all the details . . . every single one. Strange things that only she can see or hear. She's a genuine watcher . . . with a photographic memory. And it's this double-sided nature that makes her an artist: her love and enthusiasm for the artificial world of music, song and dance, and her keen fascination for the real world . . . her humanity. Her art consists of the musical interludes that she takes refuge in when she needs to . . . fragments of Selma's own musical . . . like no other musical . . . it's a collision of splinters of melodies, folk songs, noises, instruments, texts and dances that she has experienced in the cinema and in real life, using the components that she – because of her gift – can find there.

This isn't pure escapism! . . . It's much, much more . . . it's art! It stems from a genuine inner need to play with life and incorporate it into her own private world.

A situation might be incredibly painful, but it can always provide the starting point for even a tiny manifestation of Selma's art. It can be incorporated into the little world that she can control.

ABOUT THE FILM

In order to tell Selma's story the film must be able to give concrete form to her world. All the scenes that don't contain her musical fantasies must be as realistic as possible as far as acting, décor and so on are concerned, because the scenes from Selma's daily life are the model for what she adds to her musical numbers . . . and these have to be true to life. What she sees at the cinema is flawless . . . painless . . . in other words, entirely at odds with real life . . . where it's the flaws and the pain that make it shine. The intimation of humanity . . . of nature . . . of life!

So the events that form part of the story will partly be expressed by the finest, most beautiful music, recorded according to unambiguous methods – and mixed with all the muddles and mistakes that reality can contribute. These two orchestras will play together.

This is also the principle for Selma's musical. Punk is the word I would use to underline the whole thing: as I see it, punk is a collision between tradition and nature. It isn't destructive . . . it isn't solemn, because it's trying to get back to basics . . . by confronting the system with a modern, more honest view of life . . . and forcing life into something that has become stale and enclosed . . . using violent means. This is probably the only violence that Selma participates in?

The Music

The musical elements that include instruments and melodies come from the musicals that she loves. They might be fragments that are incorporated into different contexts . . . or instrumental sounds that are used in unusual ways. Selma loves the cheapest musical effects: riffs and other clichés . . . and she uses them in ways that have nothing whatever to do with good taste . . . but these elements are mixed with the sounds of life, and through this she becomes far from banal. She loves the simple sounds of living expression . . . hands, feet, voices, and so on . . . (the sighs caused by hard work?) . . . the noise from machines and other mechanical things . . . the sounds of nature . . . and above all the little sounds caused by chance . . . the creak of a floor when a floorboard develops a defect. Her music extols dream on the one hand, life on the other. She uses her own daily life to create music. Mostly to use this positively . . . but occasionally to sing out her pain . . . It's important that the artificial is allowed to remain and sound artificial . . . we have to be aware of where things come from . . . the clichés from musicals . . . and even more important: the sounds from the real world . . . they should never be 'refined' . . . the closer to reality the better . . . we prefer a rhythm created by hand using a rattling window than a sampled version of the same thing . . . if sampling is to be used here, then it must take its place on the artificial side. The music should sway from one side to the other . . . let there be occasions when only natural noises reign (stomp).

In any case, there will be an explosion of feelings and above all a celebration of the joy that fantasy can bring. The sounds of reality do not only come from machines and daily routine . . . they also come from creative people like Selma who can use anything and everything in every scene as an instrument! This is an area where Selma is superior. She can weave gold from mud. She can hear music in noise . . . and when she shows it to us . . . we can also hear . . . that the noise contains life and it is as beautiful as any traditional, celebrated masterpiece from the stage. Both sides are there . . . alike and not alike.

The Dancing

The principle is the same: Selma exploits and loves grand effects: poses, homogeneity . . . glamour . . . but she combines all this with real people . . . with real movements and faults. With the chaos of life. With acting. Efficiency and inefficiency. Her use of effects is a challenge to good taste . . . and her consideration of life's vicissitudes is immense. Every arena is utilized. She can see possibilities in every unexpected thing. The dancers can use whatever they like in their dance and their music. She has worked in a factory for a long time and takes pleasure in the slightest human gesture. She knows what a body can do . . . when it does its best to attain perfection in dance, like in the big films, and she knows how the joy and pain of everyday life can be expressed in movement. Selma dances like a child . . . for herself . . . in ecstasy . . . it might look terrible . . . but suddenly, in a fraction of a second, the whole room is in harmony . . . and she is its queen.

The dance has no façade . . . it faces every direction . . . it has no boundaries . . . a fingertip touching a surface is dance! (If we should need explanations or preparations for a shift from reality . . . we can show it in the non-musical episodes.)

The Songs

The songs from the musicals provide the bass . . . and they've got rhythm! They're primitive . . . they're Selma's naïve way of telling a story through a song . . . but sometimes her fascination with sounds, rhythms, words and rhymes fights through . . . then she starts to play with it and forgets everything. The songs are Selma's dialogue with herself . . . even if sometimes they are put in other characters' mouths, who express her words, her doubts, fears, joys, and so on. They are naïve songs, with all the well-used words from popular music . . . but often things don't work for her . . . and certain deeper truths seep out . . . When that happens Selma is quick to turn it all into a game again . . . playing with words . . . or fragments of words . . . like a child! . . . sheer astonishment at letting sounds come out of her mouth!

And remember she enjoys mimicry . . . she can sound like a machine or a violin. A mistake can suddenly also be used as an effect . . . a mispronounced word can gain its own meaning when thirty people pronounce it the same way!

The Décor

Super-realism! Neither more nor less. No one should be able to say that this is a film that wasn't made on location . . . and that these places have never been documented by a camera before. Everything in these places and that is used in dance or music . . . must be there *because of the story or the location or the characters*. We are working against the principle of musicals entirely here . . . there are NOT suddenly ten identical things to use in a dance. The same applies to costume . . . there shouldn't be a troupe of dancers wearing the same clothes. The costumes are also an expression of realism, and they say something about the person wearing them.

And, as usual, it's the sudden gaps in logic that make things credible and alive! That make everything human! And this all has its origin in Selma . . . She is the person seeing and speaking!

240

15

Dogville

SYNOPSIS

The beautiful fugitive, Grace, arrives in the isolated township of Dogville on the run from a team of gangsters. With some encouragement from Tom, the self-appointed town spokesman, the little community agrees to hide her, and in return, Grace agrees to work for them. However, when a search gets underway, the people of Dogville demand a better deal in exchange for the risk of harbouring poor Grace, and she learns the hard way that, in this town, goodness is relative. But Grace has a secret and it is a dangerous one. Dogville may regret it ever began to bare its teeth . . .

* * *

LARS VON TRIER: I like the idea of calling *Dogville* a 'fusion film'. Unfortunately fusion is a really dull idea, but I can't think of anything better. You know the term 'jazz fusion'? It's pretty terrible, a big mixture of different styles forced into the same monotonous beat. Like fusion cookery, which is a sort of mix of a whole load of different dishes. In the absence of anything better, I would still characterize *Dogville* as a fusion film.

The most reactionary attitude to art has always been the question 'What is art?' Followed by the statement 'This isn't art!' Limiting it, labelling it. In the same way, people have tried to contain and limit film – and literature too, for that matter. I'm trying to challenge that now by creating a fusion between film, theatre and literature. That doesn't mean filming a performance in a theatre, though. *Dogville* lives its own life, according to highly specific value criteria within the genre which, as of now, can be called 'fusion film'. It's important not to get bogged down in questions of what is cinematic or non-cinematic, because it seems like we've reached a position where everything is possible. The cinematic has been purified to the point where it has all become completely lacking in interest. There, a bit of cinema philosophy!

Naturally, everyone is going to abandon conventional film-making now and start making fusion films! This is the only sort of film that will be made from now on! So it's good to have a name for it . . . But, joking aside, that's what I was trying to explore in *Dogville*.

But this time you didn't write a new manifesto before you started filming?

No, it's something I've worked out only recently, once the shoot was already finished. But the real essence of the whole thing is that the elements that have been taken from theatre and literature are not just mixed up with the forms of expression offered by film. The whole thing has to function as a cohesive fusion, thoroughly blended. It isn't just a case of mixing exotic spices into a Danish dish to give it a bit of oomph. It should be a thoroughly blended and harmonious emulsion.

There are elements in Dogville *which are reminiscent of classic Anglo-Saxon literature, from Fielding to Dickens, with the omniscient narrator's voice and the division into chapters, where the chapter headings give an idea of what is about to happen.*

That's true, but it's more likely I had a book like *Winnie the Pooh* in mind when I was writing the screenplay. There, at the beginning of each chapter you read things like, 'In which Pooh and Piglet go hunting and nearly catch a Woozle', for instance. Things like that, which really get your imagination going. One of my favourite films is *Barry Lyndon*, which is also divided into chapters, although I don't remember if there are any clues as to what the chapters are going to contain. The screenplay of *Dogville* is divided into scenes. It might say, 'The scene where this or that happens . . .' 'Scene' is a word with a lot of meanings, and I chose it on purpose. But later on we switched to calling the scenes chapters, partly because of the word's literary associations.

27 *Dogville*: Nicole Kidman as Grace

There are also certain smart dramaturgical reasons for using this narrative technique. You give your audience certain expectations concerning what is about to happen, but then something different to what it expects happens. The introductory words help to build the arc you have to set up if you're going to conjure up a cinematic experience. It becomes part of the framework.

If we look at the parallels to the theatre instead, Dogville *is very reminiscent of Brecht and instructional works of his like* The Good Woman of Setzuan *or* Mother Courage.

The film was certainly inspired by Brecht. I would prefer to call it second-hand inspiration, though. My mother was really keen on Brecht. She left home when her father broke her Kurt Weill records, old 78s. She was only sixteen then, but Weill was her great musical passion and she couldn't bear what her father had done. Brecht was something of a domestic god when I was growing up, whereas my generation has tended to view him as a rather old-fashioned genius. Fashions and tastes are constantly changing, of course.

But of course *Dogville* is inspired by Brecht. One of the starting points was actually Pirate Jenny's song in *The Threepenny Opera.*

I've mostly heard it in a version composed only recently. The erstwhile Danish pop star and musician Sebastian composed some new music to the songs in *The Threepenny Opera* a few years ago, where you can still feel Weill's influence, although there's a good deal more noise. I listened to that a lot and was really seduced by the great revenge motif in the song: 'And they asked me which heads should fall, and the harbour fell quiet as I answered "All!"' I was really taken by the Danish version of the text. But seeing as *Dogville* was going to be made in English, I watched the English version, and it's really lame. A lot weaker, missing a lot of the different nuances. In the Danish version Jenny is washing glasses – '*Pas på dit glas, mit born*' ('Watch your glass, my child'). In the English version, I think she's mopping the floor.

It was those words in the Danish version of the song that gave me the idea of the Henson family in *Dogville* being involved with glass. So I kept that in, even though the film is in English and there's no mention of glasses in Pirate Jenny's song in the English version.

There's a distancing effect in the way you so clearly state 'this is a film'. You get that right from the first caption in the film, and at the end the narrator says, 'This is how the film ends,' not 'This is how the story ends.'

Yes, that's something I really wanted to underline. I don't know why. Maybe because of Brecht's influence. I experienced Brecht's dramas at a fairly young age and have never returned to him or his work. They exist in my memory mostly as feelings and atmospheres.

Can you say a bit more about how you got the idea of Dogville, *apart from Pirate Jenny's song?*

I think the idea came about one day when I was in a car with Jens Albinus, the actor who played the lead in *The Idiots*. We happened to be listening to that song, and I said I could see myself making a film about revenge. I thought the most interesting thing would be to come up with a story where you build up everything leading to the act of vengeance. And of course these days I've got this notion that I can only make films that are set in the USA, maybe because I was criticized when *Dancer in the Dark* came out for making a film about a country I've never been to. I can't really understand that sort of criticism. (But one reason for it might be that I criticized the American justice system in the film.) And I daresay I know more about America from various media than the Americans did about Morocco when they made *Casablanca*. They never went there either. Humphrey Bogart never set foot in the town.

These days it's hard not to pick up information about America. I mean, ninety per cent of all news and films comes from the USA. I reckon it ought to be interesting for Americans to see how a non-American who has never visited the USA regards their country. And Kafka wrote an extremely interesting novel called *Amerika*, and he'd never been there either. So from now on I only want to make films that are set in the USA. For the time being, at least.

Dogville is also set in the Rocky Mountains, a landscape that has always seemed to symbolize the USA for me. A powerful landscape, run through with deep ravines.

Did you get the idea for the form of Dogville *at the same time as the film's plot?*

No, when I wrote the screenplay I saw it as a conventionally formed film. But it felt boring. Then I went on a fishing trip to Sweden, and wasn't having any luck! Suddenly I had the idea that you could see the whole of Dogville as though laid out on a map. That the whole story could be told on an unfolded map. I'm pretty fascinated by the limitations that unity of space can give you. Another source of inspiration was one of the best things I've seen on television: Trevor Nunn's adaptation of Dickens' *Nicholas Nickleby* with the Royal Shakespeare Company. It looked like the actors were allowed to improvise from the text. It was a magnificent production. It was during the 1980s, if I remember rightly. Everyone watched it! And it's still as fresh today.

What was special about the performance was that it was supposed to look as though it had all taken place on a stage. Nunn edited in shots of the audience now and then, and used other distancing effects too, like the actors occasionally assuming the role of narrator, or the scenery and props being changed in full view. I can also see the influence of one of the classics of American theatre, a play that just about every American schoolchild gets to know at some point, Thornton Wilder's *Our Town*.

A long while before filming of *Dogville* got underway, we did a fairly comprehensive series of test shots. After these tests I decided that it shouldn't look like we were filming a theatre stage but that the whole thing should be stylized to such an extent that it couldn't take place in a theatre, although it should still have a sense of theatre to it. But still a stylization. Consequently you can do whatever you want to, of course, so you have to set limits to what you want to do. You haven't seen the finished film yet. You've seen a film where you hear the actors' voices and the narrator's voice, but there aren't any sound effects yet. There's still a lot of work to do, because on the sound side of things there isn't going to be any sort of stylization: quite the reverse. The sound that you hear in the finished film will be completely realistic. You'll be able to hear the crunch of gravel underfoot, for instance, even if there isn't any (visible) gravel on the studio floor. And the way the actors have played their scenes is nothing like theatre either.

There is also a suggestive tension in the mix of those big, wide shots, where you see all the actors at once, and the very tight close-ups of Grace (Nicole Kidman) and the other lead characters, particularly Tom (Paul Bettany).

The idea was that the actors would perform in a very realistic way, even though the scenery and external set-up are far from realistic. They're real in the same way that a child's drawing is real. If you give a small child some crayons and ask him or her to draw a house, you'll get a house made of a few simple lines. That's how our scenery works. We're establishing an agreement with the audience under which these circumstances are accepted. If that agreement is clear enough then I don't think there are any boundaries to what you can do. I haven't had the slightest doubt about that.

You can do almost anything on film now. With the help of computers I can insert a herd of elephants into a scene, or create an earthquake. But that doesn't interest me. I'd rather draw the shape of a dog on the studio floor to mark that there is a dog there, or put a crate of beer in a corner to indicate a bar.

The plot of Dogville *is largely driven forward by a narrator's voice,*

28 *Dogville*: Tom Edison (Paul Bettany) and Grace (Nicole Kidman)

rather in the style of old English novels. Was this the intention right from the start, when you first got the idea for the film?

It was there right from the very start. As usual I wrote the screen-play very quickly. It was a fairly large script, about 150 pages, but once I have the idea for a story and start writing it down, the words fall over each other and the writing process itself is quickly done. I haven't read much classic English literature. But I've read Wodehouse, for instance, who uses the same sort of subtle, know-ing tone that I've tried to get across in the text. After one screening the artist Per Kirkeby (with whom I'd worked on *Breaking the Waves*) said it reminded him of Dickens' *Great Expectations*. I've seen the film, and it too has a rather ironic narrator's commentary that reveals some of the characters' underlying motivations.

It was an incredibly tiring shoot. *Dogville* was filmed in about six weeks. That's fast. Unnecessarily fast. I could have taken longer, but at some point before we got started I recklessly declared that I'd have the job done in no time. It was tough work as well. I was running about all day long with that bloody camera on my shoulder. It might strike some people as a confusing way of using the camera, but this is how I want it. I can't defend the

29 *Dogville*: Grace (Nicole Kidman) and Chuck (Stellan Skarsgård)

technique apart from saying that I think it's the best way to shoot my films.

It's a technique and an aesthetic you've used since The Idiots.

Yes, since then I've become more and more egocentric.

And have wanted to control your films more and more . . .?

Well, I don't know about that. Well, maybe. But I think I get better contact with the actors when I'm the one behind the camera. I can communicate with them in a completely different way than when I'm standing next to Anthony Dod Mantle and he's the one moving the camera – which happened once or twice.

What did all these American Hollywood stars with whom you've adorned your film make of this technique? It must seem very strange to them.

I don't know about that. I'm sure they've had a lot of opinions about my way of working, but I think they've been pretty happy, in spite of everything. I know Nicole (Kidman) was completely in tune with what I was doing. I was asking her to do things in front of the camera that were pretty demanding, and she just did them. She evidently realized that a lot of thought had gone into this way of working, and that there was a point to doing it this way.

When did Nicole Kidman become involved in the project?

She was there right from the start, because I wrote the screenplay with her in mind as the female lead. I had seen her in *Far and Away*, which wasn't a particularly good film, and I had read an interview where she said she would like to work with me. So I thought, 'OK, I'll write a film for her.' I hadn't met her at that point. I didn't have any idea that she was as tall as she is. She's gorgeous.

You hadn't seen her in Kubrick's Eyes Wide Shut?

I don't think so. I saw *Eyes Wide Shut* fairly late on. I think I'd finished the script by then. She's incredibly good in that, though.

Yes, the film deteriorates once she's out of the picture. And you miss her presence throughout the rest of the film.

That's right. We had to wait a while for her. She was busy with other film projects when we were ready to go into production, so we postponed the start of the shoot to suit her. There are bound to be problems when you write a story with a particular actor in mind, and she isn't available. But we waited for Nicole, and I'm glad we did. I think she's incredibly good in the film, a real asset.

And the other actors? Did you choose them all, or were they suggested by your casting director?

It varied. I knew some of them from before, of course, like Stellan Skarsgård. And I'd dreamed of working with Ben Gazzara for a long time. The same with Philip Baker Hall, whom I'd seen in *Magnolia*. Some of them got in touch asking to be involved, like Jeremy Davies and Chloë Sevigny. That was great, because they're both really good. We've been lucky. But what a bunch to try and keep in check! Good grief, you can imagine! It's like a children's nursery, only twenty times worse!

You filmed Dogville *in sequence. What are the advantages of doing that, do you think?*

I'd sooner talk about the disadvantages first, because they're clearer. Often it takes me a while to get into a new film, to find the right style and form for it. When you film scenes out of sequence you don't notice the problems so much. But here the weaknesses were much clearer. I think, for instance, that from the point of view of the acting the film is weaker at the start, but the intensity of the acting gets more pronounced the further you go. Of course that's also due to the story, which gets more dramatic and critical as it develops. The acting is also better when the actors are relaxed, and I probably wasn't in a position to create the necessary calm, supportive atmosphere at the start of the shoot.

But I'm so bloody ambitious. My ambition in this case was not just that the entire film should take place on a black floor almost entirely without scenery and include a number of Hollywood stars, but also that it should be filmed in the shortest possible length of time. Filming was finished in six weeks, and that's sheer madness. It was something I had made up my mind about, and I was ready to do anything to make sure it happened. I demand far too much of myself, and in the end it becomes a question of honour. That's why I think it makes good sense to make three films in a row in exactly the same way, so I'm not forced to turn every cinematic concept upside down yet again. Maybe it makes things a bit more relaxing for me.

But the advantages, to move on to them, are fairly obvious. It's a big advantage for the actors to be able to follow their characters and see them develop as the story progresses, and not to have to jump back and forth in their characterization. But, as I said, we should have had twelve weeks for the shoot instead. We lost quite a few days when Katrin Cartlidge had to leave the set. I had to record all her scenes again with Patricia Clarkson, who took over the role at four days' notice and made something very different but also very personal out of it.

And now Katrin is dead. I miss her terribly.

To go back to Brecht, do you see Dogville *as a morality play?*

Perhaps I do. I often seem to manage to make things quite unclear in my stories, so that the final message is thankfully not entirely obvious. But morality? I'm not sure about that. When all's said and done, most films are about the fact that man is ultimately an animal who cannot control himself or his environment, but is governed instead by his insatiable desires – and by his stupidity. That's true of most characters, heroes and villains alike. Fortunately I don't know any more about man and his nature than anyone else, so I can only come up with a story and shape it according to my own thoughts.

At the beginning of Dogville *the narrator says of the male lead, Tom: 'Although he did not blast his way through the rock, Tom tunnelled through what could be even harder, namely the human soul, deep into where it glittered.' Is this what you want to say with the film?*

(*Laughter.*) In that case you could say that Tom is a sort of self-portrait. As the Danish author Klaus Rifbjerg once put it: 'I chop myself up into a number of smaller pieces, and there I have the characters in my story.' I think that applies to me too. At any rate, it's true of Grace and Tom. I can argue from both their points of view.

Do you know the child's game where you have to adopt a point of view and argue purely from that opinion? It was a good game, and it was best when you had to argue in support of a point of view that was completely opposed to what you yourself thought. Arguing for inappropriate and wrong points of view. That's why it was such fun writing the speech given by Grace's father (James Caan) at the end of the film, where he expounds the shortcomings of humanism. I was just trying to persuade myself of the opposite of what I personally stand for. It was great fun! I'm very happy with the exchange between Grace and her father, where he says people are like dogs, and she replies that dogs only act according to their nature and that we must understand and forgive them. And her father replies: 'Dogs can be taught a lot of good things, but not if we forgive them every time they follow their nature.'

I possess a certain amount of self-irony, and I think maybe I've bestowed that upon the character of Tom. Like when he's sitting looking at the view and daydreaming, and the narrator comments that 'there are opportunities waiting on the horizon, which is a suitable place for them'. You don't have to prove anything. You know that the opportunities are elsewhere; it's far too much trouble to try to reach them.

Tom is a remarkable mixture of idealism and calculation.

Yes, he's thoroughly cynical. But then so am I! My very first film, the short film *The Orchid Gardener*, opened with a caption stating that the film was dedicated to a girl who had died of leukaemia, giving the dates of her birth and death. That was entirely fabricated! A complete lie. And manipulative and cynical, because I realized that if you started a film like that, then the audience would take it a lot more seriously. Obviously. Death and sickness are things we have great respect for.

The word 'arrogance' occurs a lot in the film, both in the dialogue and in the narration, with various meanings and in different tones.

That's true, and perhaps the word is repeated a bit too often. My biggest problem with the story was trying to explain Grace's change of attitude at the end. Admittedly the people of Dogville, who have long exploited her, become more and more demanding and cruel, but I still had trouble explaining Grace's conversion.

Yes, up to then she has acted as a 'Goldheart' character, like the tragic heroines of your 'Goldheart' trilogy, Breaking the Waves, The Idiots *and* Dancer in the Dark.

Yes, Grace acts good-heartedly, but she isn't – and will not be – a 'Goldheart' figure. She has to possess a capacity for something else. I tried two or three tricks to get it to work, but I don't know if it does. This is where the concept of arrogance comes in, a refusal to discuss things and analyse them. So I was happy to let Grace's father accuse her of being arrogant. She can't understand this and asks her father how he can say that. And he replies that she is so irreproachably moral that no one can compete with her for righteousness. She feels superior to the other townspeople, who can't see the difference between right and wrong.

30 *Dogville*: Grace (Nicole Kidman), Gloria (Harriet Andersson), and Ma Ginger (Lauren Bacall)

There is a similar discussion earlier in the film, between Grace and Tom, where arrogance is a keyword but the conclusion is different.

Of course. Writing a script is extremely simple. You construct your story and then you introduce a discussion of the key issue at three chosen points, and you vary the conversations accordingly. It's quite mechanical. But it works well once you've found a way of dealing with the mechanics.

In your 'Goldheart' trilogy you had women who sacrificed themselves for a man, an idea and for a task. There's a different perspective in Dogville. *The female lead, Grace, may be willing to sacrifice herself, but there is a limit to her willingness to be sacrificed, and her protest is violent. You've evidently had enough of martyrs now.*

Yes, I wanted to make a film about vengeance, and women's vengeance is considerably more interesting to deal with than men's. (Pirate Jenny is also a vengeful woman, of course.) Women's vengeance is more exciting. In some strange way it seems that women are better at embodying and expressing that part of me.

The feminine part of me, perhaps! I find it easier to excuse myself and my thoughts if I allow them to be expressed through a woman. If I expressed the same thing through a man, you would only see the brutality and cruelty.

Looking more closely at cynicism ... This business of making films in English, is that because you want to guarantee a bigger audience than when you made films in Danish?

Well, my most recent films are set in the USA, of course, so it is natural for them to have English dialogue. And because they're set in the USA, I'd like an American audience to be able to see them. But one important feature of *Dogville* is that I wanted the narrator's voice to be recorded by a British actor. I don't want to hide the fact that the USA is being observed from the outside in this film.

You're also planning a sequel to Dogville.

I am. One of my problems is that I would really like to start a new experiment in form with each new film. But now I want to complete this experiment in a trilogy. Making three three-hour films in this style, that would be pretty monumental!

I've already written another script, called *Dear Wendy*, but I've passed that on to Thomas Vinterberg, because it's a story that has to be told in an entirely naturalistic style. I got tired of it, basically, because I think this new world I've created with *Dogville* is so inspiring that I want to carry on living in it for a bit longer. It's entirely uncharted territory. There's a lot of potential here that I want to carry on exploring.

Naturally there are problems involved in making three films in exactly the same way stylistically. But the idea is to develop Grace's story. I've written the next part, called *Manderlay*, which is set in the southern States, and I've got it in mind to set the last part in a big city, Washington or somewhere like that. The trilogy could be described as a depiction of a woman's development to maturity. Nicole (Kidman) has indicated that she would be interested in continuing to work together and playing the part again. It's possible that she'll change her mind when she's read the next script, but I hope she won't. It would be nice to do three films that connect directly to one another. The next part starts two days after the end of *Dogville*, so all three films will be set during the great depression of the 1930s.

I like these long stories. It's like reading a good book and leafing ahead and realizing that you've got lots and lots of pages left to read . . .

Filmography

SHORT FILMS

Between 1967 and 1971 Lars Trier made a number of short films in super-8, the earliest about a minute long, the later ones seven minutes long. The films are called *Turen til Squashland* (*Trip to Squashland*), *Nat, skat* (*Goodnight Darling*), *En røvsyg oplevelse* (*A Strange Experience*), *Et skakspil* (*A Game of Chess*), *Hvorfor flygte fra det du ved du ikke kan flygte fra?* (*Why Run from Something You Know You Can't Escape?*) and *En blomst* (*A Flower*).

Orchidégartneren (*The Orchid Gardener*, Denmark, 1977). Prod: Lars von Trier, Filmgruppe 16. Script: Lars von Trier. Photography: Hartvig Jensen, Mogens Svane, Helge Kaj, Peter Nørgaard, Lars von Trier (16mm, b/w). Editing: Lars von Trier. Music: flute solo by Hanne M. Sondergaard. 37 minutes.
Lars von Trier (Victor Morse), Inger Hvidtfeldt (Eliza), Karen Oksbjerg (Eliza's friend), Brigitte Pelissier (third girl), Martin Drouzy (gardener), Yvonne Levy (woman on bicycle), Carl-Henrik Trier (old Jew), Bente Kopp (woman in film), Jesper Hoffmeyer (narrator).

Menthe – la bienheureuse (Denmark, 1979). Prod: Lars von Trier, Filmgruppe 16. Script: Lars von Trier, free adaptation of Pauline Réage's *Story of O*. Photography: Lars von Trier, Hartvig Jensen (16mm, b/w). Editing: Lars von Trier. Music: Erik Satie. 31 minutes.
Inger Hvidtfeldt (woman), Annette Linnet (Menthe), Carl-Henrik Trier (gardener), Lars von Trier (chauffeur), Jenni Dick (old lady), Brigitte Pelissier (woman's voice).

Between 1979 and 1982 Lars von Trier made a number of test films on film and video during his time at the Danish Film School. The earliest are entitled *Produktion I*, *Produktion II*, *Videoøvelse (monolog)* (*Video Practice*), *Videoøvelse (dialog)*, *Lars & Oles Danmarksfilm*, *Produktion III: Marsjas anden rejse* (*Production III: Marsja's Second Trip*), *Produktion IV: Historien om de to ægtemænd med alt for unge koner* (*The Story of the Two Husbands Whose Wives Were Far Too Young*) and *Danmarkøvelsen (Lolita)* (*Denmark Practice – Lolita*).

Nocturne (Denmark, 1980). Prod: Lars von Trier. Script: Lars von Trier. Camera script: Lars von Trier, Tom Elling. Photography: Tom Elling (16mm, b/w and col.). Editing: Tómas Gislason. 8 minutes.
Yvette (woman), Annelise Gabold (woman's voice), Solbjørg Højfeldt (voice on telephone).

Den sidste detalje (*The Last Detail*, Denmark, 1981). Prod: Den Danske Filmskole. Script: Rumle Hammerich. Photography: Tom Elling (35mm, b/w). Editing: Tómas Gislason. Music: Alban Berg, 'Lulu suite'. 31 minutes.
Otto Brandenburg (Danny), Torben Zeller (Frank), Gitte Pelle (woman), Ib Hansen (gangster boss), Michael Simpson (henchman).

Befrielsebilder (*Liberation Pictures*, Denmark, 1982). Prod: Den Danske Filmskole. Script: Lars von Trier. Camera script: Tom Elling, Lars von Trier. Photography: Tom Elling (35mm, col.). Art Direction: Søren Skjær. Wardrobe: Manon Rasmussen. Editing: Tómas Gislason. Music: Mozart's string quartet in C major, K465, 1st movement. 57 minutes.
Edward Fleming (Leo), Kirsten Olesen (Esther).

FEATURE FILMS

Forbrydelsens element (*The Element of Crime*, Denmark, 1984). Prod: Per Holst/Per Holst Filmproduktion in co-operation with Det Danske Filminstitut. Script: Lars von Trier and Niels Vørsel.

Camera script: Lars von Trier, Tom Elling, Tómas Gislason. Photography: Tom Elling (35mm, tinted b/w, sodium lit col.). Art Direction: Peter Høimark. Wardrobe: Manon Rasmussen. Editing: Tómas Gislason. Music: Bo Halten; the song 'Der Letzte Turist in Europa' by Mogens Dam and Henrik Blichman. 103 minutes.

Michael Elphick (Fisher), Esmond Knight (Osborne), MeMe Lai (Kim), Jerold Wells (Kramer), Ahmed El Shenawi (psychiatrist), Astrid Henning-Jensen (Osborne's housekeeper), Janos Hersko (pathologist), Stig Larsson (pathologist's assistant), Lars von Trier (receptionist 'Schmuck of Ages'), Preben Lerdorff Rye (girl's grandfather), Camilla Overby (first girl), Maria Behrendt (second girl), Mogens Rukov (archivist).

Epidemic (Denmark, 1987). Prod: Jakob Eriksen/Element Film I/S in co-operation with Det Danske Filminstitut. Script: Lars von Trier and Niels Vørsel. Photography: Henning Bendtsen (35mm), Lars von Trier, Niels Vørsel, Kristoffer Nyholm, Cæcilia Holbek Trier, Susanne Ottesen, Alexander Gruszynski (16mm, b/w). Art Direction: Peter Grant. Wardrobe: Manon Rasmussen. Editing: Lars von Trier, Thomas Krag. Music: Wagner, overture to 'Tannhäuser', the song 'Epidemic, We All Fall Down' by Peter Bach, Lars von Trier and Niels Vørsel. 106 minutes.

Lars von Trier (Lars/Doctor Mesmer), Niels Vørsel (Niels), Claes Kastholm Hansen (film consultant), Susanne Ottesen (Susanne), Ole Ernst, Olaf Ussing, Ib Hansen (doctors in film within film), Cæcilia Holbek Jensen (nurse), Svend Ali Hamann (hypnotist), Gitte Lind (medium), Udo Kier (Udo), Anja Hemmingsen (girl from Atlantic City), Kirsten Hemminsen (woman from Atlantic City), Michael Simpson (chauffeur and priest).

Medea (Denmark, 1988). Prod: Bo Leck Fischer/Danmarks Radio. Script: Lars von Trier after Carl Th. Dreyer and Preben Thomsen. Photography: Sejr Brockmann (video, copied to film and copied back to video, col.). Art Direction: Ves Harper. Wardrobe: Annelise Bailey. Editing: Finn Nord Svendsen. Music: Joachim Holbek. 75 minutes.

Kirsten Olesen (Medea), Udo Kier (Jason), Ludmilla Glinska (Glauce), Henning Jensen (King Creon), Baard Owe (King

Aegeus), Solbjørg Højfeldt (nurse), Preben Lerdorff-Rye (tutor), Johnny Kilde, Richard Kilde (Medea and Jason's sons).

Europa (Denmark, 1991). Prod: Peter Aalbæk Jensen, Bo Christensen/Nordisk Film in co-operation with Gunnar Obel, Gérard Mital Productions, PCC, Telefilm GMbH, WMG, Svenska Filminstitutet, Det Danske Filminstitut. Script: Lars von Trier and Niels Vørsel. Camera script: Lars von Trier and Tómas Gislason. Photography: Henning Bendtsen, Edward Klosinski (Poland), Jean-Paul Meurisse (35mm, b/w and col. CinemaScope). Art Direction: Henning Bahs. Wardrobe: Manon Rasmussen. Editing: Hervé Schneid. Music: Joachim Holbek. 113 minutes.
Jean-Marc Barr (Leo Kessler), Barbara Sukowa (Katarina Hartmann), Ernst-Hugo Järegård (Leo's uncle), Jørgen Reenberg (Max Hartmann), Udo Kier (Larry Hartmann), Eddie Constantine (Colonel Harris), Erik Mørk (priest), Henning Jensen (Siggy), Leif Magnusson (doctor), Lars von Trier (Jew), Cæcilia Holbek Trier (maid), Holger Perfort (Mayor Ravenstein), Anne Werner Thomsen (Fru Ravenstein), Janos Hersko (a Jew), Talia (his wife).

Riget (*The Kingdom*, Denmark, 1994). Part 1: 'Den vita flocken' ('The White Flock'), Part 2: 'Alliansen kallar' ('The Alliance is Calling'), Part 3: 'En främmande kroppsdel' ('A Strange Bodypart'), Part 4: 'De levande döda' ('The Living Dead'). Prod: Ole Reim/Zentropa Entertainments ApS and Danmarks Radio in co-operation with Sveriges Television (Malmö), WDR, ARTE, Nordisk Film and TV-fond. Exec. prod.: Pater Aalbæk Jensen, Ib Tardini. Script: Lars von Trier and Niels Vørsel. Photography: Eric Kress, Henrik Harpelund. Wardrobe: Annelise Bailey. Editing: Jacob Thuesen, Molly Malene Stensgaard. Music: Joachim Holbek. 63 minutes, 65 minutes, 69 minutes, 75 minutes.
Ernst-Hugo Järegård (Stig C. Helmer), Kirsten Rolffes (Fru Sigrid Drusse), Holger Juul Hansen (Einar Moesgaard), Søren Pilmark (Jørgen Krogshøj), Ghita Nørby (Rigmor Mortensen), Jens Okking (Bulder), Birgitte Raabjerg (Judith Petersen), Baard Owe (Bondo), Solbjørg Højfeldt (Camilla), Peter Mygind (Mogge), Udo Kier (Aage Krüger), Morten Rotne Leffers (dish-washer), Vita Jensen (dish-washer), Henning Jensen (hospital manager), Laura

Christensen (Mona), Metter Munk Plum (Mona's mother), Lars von Trier (himself).

Breaking the Waves (Denmark, 1996). Prod: Peter Aalbæk Jensen, Vibeke Windeløv/Zentropa Entertainments ApS in co-operation with Trust Film Svenska AB, Liberator Productions S.a.r.l., Argus Film Produktie, Northern Lights A/S, La Sept Cinéma, Sveriges Television, VPRO Television, with support from the Nordic Film and Television Fund, Det Danske Filminstitut, Svenska Filminstitutet, Norsk Filminstitutt, Dutch Film Fund, Dutch CoBo Fund, Finnish Film Foundation, Canal +, DR-TV, Icelandic Film Corporation, Lucky Red, October Films, TV 1000, Villialfa Filmprod OY, Yleis Radio TV-1, ZDF/ARTE. Exec. prod.: Lars Jønsson. Script: Lars von Trier. Photography: Robby Müller (35mm, col., CinemaScope). Chapter illustrations: Per Kirkeby (digital video, copied to film). Art Direction: Karl Juliusson. Wardrobe: Manon Rasmussen. Editing: Anders Refn. Music: 'All the Way from Memphis' (Mott the Hoople/Ian Hunter), 'Blowin' in the Wind' (Bob Dylan), 'Pipe Major Donald MacLean' (Peter Roderick MacLeod), 'In a Broken Frame' (Python Lee Jackson), 'Cross-Eyed Mary' (Jethro Tull/Ian Anderson), 'Virginia Plain' (Roxy Music), 'Whiter Shade of Pale' (Procul Harum), 'Hot Love' (T. Rex/Marc Bolan), 'Suzanne' (Leonard Cohen), 'Love Lies Bleeding' (Elton John), 'Goodbye Yellow Brick Road' (Elton John), 'Whiskey in the Jar' (Thin Lizzy), 'Time' (Deep Purple), 'Life on Mars' (David Bowie), 'Your Song' (Elton John), 'Gay Gordons' and 'Scotland the Brave' (Tom Harboe/Jan Harboe/Ulrik Corlin), 'Happy Landing' (P. Harman) and 'Siciliana' (Johann Sebastian Bach). 158 minutes.
Emily Watson (Bess McNeill), Stellan Skarsgård (Jan), Katrin Cartlidge (Dodo), Jean-Marc Barr (Terry), Adrian Rawlins (Dr Richardson), Sandra Voe (Bess's mother), Jonathan Hackett (priest), Udo Kier (man on trawler), Mikkel Gaup (Pits), Roef Ragas (Pim), Phil McCall (Bess's grandfather).

Riget 2 (*The Kingdom 2*, Denmark, 1997). Part 5: 'Mors in tabula', Part 6: 'Flyttfåglarna' ('Migrating Birds'), Part 7: 'Gargantua', Part 8: 'Pandemonium'. Prod: Svend Abrahamsen, Peter Aalbæk Jensen, Vibeke Windeløv/Zentropa Entertainments ApS and Danmarks Radio TV-Drama in a co-production with Liberator Productions S.a.r.l., Norsk Rikskringkastning, Sveriges Television (Malmö), La Sept ARTE, RAI Cinema Piction and the MEDIA Programme of the European Union. Script: Lars von Trier and Niels Vørsel. Photography: Eric Kress and Henrik Harpelund. Art Direction: Jette Lehmann, Hans Chr. Lindholm. Wardrobe: Annelise Bailey. Editing: Molly Malene Stensgaard. Music: Joachim Holbek. 63 minutes, 79 minutes, 76 minutes, 78 minutes.

Ernst-Hugo Järegård (Stig C. Helmer), Kirsten Rolffes (Fru Sigrid Drusse), Holger Juul Hansen (Einar Moesgaard), Ghita Nørby (Rigmor Mortensen), Søren Pilmark (Jørgen Krogshøj), Jens Okking (Bulder), Birgitte Raaberg (Judith Petersen), Baard Owe (Bondo), Solbjørg Højfeldt (Camilla), Peter Mygind (Mogge), Udo Kier (Aage Krüger and Lillebror), Erik Wedersøe (Ole), Morten Rotne Leffers (dish-washer), Vita Jensen (dish-washer), Henning Jensen (hospital manager), Ole Boisen (Christian), Louise Fribo (Sanne), Otto Brandenburg (caretaker Hansen), Stellan Skarsgård (lawyer), Klaus Pagh (bailiff), Lars Lunøe (health minister), Michael Simpson (man from Haiti), Lars von Trier (himself).

Idioterne (*The Idiots*, Denmark, 1998). Prod: Peter Aalbæk Jensen, Vibeke Windeløv, Sven Abrahamsen/Zentropa Entertainments ApS and Danmarks Radio TV-Drama in co-operation with Liberator Productions S.a.r.l., La Sept Cinéma, Argus Film Produktie, VPRO Television, Holland, ZDF/ARTE, SVT-Drama, Canal +, RAI Cinema Fiction 3 Emme Cinematografica, with support from the Nordic Film and Television Fund. Script: Lars von Trier. Photography: Lars von Trier, Kristoffer Nyholm, Jesper Jargil, Casper Holm (video, transferred to 35mm film). Editing: Molly Malene Stensgaard. Music: Kim Kristensen, 'The Swan' (Camille Saint-Saens), 'Vi er dem de andre ikke må lege med' ('We're the Ones the Others Won't Play With', Kim Larsen and Eric Clausen). 117 minutes.

Bodil Jørgensen (Karen), Jens Albinus (Stoffer), Anne Louise Hassing (Susanne), Troels Lyby (Henrik), Nikolaj Lie Kaas (Jeppe), Henrik Prip (Ped), Luis Mesonero (Miguel), Louise Mieritz (Josephine), Knud Rømer Jørgensen (Axel), Trine Michelsen (Nana), Erik Wedersøe (Stoffer's uncle), Michael Moritzen (man from the council), Anders Hove (Josephine's father), Claus Strand-berg (factory foreman), Lone Lindorff (Karen's mother), Hans Henrik Clemensen (Anders, Karen's husband).

Dancer in the Dark (Denmark, 1999). Prod: Peter Aalbæk Jensen, Vibeke Windeløv/Zentropa Entertainment ApS in co-operation with Trust Film Svenska AB, Liberator Productions S.a.r.l., Pain Unlimited, Cinematographers, What Else Prod., Icelandic Film Corporation, Det Danske Filminstitut, Svenska Filminstitutet, with support from the Nordic Film and Television Fund. Exec. prod.: Lars Jönsson. Script: Lars von Trier. Photography: Lars von Trier and Robby Müller. Art Direction: Karl Juliusson. Wardrobe: Manon Rasmussen. Choreography: Vincent Paterson. Editing: Molly Malene Stensgaard. Music: Björk.

Björk Gudmundsdóttir (Selma), Catherine Deneuve (Kathy), Peter Stormare (Jeff), Vladan Kostig (Gene), David Morse (Bill), Cara Seymore (Linda), Jean-Marc Barr (Norman), Jens Albinus (Morty), TJ Rizzo (Boris), Vincent Paterson (Samuel), Katrine Falkenberg (Suzan), Stellan Skarsgård (doctor), Udo Kier (Dr Porkorny), Lars Michael Dinesen (defence lawyer), Zeljko Ivanek (district attorney), Joel Grey (Oldrich Novy), Lars von Trier (angry man), Paprika Steen (woman on nightshift).

Dogville (Denmark/Sweden/Britain/France/Germany/Holland, 2003). Prod: Vibeke Windeløv/Zentropa Entertainment ApS and Film-mek in co-production with Memfis Film International AB, Troll-hättan Film AB, Slot Machine Sarl, Liberator Sarl, Isabella Films International, Something Else BV, Sigma Films Ltd, Zoma Ltd, Pain Unlimited Gmbh, ArteFrance Cinema, France 3 Cinema. Executive producer: Peter Aalbæk Jensen. Co-producers: Gillian Berrie, Bettina Brokemper, Anja Grafers, Els Vandevorst. Co-executive producers: Lene Børglum, Peter Garde, Lars Jönsson, Marianne Slot. Script: Lars von Trier. Director of photography: Anthony Dod Mantle. Production designer: Peter Grant (creative consultant: Karl Juliusson). Costume designer: Manon Ras-mussen. Editing: Molly Malene Stensgaard.

Nicole Kidman (Grace), Harriet Andersson (Gloria), Lauren Bacall (Ma Ginger), Jean-Marc Barr (The Man with the Big Hat), Paul Bettany (Tom Edison), Blair Brown (Mrs Henson), James Caan (The Big Man), Patricia Clarkson (Vera), Jeremy Davies (Bill

Henson), Ben Gazzara (Jack McKay), Philip Baker Hall (Tom Edison Sr.), Siobhan Fallon Hogan (Martha), John Hurt (Narrator), Zeljko Ivanek (Ben), Udo Kier (The Man in the Coat), Cleo King (Olivia), Miles Purinton (Jason), Bill Raymond (Mr Henson), Chloë Sevigny (Liz Henson), Shauna Sim (June), Stellan Skarsgård (Chuck).

Index

269